TEACHERS *Can* BE FIRED!

TEACHERS *Can* BE FIRED!

The Quest for Quality

A Handbook
for Practitioners
in Elementary, Middle,
and Secondary Schools
and Community
Colleges

Hans A. Andrews

CATFEET
PRESS

Chicago

PRESS

CATFEET PRESS™ and the above logo are trademarks of Carus Publishing Company.

© 1995 by Catfeet Press™

First printing 1995

Printed and bound in the United States of America.

Library of Congress Cataloging-in-Publication Data

Andrews, Hans A.
    Teachers can be fired! : quest for quality : a handbook for
practitioners in elementary, middle, and secondary schools and
community colleges / Hans A. Andrews.
        p.   cm.
    Includes bibliographical references and index.
    ISBN 0-8126-9280-2. — ISBN 0-8126-9281-0 (paper)
    1. Teachers—Rating of—United States—Handbooks, manuals, etc.
2. Teachers—Dismissal of—United States—Handbooks, manuals, etc.
3. Community college teachers—Rating of—United States—Handbooks,
manuals, etc. 4. Community college teachers—Dismissal of—United
States—Handbooks, manuals, etc. I. Title.
LB2828.A53 1995
371.1′44′0973—dc20   95-5905
                                                              CIP

In Memory
of Grace L. Andrews
Mother, Grandmother, Friend

CONTENTS

──── Acknowledgments ────

Special thanks to Dr. Ralph C. Bedell, Professor Emeritus (deceased), University of Missouri–Columbia, for his advice and encouragement for over 20 years. He continually pressed his philosophy that one must tell and continue to retell his or her story if it is important for improvement of education. Bourne (1988) quoted Bedell in an interview in his strong support of applied research: "If your research doesn't result in practice, your research is no good, and if your practice is not based on research, your practice is no good" (p.138).

Thanks also goes to Dr. Alfred Wisgoski, President of Illinois Valley Community College for his support and guidance in the development of an effective evaluation system; and to Evelyn Moyle, Carol Bird, and Jan Vogelgesang for their many hours of research support. Mr. Bruce Mackey has provided this author with much exceptional guidance through his legal counsel for over 15 years.

Special thanks to my wife Carolyn who has experienced my emotional ups and downs in carrying out effective evaluation practices over a 25-year period. Thanks to Kris Curley and Judy Day for outstanding secretarial support in producing the finished manuscript.

Recognition is also extended to Lou Borio, Lewis Cushing, Samuel Rogal, John Knight, William Uebel, Carol Haas, John Erwin, Harold Barnes, Linda Knight and Ed Anderson who as Division Chairs, and John Allen, Associate Dean of Instruction, have made effective faculty evaluation at Illinois Valley Community College the model program it has become.

INTRODUCTION

The Total Quality Management (TQM) movement in business and industry has moved rapidly into the American educational system. But, for the most part, it has stopped at the classroom door. Some of the pioneers in introducing more effective management to the schools even proclaim proudly that they have no intention of interfering with what goes on in the classroom.

Yet all of a school's non-instructional activities exist purely in order to support instruction. If the quest for quality makes sense in every other productive activity, can there be any reason why it would not be appropriate in the arena of instruction?

No car manufacturer would apply TQM principles to the car body, the tires, and the upholstery, and overlook the quality workmanship that goes into the engine. A car with an unreliable engine is a bad car, because the customer says it is a bad car. Similarly, the education system's student-customers and taxpayer-customers will not recognize a quality educational product if the system's support services are made more efficient while what goes on in the classroom is left alone to muddle along.

Unless we can *guarantee quality teaching in every classroom,* the various improvements in registration procedures, mail distribution, physical maintenance, payroll, and printing services will pale into insignificance. Yet, as Seymour (1991) found in his survey of the leading "pioneering" colleges, this is precisely what has been happening in most cases.

The argument of this book is that the quality of teaching can be improved by a rational system of faculty evaluation. I understand 'Quality Faculty Evaluation' as the totality of practices which lead to those predetermined instructional goals jointly agreed to by faculty, administrators, and board members. Quality faculty evaluation starts from a clear understanding of what the outcomes of evaluation should be, and of issues and procedures which produce those outcomes.

The evaluation of teachers should recognize superior teaching performance, reward it, and help to motivate it. Where teaching is inadequate, evaluation should identify the weaknesses and indicate the steps to be taken to correct them. In the case of the small minority of teachers whose performance is sub-standard and cannot be remedied by appropriate measures, evaluation provides a solid base, both legally and in the ethics of fairness, for the dismissal of teaching staff, whether tenured or not.

In this book I present what I believe to be a strong case that supervisory/administrative evaluation is crucial to the improvement of faculty, and is superior to alternative methods (peer evaluation and student evaluation). This view differs from that of the majority of senior university professors who have written on this topic.

Contrary to a widespread but ill-founded opinion, there is plenty of evidence that the majority of teachers will accept and welcome vigorous evaluation, provided that certain conditions are met: the goals and procedures of the evaluation have to be objective and clearly spelled out in advance, teachers' input has to be taken seriously at every stage, and the evaluators themselves have to be demonstrably knowledgeable and competent.

Supervisory/administrative evaluation of faculty is seldom found in four-year colleges or universities. It has therefore not been easily available for study and has not been promoted by faculty or administrators at that level. The situation in these institutions is often complicated by the demands of research. But in elementary, middle, and senior high schools, and community colleges, *classroom teaching is the predominant job requirement.* Here, there can be no doubt that the preparation and delivery of classroom instruction are so important that they need to be monitored and evaluated by instructional leaders.

This book aims to promote clear thinking about evaluation and educational outcomes. It should assist department and division chairpersons, principals, assistant principals, and deans and vice presidents of instruction to implement the best system of quality control they have available. I hope it will also help teachers, board members, parents, and others interested in the fate of education in our society to understand what can go wrong in the management of instruction.

Before we can establish a system of effective teacher evaluation, we need to face certain questions squarely, and come up with straightforward answers. What objective and relevant observations can be made of a teacher's classroom performance? What rewards, if any, will exceptionally competent faculty receive for their efforts? How will help be given to those faculty who need to improve? What will be proposed for the slouchers? What will happen to those faculty who refuse to change or cannot improve? Will the evaluation system provide the depth of documentation required to make administrative actions legally defensible? Can the system hold up if attacked by attorneys on behalf of disgruntled faculty members? These and other issues will be addressed in the following chapters.

GETTING THERE FROM HERE: GOOD AND BAD EVALUATION METHODS

My last evaluation was very complimentary, but it was based on nothing more than casual observations on how I interact with kids. What if I wasn't an effective teacher? My principal doesn't make in-class evaluations and isn't familiar with the classroom. He doesn't hold conferences; he just writes everyone a complimentary evaluation. For the last two years, he's missed the district deadline and predated his evaluations.

A Teacher

In this chapter I want to acquaint readers with some of the themes which will recur throughout this book, and which I will discuss more systematically in later chapters.

Contrary to a widespread preconception, there is good evidence that teachers are inclined to favor effective supervisory evaluation, provided that it meets certain standards of fairness and objectivity. There is strong support among teachers for the view that the small minority of true incompetents should be weeded out. Teachers are, however, often fearful that evaluation may be capricious or inept, as indeed it often is. There is widespread agreement that present evaluation methods are most commonly ineffectual at best. Because many evaluation systems currently in use can barely be taken seriously, they usually do not lead to the removal of incompetent faculty, who remain in the schools, giving rise to 'horror stories' about teachers.

Contrary to another myth, tenure does not guarantee a teacher against dismissal for poor performance, and dismissal of tenured faculty has been upheld by the courts. Yet firing teachers is a last resort. Far more often, a good faculty evaluation system should indicate ways in which excellent performance can be recognized and shortcomings can be remedied.

Faculty evaluation requires time, application, and expertise. It needs to be documented fully at each stage. In later chapters we will see that faculty input into and support for the evaluation process is vital, and we will explore in detail how these can be secured.

THE IDEAL FACULTY EVALUATOR

Turner (1986) drew a composite picture of an ideal evaluator of faculty: "The evaluator is genuinely interested and concerned. He's a common sight in the classroom making many formal and informal visits throughout the year. He spends plenty of time observing, knows the classroom and students well, and is on hand to point out the teacher's strengths and weaknesses. He talks with the teacher before and after each evaluation, gives specific suggestions, and welcomes the teacher's input. The situation is relaxed and comfortable; the evaluation, nonthreatening and fair. The principal's purpose is to help the teacher improve her teaching, period" (p. 58). This picture was put together from over 1,000 teachers' responses to a poll on teacher evaluations.

A picture also emerged of the most disliked evaluator, the one who alienates teachers from the evaluation process. Evaluators who conform to this "bad" stereotype:

1. Spend 15 minutes in the classroom once a year;
2. Are more concerned with how the bulletin board looks than how a teacher interacts with her students;
3. Offer no feedback, no suggestions for improvement, and no interest in what the teacher has to say.

Receiving high marks from such an evaluator means little or nothing to the teachers who have a supervisor with this profile. Over 52 percent of the teachers who responded to the survey conducted by *Learning 86* magazine felt that their evaluations had had either a "negative effect or no effect" on their teaching.

Norland (1987) found that the secondary school faculty evaluation system in Dixon, Illinois, is based "on the philosophy that effective evaluation of teachers and administrators is reflected in improved student learning." A good evaluation system must:

1. Establish the importance of performance evaluation.
2. Be manageable.
3. Be legally defensible.
4. Be positive.
5. Provide data for personnel decisions.
6. Provide for consistency from evaluator to evaluator.

7. Provide for the development of intensive assistance plans where appropriate.
8. Provide for recognition where appropriate (p. 27).

My dialogues with faculty and administrators on "legally defensible" faculty evaluation have confirmed my view that support exists among teachers for fair and meaningful evaluation of teaching. There is a need for both faculty and administrators to have a clearer understanding of what can be accomplished through effective classroom evaluation and how it can be made less threatening for the large majority of the faculty involved.

A JUNIOR HIGH SCHOOL

During a visit with the junior high school faculty in Spring Valley, Illinois, I learned some of the things they hoped would come out of an improved evaluation system:

1. Improved instruction;
2. Better communication between administration and teachers;
3. Elimination of poor teachers who do not follow remediation procedures;
4. A chance to see your weaknesses and the opportunity to improve on them in a constructive way;
5. An opportunity for administrators to see the realistic situations that a teacher encounters;
6. Improved public relations when incompetent teachers are removed;
7. Improved cohesiveness of the faculty;
8. Upgraded community opinion of the teaching profession.

The faculty members wanted significant improvements and outcomes, but they were keenly concerned about the anonymity of their responses. Faculty are often anxious that their honesty might cause them problems if their responses become known.

ELEMENTARY SCHOOL

Johnson et al. (1985) surveyed 935 teachers in 15 elementary schools on school climate as it related to evaluation. They found that teachers' attitudes were much more positive about evaluation if there was high morale in the school. Other factors correlated to positive attitudes included getting along well together within the school, a principal whose behavior was personal and direct, and a school staff committed to quality teaching and learning.

As far back as 1911 the quality of teaching was being documented and the "causes of failure among elementary school teachers" was the subject of a study by Littler (1914). He surveyed 50 county, 50 city, and 50 town and village superintendents and another 50 ward principals in Illinois, and an additional group of superintendents in Iowa, Indiana, Wisconsin, and Missouri. In total, 400 requests were sent to these schools and a follow-up response of 281 replies were received. The replies represented some 676 elementary teachers who had been dismissed for a number of reasons. The main reasons are given in Table 1 below:

Littler compared his study to one by Ruediger and Strayer, published in the Journal of Educational Psychology in May of 1910, which looked at "merit" qualities in elementary teachers. The "merit" qualities of the best elementary teachers were ranked as follows:

1. Discipline
2. Teaching Skill
3. Initiative
4. Personality
5. Studiousness
6. Follow Suggestions
7. Health

TABLE 1

Causes of Failure among Elementary School Teachers (1911)

Reason for Failure	Number	Percent of Total
1. Lack of Discipline	105	15.53%
2. Lack of Proper Personality	100	14.79%
3. Lack of Interest in Work or Too Much Interest in Outside Work	71	10.50%
4. Lack of Scholarship	53	7.83%
5. Lazy—Made No Daily Preparation	48	7.10%
6. Lack of Preparation	29	4.29%
7. Lack of Instructional Skill	29	4.29%
8. Lack of Pedagogical Training	26	3.86%
9. Failure to Cooperate	25	3.69%

The role of discipline and other teaching skills will be outlined later in this book in terms of elementary schools in the 1990s.

COMMUNITY COLLEGES

Filan (1992) did a national survey to find those topics that instructional leaders felt to be of the greatest concern and should be addressed at the First National Conference for Community College Chairs. "Faculty evaluation" was the choice checked most often. This choice was selected by chairpersons who were found to have primarily a faculty role. The possible conference topics checked most often were:

(1) Faculty evaluation   298
(2) College and division/department strategic planning   284
(3) Curriculum design   268
(4) Conflict management   255
(5) Budgets: developing, managing, etc.   236
(6) Dual role of the chair   232

As the presenter at this conference on faculty evaluation, I found that community college chairpersons throughout the U.S. and Canada want quality faculty evaluation, but that they have very little training to support this objective.

I also led a discussion with over 45 faculty and division chairpersons at a Colorado community college. At the end of the first day I asked for feedback on how the session was progressing. The largest number of responses voiced the desire to become focused more directly on the evaluation problems at the respondents' college and on how to change them. Small groups discussed "what can be salvaged from your present system?" and "what needs to be done to strengthen evaluation at your college?" The participants summarized the following responses:

What can be salvaged from our present system?
1. "Nothing!"
2. Student evaluation, but in a revised form
3. Supervisor form, re-evaluated

What needs to be done?
1. Include 'teaching' in annual evaluation
2. Don't visit and evaluate only when problems exist

3. Eliminate the 'fear' of being observed
4. Revise faculty evaluation form to focus on teaching
5. Develop a consistent approach (throughout the system)
6. Define expectations and define quality teaching
7. Develop a uniform part-time faculty handbook for classroom visitations
8. Have a board/president policy approved
9. Keep in mind the system must be fair
10. Determine the primary purpose of what the evaluation system should do: improve instruction.

The need to move away from the present inept attempt at faculty evaluation was unanimous. Each of the small groups agreed on what was needed to improve instruction in effective ways: develop an evaluation system that is fair, includes all departments, is established for both full- and part-time faculty, has consistency, defines what quality teaching is, and then measures it. This prescription highlighted the frustration this group had been living with for a number of years.

The question "what motivates you to want to improve your evaluation practices?" solicited the following responses:

■ We are tired of teacher bashing, and we need professionalism to gain the status teachers deserve. We need to police ourselves.
■ Get the deadwood out and regain our pride.
■ The consensus is that the current system doesn't work. It is not fair and consistent.
■ We really do believe that a revamped system could improve instruction.

When discussing how they feel about in-class observations, the needs to reduce fear, ensure consistency and fairness, and have well-trained evaluators were brought out. There was a consensus that the faculty, "must be convinced that the evaluator is well-trained and competent in order to create trust."

These two experiences reinforced the research of Andrews and Licata (1990a), who found faculty leaders supportive of using a quality evaluation system to improve instruction. They did not, however, feel that their current evaluation system was nearly as effective as it should be. In a survey of those faculty leaders in the North Central accreditation region of the country, 158 responses were received for a rate of 51 percent. Individual faculty development was the number one stated reason for post-tenure evaluation by 59 percent of these faculty leaders. Only 27 percent rated their system as "very effective" or "effective."

This compared with administrative leaders which as a group had 56 percent rating evaluation as "very effective" or "effective."

The 73 percent of faculty leaders who gave responses of "uncertain" or "ineffective" when asked to describe the effectiveness of their systems listed the following major reasons:

1. Pays only "lip service" to faculty development;
2. Has no mechanism to measure competence/incompetence;
3. Does not have adequately train evaluators.

Both faculty and administrators did support the premise, "there should be post-tenure evaluation for tenured faculty." In this part of the study 96 percent of the faculty and 100 percent of the administrators agreed or agreed strongly with the statement.

CONCERN ABOUT POOR INSTRUCTORS

Faculty and administrative respondents in the Andrews and Licata study were asked to give their opinions as to whether evaluation in their colleges *"should* lead to the weeding out of incompetent faculty." There was strong agreement by both groups that it should. On the other hand the statement, "post-tenure evaluation *does* lead to the weeding out of incompetent faculty," showed a definite split in responses. Faculty responded with a strong 77 percent "disagree or strongly disagree" compared to a 58 percent response from administrators.

A number of other researchers and authors on evaluation have identified problems within evaluation systems and with personnel involved in making decisions on poor teachers. McDaniel and McDaniel (1980) see the principal in two conflicting roles: consultant as well as evaluator. They show that a principal who has trouble reconciling or finding some balance to these roles will usually lean toward, "the positive role of consultant rather than the negative role of evaluator" (p. 35). They suggest that teacher deficiencies usually show up during the first year of teaching.

Phay (1981) encourages schools to maintain high standards when selecting teachers, to ensure students the best learning opportunities. Boards have this responsibility as well as the responsibility to dismiss a teacher as soon as deficiencies are noticed. This should be in the first year if excellence is not forthcoming in the evaluations (p. 10–16). Gaynes (1990) also sees the first year as key to making continuation or dismissal decisions. The principal needs to actively monitor and evaluate all probationary teachers. Only the best teachers should be kept in the classroom (p. 30–32).

Van Sciver (1990b) expressed concern that administrators may not give top priority to understanding the evaluation instruments and finding time to evaluate teachers. He says that this is "ironic, for schools exist first and foremost to educate our children." He went on to say that "allowing other concerns to intrude on the effectiveness of that mission seems counterproductive" (pp. 318–19).

Huddle (1985) found that faculty believe a sound teacher-evaluation process is vital, legally & pedagogically, in identifying, helping, and (if necessary) dismissing ineffective teachers. Faculty support was found to be possible if certain conditions are met: (a) a consistent, objective, and fair evaluation process if effective incentives or merit plans are to be used for teachers; and (b) peer supervision or coaching to decrease teachers' feelings of isolation.

Incompetent teachers were found to be relatively few by Bridges (1985). The number of students being taught by these teachers was, however, substantial. Parental complaints were found to play a major role in signaling that something may be radically wrong in the classroom of a certain teacher. Too often Bridges found the administrator leaving the teacher alone. When a meeting is called to discuss problems, there are two distinct purposes that need to be considered. One is where the administrator is trying to "salvage the teacher." He found few such teachers actually being salvaged and suggests that the "incompetent veteran teacher is near impossible to make a good teacher." The second stage, where the administrator tries to get rid of the incompetent teacher, is not easy when dealing with a tenured teacher. Non-tenured dismissals do not offer nearly as much of a challenge. Bridges found in California that poor tenured teachers were being "eased out" about 20 times as often as those dismissed.

Bridges concluded that granting of tenure may well be the most important single decision facing administrators and governing boards everywhere. They found incompetent teachers being allowed to continue indefinitely, and unless the public and student pressures became almost intolerable, little or no action was taken to dismiss such poor instructors. Bridges points to the fact that most states have laws that make it possible to move toward termination of those faculty found incompetent. Such termination, however, requires a well-defined evaluation system and adequate team support of the administration and governing board wanting to deal with the problem of poor teaching. He concluded with showing that even "coaching out" incompetent faculty would have a better chance of succeeding when a school has an evaluation system that commits the administration to evaluating a teacher over a period of time and allows the person ample time to improve (p. 24).

TENURE

Wheeler et al. (1993) provided a definition of tenure:

> TENURE: An employment status conferred upon a teacher by state law or institutional regulation after successful completion of a probationary period. Tenure provides substantial but not complete protection against arbitrary or capricious dismissal and entitles the teacher to due process procedures and other protections that may not be available to the non-tenured teacher (p. 26).

Nisbet (1973), in his discussion on tenure and the abuse that exists in the granting of it, found that tenure does indeed mean a guarantee of a lifetime job for most teachers. Very few faculty are ever dismissed from tenured positions, and Nisbet stated that there are many institutions where a tenured faculty member has never been dismissed. He concluded: "To argue that tenure is not a refuge for the lazy, incompetent and delinquent, that "with cause shown" such individuals may be dismissed, hardly carries conviction when, as the record makes plain, tenure *is* such a refuge" (p. 47).

He also describes the frustration a new university president who, along with board members and a substantial number of faculty members, wishes to make significant improvements: "What must be the emotions running through the mind of such a president as he looks at the layer on layer of mediocrity, sloth, incompetence and disdain for effort, the heritage of years, and at the budgetary and appointment problems made inevitable by inability to reduce these layers, protected as they are by an iron doctrine of tenure?" (p. 53).

DaMarto (1990) discussed the impact of a recent law that has attempted to assist in the removal of incompetent teachers during the non-tenure probationary period. California passed SB 813, and in a survey of 65 responding school districts, the consensus was that "the number of ineffective teachers granted tenure since SB 813 has decreased" (p. 35).

QUESTIONABLE SYSTEMS: QUESTIONABLE RESULTS

In a study by Wise et al. (1984) the conclusion was reached that most secondary school teacher evaluation systems in use were not suitable for rating teachers for the merit pay or master teacher programs that were considered key in the reform movement to improving education.

They found that most school districts did not have highly developed teacher evaluation systems, and "even fewer put the results into action." There was more emphasis on conforming or compliance with procedures and with a minimal commitment of resources. These researchers stated that educators tend to believe that teacher evaluation "requires no more than finding the right checklist," which the principal fills out once a year while they are sitting in the back of the class of a faculty member.

Looking back over the years Seldin (1982) described the failure of evaluation systems on several points: (1) failing to distinguish between poor, adequate, and good teaching; (2) failing to motivate teachers to improve their performance. In some cases the teachers, or only one teacher, wanted the system to fail and that was sufficient to ensure failure. The same could happen if administrators, or one administrator, wanted it to succumb. He summarized that even if evaluation practices are won on paper it does not ensure that the proper performance will be forthcoming on behalf of administrators or some professors if they have "a lack of interest, inability, or covert opposition" (p. 93).

Another concern Seldin presented was that the evaluation program may start out flawed by being so vague or loose that no one may know how it works. He said it can also become "so comprehensive and detailed, down to assigned weights to publications, classes, professional and community activities, that it will not work" (p. 94). Cohen and Brawer (1982) also found evaluation procedures being developed into "labyrinthine complexity" (p. 75). Scott (1975) showed that administrators could be ineffective enough to cause the collapse of an evaluation system by having irregular ratings schedules, unclear instructions on forms, and inconsistent standards. Seldin concluded that, "how the evaluation program is developed and administered can be almost as important to program success as program content" (p. 94).

AN IDEAL TEACHER EVALUATION SYSTEM

"Good, better, best. Never let it rest. Until good becomes better and better becomes best!" This was suggested as the slogan for teacher evaluation by Hunter (1988a, p. 32). She delineated her view of an ideal system on which sophisticated supervisors and evaluators should base their teacher evaluations:

1. Teaching is seen as a learned profession, not a genetic endowment.
2. Many principles governing effective teaching are described, taught, observed, and documented in practice.
3. It is understood that *artistry,* beyond the *science* of teaching, exists

and can be observed, but it doesn't seem to be reliably acquired through direct instruction.

4. All teachers (and all administrators) continue to grow in professional effectiveness and artistry, and this is required as a condition of continued employment.

5. Increasing the quality of educational practice is encouraged, stimulated, and demanded by formative and summative evaluation.

6. Career opportunities and psychological incentives for continuing growth are available to excellent teachers. Stimulation and incentives for growth are provided for "average" teachers. Compassionate but rigorous and effective remediation is required for teachers who need it. Removal with dignity takes place for those very few teachers for whom remediation is not effective.

7. Daily teaching is seen as the most critical professional duty of a teacher.

8. Peer coaching is used to provide a formative process, which results in increased professional effectiveness and artistry.

9. The purpose of the district's evaluation is summative, based on a year's professional performance; the summative evaluation certifies a professional as belonging to a category from outstanding to unacceptable. Summative evaluation is viewed as extremely important but is only a small part of the total time devoted to staff development. It is the final assessment of the district's and the teacher's efforts.

10. The summative evaluation is fair and just because it has the following three qualities: First, it is based on many performance samples (not on one observation or on hearsay); second, it is conducted only by an adequately trained evaluator; last, it is based on stipulated criteria with meanings common to teacher and evaluator.

11. The evaluators are competent and demonstrate expertise in two key areas: They possess knowledge of the research-based, cause-effect relationships between teaching and learning, and they demonstrate competence in observation and conferencing skills (pp. 34–35).

HOPE: QUALITY EVALUATION SYSTEMS EMERGING

Thirty-two school districts surveyed by Wise et al. (1984) were considered as having highly developed evaluation mechanisms in place. Of these, they found four districts—Salt Lake City, Utah; Lake Washington, Washington; Toledo, Ohio; and Greenwich, Connecticut —that were best able to identify incompetent teachers and to improve teacher performance. These districts spent the most administrative time, money, and care in the implementation of faculty evaluation. These "exemplary" systems made sure their evaluators were competent, sought cooperation from both teachers and administrators, and tailored a system of evaluation to fit their particular district's educational and political characteristics (p. 63).

Over a nine year period the Salt Lake City district removed 37 teachers who were found to be incompetent. The Lake Washington upper-middle-class suburban district used a highly structured system, with both pre- and post-observation conferences and personal development plans. Over a five-year period 56 faculty were "counseled out" of their system (p. 100).

These researchers concluded that the movement toward merit pay and master teacher programs that were widely being discussed and implemented in a number of states during the 1980s would surely be doomed if teacher evaluation was not a key element in the process.

This discussion is important as it runs counter to popular opinion that faculty are resistant to evaluation. The research and experiences of this author and others simply do not support such opinions. There is, however, a great deal of anxiety that centers on who is going to be doing the evaluating for in-class administrative evaluation of faculty. Faculty have a right to expect quality evaluation on the part of the evaluator as much as the evaluator and school have a right to expect quality in teaching by the faculty members being evaluated.

RIGHTS OF THE INSTITUTION IN EVALUATION

A "bill of rights for faculty evaluation" for school districts has been proposed by Strike (1990). It places the role of evaluation in the hands of the institution and underlines its need to gather information on how to improve instruction:

1. Educational institutions have the right to exercise supervision and to make personnel decisions intended to improve the quality of the education they provide.
2. Educational institutions have the right to collect information relevant to their supervisory and evaluative roles.
3. Educational institutions have the right to act on such relevant information in the best interest of the students whom they seek to educate.
4. Educational institutions have the right to the cooperation of the teaching staff in implementing and executing a fair and effective system of evaluation.

RIGHTS OF FACULTY IN EVALUATION

Andrews (1986c) suggested a "faculty evaluation bill of rights" which was developed out of many contacts with faculty from elementary schools up through the community college level:

1. Competent evaluators should be expected and used.
2. The evaluators and faculty members should have a clear understanding of the evaluation system and instruments to be used.
3. Consistency should be expected.
4. Fairness is a "must" element of the system.
5. Both verbal and written evaluations should be part of the feedback to teachers.
6. Teachers should be allowed to express disagreement, both verbally and in writing.
7. Feedback from the evaluator should be expected to occur in a reasonably short time.
8. Positive types of recognition for excellence in one's work should be given.
9. A reasonable amount of time should be given for those areas of teaching that may need some form of remediation due to a weakness.
10. Mutual respect between faculty and administrative professionals should permeate the process.
11. Privacy of results should be expected—except when an open meetings act may call for board action on a "notice to remedy", or on a dismissal of personnel action being recommended.

While such a "bill of rights" is not intended to be legislated, it can provide for much of the professionalism that is necessary to ensure trust, support, and positive expectations from faculty. It may also be adopted as a board philosophy statement.

FACULTY UNION LEADERS SUPPORT QUALITY EVALUATION

Futrell (1986), while president of the National Education Association (NEA), saw faculty as supportive of having their supervisors evaluate them, providing that such evaluation is professionally carried out. The faculty bill of rights includes several of the ingredients Futrell suggested faculty should expect.

The American Federation of Teachers (AFT) president, Albert Shanker indicated that poor administrators are responsible for poor instructors being kept in place rather than being dismissed. According to Shanker:

The machinery for dealing with incompetent teachers is in place in every community and has not been compromised by any negotiated settlement.

One cannot deny that this is often an unwieldy, time-consuming, thankless process. And the truth is that most teachers are as troubled by the situation as are supervisors. Incompetent teachers reflect badly on the profession and their fecklessness usually ends on the back of their colleagues. (Shanker 1985)

Chait and Ford (1982) did not find that the AAUP had an official position on post-tenure evaluation. They believed, however, that the AAUP would denounce the process if it were employed to terminate tenured faculty without cause. The chance for remediation and due process would have to be key elements if post-tenure evaluation were to be sanctioned.

THE EVALUATORS: COMMITMENT AND COMPETENCE

Eble (1971) described faculty as believing that tenure really had neither positive or negative effect on the effectiveness of teaching. Later on he described the process of effective administrative evaluation as being ignored due to the time constraints and lack of initiative by administrators. It takes considerably more time than many administrators wish to give in documenting incompetent tenured faculty. He concludes that time, not tenure, is the culprit (Eble 1973).

In a report by the National Commission on Higher Education Issues (1982) several conclusions were put forth relative to post-tenure evaluation:

(1) It should ensure that the tenured faculty member has maintained the appropriate level of competence and is performing at a satisfactory level.
(2) The responsibility lies with faculty and administration to see that unsatisfactory performance is remedied.
(3) Ultimately, "incompetent faculty members must not be protected at the expense of the students or the maintenance of quality" (p. 10).

Bridges (1990) shows that if a teacher is worked with through good faith efforts, but cannot be considered for future employment due to a lack of improvement, "the administration must be able to justify its dismissal decision to an impartial third party" (p. 154). These third parties are court judges, hearing officers, or a commission on professional competence. It is here that credible evidence is most important for the decision being made and for the institution. The administration is under pressure to justify its decision. Written records that document a pattern of poor performance are necessary. The emphasis is definitely on the pattern rather than isolated incidents which might be considered remediable. It is when the administration is unable to document a pattern of deficiency and defects in the teaching or other job responsibilities that dismissal is not allowed by those who must sit in judgment of the evidence.

Wise et al. (1984) point out that the best thought-out process and support for that process will flounder if the responsible evaluator lacks the "necessary background, knowledge, and expertise" (p. 86). Desirable evaluator qualities, they suggest, are (1) the ability to make sound judgments about teaching quality; and (2) the ability to make appropriate, concrete recommendations for improvement of teaching performances.

SUMMARY

Supervisory faculty evaluation can be both an accountable and acceptable means for evaluating faculty with the objective of improving instruction for students. Faculty at the elementary, junior high, senior high, and community and junior college levels have been found in research studies to support such an evaluation process. Support is dependent upon skilled and trusted administrative evaluators. It is also dependent upon the development of trust, faculty input into the system, and administration of the process in a manner that is consistent and fair.

Recognition of quality instruction and support for improvement are key elements in successful evaluation programs. There is a strong need for recognition plans for those faculty who are working hard and providing a high level of quality in their teaching. This continually comes through when faculty are asked about evaluation. They are looking for a system that recognizes good performance as well as identifying shortcomings.

There are major differences in how governing boards, arbitrators, and the court system deal with non-tenured and tenured dismissals. Non-tenured dismissals, when challenged in the appeals process, have been upheld in most cases. A solidly conceived and administered evaluation system strengthens the legal position of administrators and governing boards. Tenured faculty dismissals are much more difficult to accomplish. Incompetence is difficult to document and documentation can prove to be a very time-consuming process. Incompetent faculty are often left in an elementary or secondary school district or community college because of lack of motivation on behalf of the administration.

Poor instruction has been found to be left untreated in most studies looking at why poor faculty remain in schools. The law in most states supports sound evaluation systems. Faculty union leaders agree that the mechanisms for dealing with poor and incompetent teaching are in place and ready for competent administrators to use when needed. Faculty support is vital in those schools and colleges wishing to initiate administrative evaluation systems.

SUGGESTED EXERCISES

1. Discuss what would help make supervisory evaluation successful in your school. What elements should be included in a supervisory system so that faculty will lend support to it?
2. What personal characteristics should a supervisor have in order to gain faculty support for an in-class evaluation system?

2

SHORTCOMINGS OF STUDENT AND PEER EVALUATION SYSTEMS

Choice of a faculty evaluation method is crucial if a school system is to pride itself on having *quality control* of the instruction that takes place. In this author's judgement, supervisory evaluation is the most effective. Contrary to popular myth, teachers will welcome supervisory evaluation as long as they perceive it to be fair. Mary Futrell, past executive director of the National Education Association (NEA), found that administrative or supervisory evaluation is acceptable if it is carried out in a professional manner:

> Most teachers agree that they should be evaluated, but teachers do not want evaluations done by someone standing outside the classroom door or by someone who turns on the public address system and listens in a classroom, or by someone who steps into a classroom to deliver a message and later calls that stopover an evaluation. Teachers want to know what evaluation instrument will be used. They want the evaluators to come into the classroom for at least a full class period of time and within five days, they want feedback—in writing and orally—and a chance to respond. (1986, p. 58)

EVALUATION SYSTEMS CURRENTLY IN USE

Supervisory evaluation is the primary system used in elementary, middle and secondary schools. A significant number of community and technical colleges also use this type of evaluation system. Although many community colleges use student evaluations in combination with other methods, only a few have selected student evaluation as their sole method of evaluation. In a study of nearly 200 community and technical colleges in the North Central region of the United States, Andrews and Licata (1988–89) report the following breakdown of the types of evaluation systems:

(1) Administrative evaluation	33 percent
(2) Combined student and administrative	33 percent
(3) Combined student, peer and administrative	16 percent
(4) Student evaluation only	7 percent
(5) Not reported	11 percent

A second community and technical college study by Erwin and Andrews (1993) found 283 colleges (80 percent) within the same North Central region reporting the following types of evaluation:

(1) Evaluation by students	204
(2) Evaluation by supervisor	160
(3) Evaluation by faculty (peers)	50
Total	414

The total of 414 responses by the 283 respondents indicates that there were a number of these colleges using a combination of 1, 2, and 3 above.

The university system, by contrast, has largely focused itself upon student evaluations and to some degree upon peer evaluation (faculty evaluating each other).

A fourth evaluation type, *self,* is used in a number of colleges. Centra (1977) found self evaluations were given little value by division chairpersons when making tenure and promotion decisions. In a study of 343 teaching faculty from five different colleges (Centra, 1973) it was found that self evaluation outcomes when compared with student ratings had a median correlation of only .21. They were even more generous than students in their evaluations, with 30 percent of the teachers in the study ranking themselves higher than the ratings given by their students. Centra asserted that if these faculty had felt the ratings would be used in determining promotions, self-ratings would have been even higher. He concluded that self-evaluations may be useful for an individual to improve his or her instruction, but they are of "limited use for administrative purposes" (p. 71).

This chapter looks at the research behind student and peer evaluation systems with respect to their impact on the quality of instruction. Each of these systems has the goal of improving instruction. Some of them are used in place of an administrative or supervisory evaluation system. Sometimes they are used in conjunction with the supervisory system. Do they improve instruction as they are purported to do?

STUDENT EVALUATION

Research finds student evaluation to be the most studied and discussed type of faculty assessment. Why should this be? With the movement toward greater accountability, the university system and many community colleges found that they could obtain a significant amount of feedback on their faculty members' teaching by asking students. Such evaluation is usually designed to yield numerical outcomes that make it much less subjective than written narrative reviews by supervisors. Numerical data are much easier for researchers to compare, rank and analyze and for administrative personnel to review. According to Cashin (1988), there were at that time over 1,300 published articles and books on student evaluation.

Stodolsky (1990) expressed her concern that too much emphasis has been placed on trying to ensure reliability and objectivity, at the expense of attention to validity and definitions of teaching. She held that "selection of a system should be determined by the match between the school district's view of teaching and the adequacy with which the instrument reflects that view" (p. 181).

RESEARCH ON STUDENT EVALUATION

Cashin (1983) listed several defects in the utilization of student evaluation ratings. He said that students are not qualified as curriculum experts and are not able to judge whether a teacher is knowledgeable in his or her field of study. Students tend to be inflexible in accommodating a variety of teaching methods and approaches (pp. 60–61).

Possibly the most comprehensive reporting on student ratings has been accomplished by Centra (1979) in which he concluded: (1) students seem to rate elective courses or courses in the major area more highly than courses taken to fulfill a college requirement; (2) students are generally lenient in their judgment, therefore students' ratings may be misleading as to the effectiveness of some teachers (pp. 152–53). He supported his premises with a study from the Educational Testing Service (1975, p. 153) which found that out of almost 400,000 teachers in a national sample, there were only 12 percent receiving less than "average" ratings from student reviews. Centra saw this leniency as adding to what might already be an inflated feeling of how well some faculty felt they were doing. Fraher (1982) said that students expect their teachers to be "excellent", and when students rate a teacher as "average" or "good" the teacher should not take it as a compliment, as they often do. (pp. 123–24).

Centra (1979) outlined the following limitations that should be considered when using student ratings:

1. Because most student rating instruments elicit numerical responses that can be scored and quantified, it is easy to assign them a precision they do not possess.
2. Student ratings may be given too much weight in relation to other criteria.
3. It may be possible for teachers to influence ratings but not student learning. The teacher who is lenient in assigning grades and out-of-class work is not improving learning, yet may be better rated by some students.
4. The manipulations of ratings by teachers must be considered when ratings are used for personnel decisions.
5. Student ratings have misled some institutions into thinking that nothing more is needed to upgrade instruction. While some teachers can use the rating information to make needed changes, others need faculty and instructional development services.
6. Because of the positive bias in student ratings, teachers who need to improve may not realize their weaknesses (pp. 44–45).

Use of student evaluations for personnel decisions

Even though the student evaluation system has significant problems and limitations, many colleges and universities use student evaluations for both tenure and promotion purposes. This type of evaluation has also migrated into the community college and secondary school faculty rating system. Centra found two-year colleges using student ratings almost as much as the four-year colleges (p. 9).

Selden (1984) estimated that somewhere near 70 percent of the American colleges and universities he surveyed were collecting student ratings of their faculty members (p. 48). A survey by Ory and Parker (1989) of 40 large research universities concluded that all 40 of them used student ratings in their teacher evaluation process. These studies show that what was once a process to help students select courses more effectively has now become "a powerful source of information that is consistently used by administrators to make personnel and program decisions" (p. 383).

Ory (1990) traced student gathering of information on teachers back as far as the 1920s. This information was used in the selection of courses and instructors. In the 1960s, students were demanding greater participation in all areas of college life. Some administrators at that time began to consider extremely low student ratings in promotion, teaching assignments, and tenure decisions. In the 1970s, this type of data became an accountability tool for administrators (pp. 63–64).

Use of student evaluations to support legal actions

Eble (1984) explained that "tangible measures of judgment get preference, not because they may be better, but because they afford written evidence that may stand up in court" (p. 177).

I was unable to find any court cases over a 22-year period to substantiate the view that such student evaluation leads to the termination of those faculty performing poorly. During this period of time, faculty evaluation has been a subject of much research and many legal cases. Part of the problem of the "written evidence that may stand up in court" is that the evaluations received from students are *anonymously* completed. There is no one available to testify in a board, arbitration or court hearing.

In *Ianello v. The University of Bridgeport* (1979) a student complained that the content in a course did not match up with the college's catalogue description, had minimal substance, and lacked testing and grading. The student lost the case because the court found the student had not presented sufficient evidence to support her claims against the instructor. It would be rare indeed that a student might win such a case, due to limited ability to collect relevant evidence and also to being only one individual in a class.

DEVELOPING ETHICAL PROCEDURES IN STUDENT EVALUATION

Ory (1990) summarized a number of procedures, which if followed, would lend ethical credibility and a much stronger degree of objectivity to student ratings. Among these procedures are the following:

1. All student rating forms should be administered in the classroom during regular class hours and under normal circumstances.
2. All students and faculty should be informed of procedures for administering student ratings.
3. The instructor should read directions (provided by the institution); see that forms are distributed; ask a student to collect the completed forms; and leave the classroom.
4. The directions should state the purposes and uses of the ratings; explain how to fill out the form; say when the instructor will have access to the results; ask students to respond honestly and fairly; assure confidentiality of responses; and remind students to work independently.
5. The student helper should collect the rating forms; place them in an envelope along with a form that indicates the number of blank forms returned; sign and seal the envelope in the presence of several classmates; and, in the presence of several classmates,

return the envelope to the evaluation office or place the envelope in a campus mailbox. Student helpers should also inform the faculty member and the evaluation office of any deviation from these procedures.

6. Faculty and student helpers should refrain from reading rating forms until results have been returned from the evaluation office, after course grades have been assigned.

7. Upon return of the results, instructors should refrain from attempting to identify respondents by analyzing handwriting or inspecting demographic information.

8. Students should have a mechanism to (confidentially) inform administrators of instructors who fail to follow procedures.

9. Institutions should have procedures for handling accusations of unethical behavior, determining their occurrence, and enforcing penalties. Administrators must strictly follow regulations when handling accusations of wrongdoing.

10. Administrators responsible for developing documents for promotion and tenure should include all available ratings. If necessary, the documentation can include information explaining aberrant ratings (pp. 72–73).

Ory made it clear that his intent was to, "encourage colleges and universities to review their procedures for administering and using student ratings of instruction and to make necessary modifications to prevent some of the unprofessional, unethical, and unlawful behavior that is occurring today." His article listed several scenarios of such abuse, and his procedures were developed to help avoid them.

A large number of secondary schools and colleges presently use and will continue to use student ratings as their most important, or one of their most important, means of evaluating their faculty for retention, promotion, or merit recommendation. It is, therefore, essential that administrators obtain the highest quality of student response and that ethical standards permeate the system.

STUDENT EVALUATIONS AND ACCOUNTABILITY

Andrews (1986b, p. 6) provided a chart to show the difference in accountability between administrative and student evaluation systems. It is presented as Table 2 below:

Evaluation of the total job versus student responses to one class, follow-up, administrators expecting no rewards (grades), and responsibility to the governing board all go to show the much greater responsibility and accountability inherent in an administrative evaluation system.

T A B L E   2

Administrative vs. Student Evaluation in Accountability and Professionalism

Professional Administrative Evaluation	Student Evaluation
1. Evaluation of the total job of the faculty member (in-class and other professional responsibilities). Follow-up visits to other classes may be made.	1. Evaluation of one class only.
2. Evaluators are grounded in teaching techniques, teaching experience, educational psychology, learning theory, observational techniques, etc.	2. Students are evaluating with no experience or training in teaching, educational psychology, or classroom observational techniques.
3. Evaluators enter the classroom to observe the teaching and learning techniques and the classroom environment.	3. Students are in the classroom for subject matter and learning needs. The evaluation task is thrust upon them with no prior preparation.
4. Evaluators will be following up classroom evaluation with both written and oral reports to the faculty member.	4. Student evaluation is a one-time event. There is no follow-up by students after their written report or in subsequent semesters or terms.
5. Evaluators expect no rewards from the instructors.	5. Students often evaluate prior to being awarded a grade for the course.
6. Evaluators have job responsibilities to the board of trustees to guarantee that quality instruction is taking place in the classroom. Accountability is to the instructor and to boards.	6. Students have no responsibilities to anyone with respect to their evaluations. They will remain anonymous and not be subject to account for their remarks.

NEGATIVE RESPONSE TO STUDENT REVIEWS

Hocutt (1987–88) raised strong questions concerning the movement toward what he termed "student poll of teaching" (SPOT). He asked that universities look at what they have done with this movement. Specifically, he asked: "Was the SPOT's rise merited?" "Has it proved its worth?" "Has it provided the universities with a good measure of teaching?" "Has it helped to improve teaching?" He defines a good teacher as "simply someone from whom students learn." He further clarifies his definition: "The best teacher of algebra is the one whose pupils learn the most algebra."

Hocutt's criticisms of SPOT include the following: (1) SPOT gives the appearance of providing objective, factual information. Worked out to two decimal places, it looks very scientific, and many people think it is. (2) SPOT does not yield an objective measure of the teacher's performance but a subjective index of the student's satisfaction. (3) No matter which study you pick (regarding SPOT), there is another on the same issue to contradict it. (4) A professor who does his own grading is in a position to use grades to influence his ratings on SPOT. Yet, once again, most universities let instructors do their own grading, so it becomes impossible to separate the part of an instructor's rating that is due to his teaching effectiveness from the part that is due to his grading policies. (5) There *seems* to be a weak relation between learning and ratings on SPOT, but much of the research has been so flawed that nobody can legitimately claim to know what this relation is or reliably estimate its strength (pp. 58–59).

In his review of research on grades Hocutt became even more critical. He said: "Cynical professors have long suspected that they can buy ratings with grades." He sees colleges giving better grades today to students who are worse than in prior decades. Part of it has to do with encouraging professors to adopt grading practices that he says have no relationship to learning. He sees it as "no accident" that the greatest "grade inflation" in educational history has paralleled the increasing use of SPOT. The average grade today is a "B", as against a "C" two decades ago. The second main way he sees SPOT harming teaching is that it has encouraged professors to give up the teaching of complex concepts and in its place teach simple facts and figures.

Seldin (1989) cautions that student assessment of teaching, as important as it might be, should be viewed as only a "part of the whole." The "whole" he refers to includes classroom observation, self appraisal, samples of instructional material, and videotaped classroom sessions.

Seldin separates out what he feels students are capable of judging: teacher's ability to communicate at their level, professional and ethical behavior in the classroom by the instructor, student-teacher relationships, what has been learned in the course, and how much interest in the subject has been stimulated. He does not feel that students are capable of evaluating the curriculum or course content, how much knowledge of scholarly background the faculty member has, or how appropriate the course objectives are. He also warns that multiple sources of information should be used rather than student ratings as the sole source. Seldin suggests that completed student evaluations go *only* to the evaluated faculty members. Research shows that this is not the case in many institutions where the faculty member's supervisors use the results as a means of making tenure, rank, and merit recommendations.

COMMUNITY COLLEGE STUDENT LEADERS ON INSTRUCTION

John Erwin and I carried out a survey of student leaders in community colleges in Illinois during the spring of 1993. The survey was conducted in preparation for a workshop with student advisory committee members of the Illinois Community College Board. The students had asked for a workshop on faculty evaluation to explore what could be done to improve teaching through faculty evaluation in their colleges. Initial responses showed students to be highly critical of the teaching they were receiving in a significant number of classes. They were asked how many *high quality* and *poor quality* faculty they felt they had had during their college time. The following is a sampling of individual responses:

1. How many *high quality* faculty have you had in college?
   12, 6, 7, 6, 3, 3, 6, 5, 6/70%, 90%, 25%
2. How many *poor quality* faculty have you had in college?
   3–4, 4, 5, 10, 1, 1, 1, 7, 1/33%, 10%, 30%

When asked what they felt were the *best teaching methods* and practices they had observed as students the following responses were included:

1. Hands-on experimentation;
2. Fun/sense of humor;
3. Stuck to the syllabus;
4. Explained exactly what is expected;
5. Giving encouragement;

6. Gathering outside sources;
7. Interaction between students;
8. Treats everyone on the same level;
9. Asks questions and has interaction with students;
10. Open-mindedness of teacher.

To the question of what were the worst teaching methods the following responses were elicited:

1. No organization;
2. No complete knowledge of the material;
3. Difficult to contact;
4. Lack of sense of humor in classroom;
5. No enthusiasm for the material;
6. Does not stay current with new information;
7. Hides behind tenure;
8. Lectures strictly from the textbook;
9. Not present during office hours;
10. Constantly late for class;
11. Leaving a matter that is complex at a level that cannot be understood;
12. When an instructor does not leave his/her personal life out of the classroom;
13. Tests that have information not discussed in class or in the book;
14. Obscenities;
15. Repeating the same material.

The question "What do you believe your college should do to improve the poor teaching practice you have received?" brought the following reactions:

- I feel the selection process of an instructor should be taken more seriously than in the past.
- Reevaluate tenure.
- Actually pay attention to teacher evaluations.
- Require teachers to attend refresher sessions.
- Confront teacher with problems.

The student leaders were asked to express the personal feelings they have when they find out they have a poor teacher for a class. The following are direct quotations from the students:

- I feel outraged and upset since I am paying for the class and the college fails to provide a qualified instructor for the class.

- I feel that I am cheated out of an opportunity along with my college education.
- Worse than that [losing the money] is when you know that another class you have to take is taught only by a poor instructor.
- I am disgusted that I wasted my time and money on this class.
- Mad as hell! Not only is it a waste of my time, money, and efforts, it is a rip off of students who do not have the money to lose.

The question "Have you discussed your concern with an administrator?" elicited some interesting responses:

- They cordially take notes and say that they will speak to that instructor and then nothing happens.
- As a result that particular instructor was dismissed from the college and the renewal of the contract was denied.
- He said he couldn't write a teacher up for the same charge twice . . . but I think that is stupid when you consider a class of 25 dissatisfied students.

This was an unusual opportunity to ask student leaders (ages 18 to 50) to respond in general terms about the instruction they have been receiving. Most research has been limited to students' responses on a single course.

PEER EVALUATION

The research on peer evaluation is similar to that found on student assessment of teaching. Centra (1979) summarized his research review and found "colleague evaluation" was even more generous than student evaluation. Some 94 percent of the peers judged the teaching of those being evaluated as "excellent" or "good." He also found them to be statistically unreliable. The highest correlation he could find in the research among ratings by different colleagues was .26 for each item. He concluded that "this low reliability casts doubts on the value of colleague ratings as they were collected in this study" (p. 75).

With this high percentage of "excellent" evaluation coming forth from peer evaluation systems, one might conclude that faculty unions would try to implement such a system in more community colleges and in elementary, middle, and secondary schools. But the literature has not been consistent on where faculty unions stand relative to classroom evaluation. While on the one hand, faculty unions wouldn't be opposed to a system that gave their members primarily favorable ratings, on the other hand, they do oppose the administration doing nothing about incompetent teachers. McNeil (1981) presented an example of this conflict:

> They hold that hiring and firing are the responsibility of the employer. In spite of their general opposition to negative assessment by school authorities, which they tend to view as deficient, leaders of some teacher organizations blame school boards and administrators for being irresponsible in hiring and evaluating incompetent teachers. (p. 276)

McNeil further concluded that these faculty organizations *do not* take responsibility for removing incompetent teachers (p. 275).

Barber (1990) lists peer review, nonthreatening collegiality, modeling, and peer sharing of quality teaching as "extremely effective ways of improving teacher performance" (p. 227). He also suggests that given their choices, the professional teachers will constantly request these options. No evidence was presented to support these evaluation options as being "extremely effective."

Most researchers agree that division or department chairpersons are in a position to be competent evaluators of faculty under their supervision. Chairpersons are regarded as peers in most university settings and vary as to whether they are peers or supervisors in community college and elementary, middle, and secondary school settings. The legal definition is usually drawn to mean supervisory if at least 51 percent of the chairperson's work is administrative and includes supervisory responsibilities.

In a highly critical look at peer evaluation, Lieberman (1985) castigated the Reagan Administration and then Secretary of Education William Bennett's attempt to promote merit pay for teachers. He cited the guidelines being developed which encouraged peer review and collaboration with institutions of higher education—"two more prescriptions for failure" (p. 107). According to Lieberman:

> The unstated assumption underlying the guidelines is that peer review has been used successfully in higher education. Aside from the fact that there is not a shred of evidence to support this assumption, the guidelines, like other peer review proposals, ignore the following considerations.
> 1. The "peers" are in no way accountable for erroneous or biased judgments of merit. On many campuses, it is impossible to ascertain what recommendations were made by peers. Even when this is not so, no professor ever suffers a loss of salary or is denied a promotion because his or her judgments rendered as a peer were poor. . . . It is bad enough that higher education uses this irresponsible procedure; for the Department of Education to encourage its adoption in K–12 education is most unfortunate.

2. Nor is it reasonable to contend that, unlike administrators, teachers who evaluate other teachers will be unbiased. In a California school district, "peers" who supported a strike were unable to identify any meritorious teachers among those who taught during a strike—even though one of the latter had been recognized as a teacher of the year by local and county organizations. (p. 107)

He added several other points to substantiate his distrust of peer review as having strong biases and lack of objectivity.

Kulik (1974) found administrative ratings more closely correlated to peer ratings than to student ratings. While no reason was given, it should lead the reader to deduce that professionals who understand quality in teaching should be in a better position to agree than students who lack such a base of professionalism. Greenwood and Ramagli (1980) found low correlation between administrative and student ratings. In another study by Rotem (1978), feedback from students was found to lack any significant effects on improving an instructor's performance: "To be effective, feedback must contain diagnostic information that helps the teacher know not only whether or not his performance is considered satisfactory, but also the particular areas in which he has to improve" (p. 317).

Teachers in the early research by Centra (1972) with unrealistically high opinions of their teaching effectiveness with students were more likely to change than those who saw themselves as being average or poor.

Bonato (1987) added to the legal considerations of student evaluations: "The weight afforded student ratings is likely to be greatly diminished if, for example, they were solicited at a time the students knew there was administrative dissatisfaction with the teacher's performance and a desire to fire the teacher" (p. 25).

The above discussion should leave the reader in a quandary as to which method or methods of evaluation to select when setting up an evaluation system. A comparison of administrative, student and peer evaluation is summarized in Table 3. It shows the outcomes expected, accountability role and quality factors of each of the three systems.

Accountability is lacking most often for student and peer evaluation. Administrative evaluation is usually considered an important component of the job description of the elementary, middle or secondary school principal, assistant principal, or college dean and division chairpersons. In addition, the administrators are considered to be professional evaluators who are well versed in teaching methodologies and competent techniques of instruction.

T A B L E   3

Comparison Summary of Types of Evaluation Systems

Type of Evaluation	Outcome Orientation	Accountability Role	Quality Factors
ADMINISTRATIVE EVALUATION	For positive reinforcement For identifying improvemen needs For developing remediation processes	Professional responsibility of administrators Required for all faculty and academic support personnel	Professionalism Experience Knowledge of teaching/ learning process
STUDENT ASSESSMENT OF INSTRUCTION	For assessment of major strengths and personal development needs. For student input into weaknesses from a learner's viewpoint only	Anonymous— no accountability Optional for most tenured faculty Required for non-tenured faculty	Amateur status Lack of experience in professional assessment "Halo" effect
"PEER" RULES IN EVALUATION	For content assessment and improvement suggestions in content, organization and depth	Non-job responsibility of peers Optional, or as suggested by administration	Tendency to resist Providing negative evaluation of peers

SUMMARY

This chapter has focused upon two types of faculty evaluation systems —student and peer—that are utilized at all levels of education from secondary school through university. The research from a number of studies finds that student assessment of faculty can provide useful feedback. It does not, however, show any evidence of leading to improved teaching. There are no face-to-face meetings to discuss the findings with students. The student evaluators remain anonymous and there is no follow-up conducted if student concerns are found. In addition, there is no documented evidence to show that student ratings lead to the administration placing faculty members into remediation or removing poor faculty. It appears that poor instruction is not identified through use of student ratings.

The literature summarized by Centra and others, in fact, points in the other direction. It points to a generous positive skewing of the outcomes of student ratings. Most students do not wish to cause faculty problems, keep them from obtaining tenure, or cause them to miss pay increases. Peer evaluation seems to have the same problem of reliability as student evaluation. Centra found peer evaluations to be even more generous than student ratings. It is seldom that peers actually go into a faculty member's classroom and conduct serious reviews of what takes place. Peer evaluation in university settings is usually comprised of a review of research and publishing activities. At the community college and secondary school, peer evaluation is more likely to take place, with the "peer" being identified as a supervisory chairperson of a department or division.

Most of the research presented agrees with the premise that student ratings should not be taken as the sole type of evaluation conducted by any institution. Researchers suggest students have some areas that they can legitimately evaluate and point out those areas in which they are not sophisticated enough to respond.

Neither student ratings nor peer evaluation lead to the remediation or dismissal of incompetent faculty members. They also lack credibility in arbitration hearings and the court system since they are almost always carried out as anonymous systems. Who, then, is to appear, speak, and face cross-examination in such hearings? These are questions for governing boards, administrators, and faculty to consider when reviewing or setting up effective evaluation systems. It is unclear whether, and to what extent, student or peer evaluation systems can be effective in improving instruction. The uncertain efficacy and reliability of these methods means that they cannot be used for summative evaluation.

SUGGESTED EXERCISES

1. Develop an evaluation system that might fit a secondary school or community college system. Consider what weight might be given to

supervisory, student, and peer evaluation if one or more combinations are considered.

2. List those concerns and/or fears that students consider when they complete a faculty rating sheet. Are they honest? Do they consider themselves threatened at the expense of honesty? Develop discussion groups using teachers and students to discuss how they feel and how much honesty is found in student comments and checklists.

3. List those concerns and/or fears that faculty consider when they complete a *peer* rating sheet.

CHAPTER

3

DEVELOPING FACULTY UNION SUPPORT
FOR ADMINISTRATIVE EVALUATION

A teacher affects eternity; he can never tell where his influence stops.

Henry Brooks Adams

The most predictable question this author receives when speaking about supervisory evaluation, whether from faculty, faculty senates, administrators or board members is, "How do faculty respond to a system of administrative evaluation of faculty?" It must be difficult for some faculty and administrators to conceive of any faculty members openly supporting a system that includes in-class observations by members of the administrative staff.

In fact, faculty union leaders in America have over the years called for faculty to carry out their job responsibilities. They have also pointed out that many administrators and governing boards lack policies and procedures to conduct effective evaluation. They suggest that these administrators and boards often hide themselves in the shadow of faculty unions and tenure to justify their not carrying our responsible faculty evaluation.

Wise et al. (1984) suggest that, "a well-designed, properly function-ing teacher evaluation process provides a major communication link between the school system and teachers. On the one hand, it imparts concepts of teaching to teachers and frames the conditions of their work. On the other hand, it helps the school system structure, manage, and reward the work of teachers" (p. 61).

THE ESSENTIAL ELEMENTS FOR GETTING FACULTY
UNION SUPPORT

There are four fundamental components of any administrative evalua-tion system that will earn the support of faculty:

33

(1) Trust. This is possibly the number one factor in setting up a system. Faculty want to trust those persons selected to supervise them in their classroom and other job responsibilities. This trust must be earned through experience working with faculty. McLaughlin (1990) says that "teacher evaluation will be no more effective than the extent to which teachers support it; and an effective evaluation system insists on trust between teachers and administrators" (p. 404). Trust is defined by Wheeler et al. (1993) as "a common understanding of the purpose and potential of teacher evaluation, and a cooperative spirit between the teacher and the evaluator for maximizing the benefits of doing the evaluation. Trust is related to such factors as confidentiality of communication, careful consideration of the accuracy of evidence from such sources as hearsay or complaints, honesty, openness, sharing, and sincerity on the part of both the teacher and the evaluator" (p. 27).

(2) Input. The best faculty understand what it takes to be effective in the classroom. It therefore behooves the administration and board to seek the input of faculty in the development of the evaluation instrument. A feeling of ownership will go a long way to encourage acceptance of the system and instrument that is arrived at in the process.

(3) Feedback. Faculty want both oral and written feedback on the supervisor's observations. They also want feedback as quickly as is practicable following classroom observations. Feedback provides an opportunity for faculty members to respond to the observations. They want to have the option of disagreeing and to have their viewpoints heard and respected.

(4) Remediation. This is important because the supervisor must spell out those things that need to be improved or changed. It also allows for a specified period of time in which to carry out the remediation items. Wheeler et al describe remediation as "those techniques or strategies designed to improve a teacher's performance with respect to general deficiencies or specific areas of weakness" (p. 22).

Licata (1986) made the following recommendations for those institutions interested in developing or modifying a plan to evaluate their tenured faculty members:

1. The purpose of the evaluation should drive all other aspects of the evaluation plan. Will the evaluation be formative or summative in nature?
2. Faculty must be involved in the design of the plan.
3. Faculty and administrators should agree upon the specifics of the plan.

4. A post-tenure evaluation plan should be flexible and individualized.
5. Faculty development programs should be linked to a post-tenure evaluation system.
6. Innovative approaches to post-tenure evaluation and institutional planning should be sought (pp. 67–68).

In the fifth item above, Licata suggested that if "institutional commitment to faculty development and provision for faculty rewards cannot be delivered, then institutions should seriously question the usefulness and effectiveness of such evaluation" (p. 68).

In their report entitled *Action for Excellence,* the Task Force on Education for Economic Growth, Education Commission of the States (ECS) (1983), presented several recommendations, which included faculty input in the development of evaluation systems:

> We recommend that boards of education and higher education in each state—in cooperation with teachers and school administrators—put in place, as soon as possible, systems for fairly and objectively *measuring the effectiveness of teachers and rewarding outstanding performance.*
>
> We strongly recommend that the states examine and tighten their procedures for selecting not only those who come into teaching, but also those who ultimately stay. . . . Ineffective teachers—those who fall short repeatedly in fair and objective evaluations—should, in due course and with due process, be dismissed. (p. 39)

THE NECESSITY OF FACULTY INVOLVEMENT

Wise et al. (1984), recognized evaluator competence as possibly being the most difficult part of the process in evaluation. Their concern centered on the fact that, no matter how well developed an evaluation process may be, a lack of background, knowledge, and expertise of the evaluator can render such a process ineffective (p. 86). Their study of four school districts with well recognized evaluation systems found that all four allowed the teachers' organizations to play a major role in designing and implementing the evaluation process. They recommended that school districts "should involve teacher organizations in the design and oversight of teacher evaluation to ensure its legitimacy, fairness, and effectiveness (p. 111).

Van Sciver (1990) suggests working with teacher union leadership and also school board members about how important quality instruction is to the school. He sees such effort as gaining support from the board when the time comes for a contract termination (p. 41).

Seldin (1982) calls for both faculty and administrators to lend their support to the development of faculty evaluation. He also points out that such a system needs to recognize that the goal is to make "improvement" and "not perfection" (p. 98).

AN INTERVIEW WITH FACULTY UNION LEADERS

The faculty senate at Miami-Dade Community College in Miami, Florida, invited this author to present a framework of effective supervisory evaluation practices at their annual retreat in 1987. In preparation for the presentation two former faculty union presidents at community college district 513 in Illinois were interviewed about the administrative evaluation system at their college. Mary Sue Myers, a physical fitness instructor, and Robert Mueller, a teacher of English and Literature, were the respondents:

Classroom evaluation of faculty

Interviewer: This college is somewhat unusual in that faculty are evaluated in the classroom by a department chairperson, associate dean and dean. Bob, would you start by commenting about how being evaluated in the classroom makes you feel. Does being evaluated in the classroom make you feel ill at ease? Some instructors have expressed such a feeling.

Robert: Yes, I think evaluation is something that we are going to have to live with. It has always been with us. As faculty members we have had input into the instrument that we are going to be evaluated on, and on the procedures involved. As a union president we have negotiated fringe benefits but have never really talked about teacher evaluation. It has been a non-negotiable item.

As far as a feeling about faculty evaluation is concerned, no matter how long you are in teaching, when you are being evaluated there is a little tenseness and *perhaps that's good.* Perhaps that gives you that edge and you go from there. Our visits are unannounced by the division chair people, also by the dean of instruction. I think it's something that at least we have been involved in developing some of the key elements that have made up the evaluation form. In that way the faculty feel that they are a little more at ease than if the evaluators were coming in with a different instrument being forced upon us.

Mary Sue: I guess my personal feeling is that it is helpful to know what is expected. When the evaluators are in evaluating I kind of know the expectations, and when I go into the classroom I *am prepared.* I feel on any day they could come in and I would feel comfortable with an evaluation. I know what the expectations are and I don't have a problem with it.

Interviewer: You would have occasion to know most of our faculty on a personal basis. Are the feelings you expressed generally the feelings of the faculty at large?

Robert: I think so. In talking, and that's what faculty do best, we do talk around coffee and I think that everyone is in agreement that, number one, the evaluation is part of our job, and number two, the instrument is fair, in that it does evaluate those areas that are important in teaching, like the course syllabus—are you following it? I think it is one of our requirements as a teacher and that it becomes our bible of instruction. I think of the faculty who have been evaluated on the form and comment about the written evaluation being far more superior to a checklist approach where you would have numbers from one to six or one to ten or whatever methodology you are going to use. I think that the written evaluation is far superior to any kind of checklist mainly because it allows for some kind of specificity; it allows for those areas that were observed. And also following a classroom visitation there is a discussion with the teacher and the person who has done the evaluating. The faculty member will sign the form, but you only sign the form after you have reviewed each item that is on the evaluation form.

That feedback is a strong point of the instrument because if I'm being evaluated and I'm having something written that I feel deserves an explanation then I'm allowed that opportunity to say that what you observed is atypical or whatever. There is room for discussion, and what I'm hearing from the faculty is that they are in agreement with that. Sue can maybe comment on that . . .

Mary Sue: I think they see the instrument as, number one, a way of improving instruction, and I think the faculty does take pride in the reputation of our students doing well. And I think this is just part of the pride that we have that we all want to do well, and we see this [evaluation] as one of the ways that will help us to do a better job. Again, it was important that, in developing the instrument, we had input. I was involved when it was being set up and I can remember some very tough discussions we had with the administration. I was representing the union at that time, but I think that we came up with some things we can all live with here.

Robert: The instrument does allow in the written format a means of remediation, and I think that that is an important part of evaluation. Is the evaluator coming into the classroom to evaluate objectively as much as she/he can or is the evaluator coming in to solidify a pre-conceived idea? In other words, if my reputation is that I'm not doing a very good job, does that slant the evaluation? I don't think he can say that would be reflected in an instrument relying on numbers. I do think that helps in the written form especially when I have the chance to go one-on-one with the person who has evaluated me. I can say, 'well, I can do this or I can do that or I can see where this area needs improvement or that one may not.' I can see where the feedback is the essential part of the instrument.

Evaluation and improved instruction

Interviewer: Do you have a feel for whether the system of evaluation has a systemwide tendency to improve instruction?

Robert: I believe that in our conversations the faculty is in agreement that evaluation here is to improve instruction. I know there is a tendency once in a while to say that, 'if they want to get me, they can get me,' which is true under any situation. The instrument isn't at fault there. If they want to, they can build a case if you are in that situation. We have had some in that situation who have been evaluated several times, given remediation dates, those had not been met, and they have been discharged from the faculty. As a union president that is a very difficult situation to be in because you are caught right in the middle. Sue was more involved with some of those than I, particularly. But I think that the instrument does allow, as I say, the feedback, which is important. And also if I'm doing something wrong, tell me, give me a chance to remediate, and then come on back and evaluate. In that way I think it's improving instruction. It's not a vendetta, it's not a solidification of a preconceived idea, it's an evaluation.

Mary Sue: I think of some things that I find even in my own teaching, even right now—and I have been recently evaluated so I'm kind of thinking they won't be back in for a while. But on the other hand, I find myself stating objectives each day that I go in. Do the students know what is expected? In summing things up, these are the kinds of things they are looking for in the evaluation and I find that I am just more careful that I do these things, and I think these are educationally sound kinds of things that we should all be doing. Some people, I think, are sometimes a little careless. So again, I think they are things to help the students, with us being better teachers. These are just some of the kinds of feelings you get as a result of being evaluated and having these things pointed out, that these are important things, and that you really should be doing them in each class.

Robert: I really think that if you're not evaluated it doesn't help you a great deal, because you really don't know and you get into your own way of doing things and you think it's working, and so on. And at least this is how I look at it: I'm happy to have someone come in and then give me that interaction to help me to become a better teacher. Here we're our own best public relations because the faculty here has traditionally been strong on the transfer successes of our people, so something good is going on in that classroom. I think the evaluation allows discussion of those methods of what's being done, what's good, what works, what doesn't work. What Sue mentioned, and it's true, the form has comments about the course syllabus: Are the students given direction? Do they know what you're covering today? What's going to be coming up the next meeting, or the next meeting? And as Sue mentioned, I think it is very true that those are sound educational principles.

Mary Sue: I guess I really don't have anything else to add here other than, I just get back to the point that educationally this is a very sound approach to things and I just think it very definitely can make better teachers out of all of us.

Removing poor faculty

Interviewer: Some of our faculty, of course, did not survive the evaluation system, and you folks were involved, in that these were colleagues, and also you were in union leadership positions. Candidly, would you tell how you felt about that sort of thing? Obviously, it couldn't have been easy.

Mary Sue: I think I was the one who was involved probably when all of this was going on. I was president of the local association for two years, and it was during these two years that there was some hard evaluating going on here. And, truly, it was personally a very hard time for me because I was involved with some of these individuals. Some of them were my close friends. I think in looking at it, I think it was helpful, both for the administration and for the faculty involved, to have me, not just me as a person, but sort of this [union leader] position. I think that I could see things happening oftentimes when we would have meetings trying to see where problems were. Oftentimes, I found that the faculty person who was involved would sit in the meeting but wouldn't really hear what was being said. Basically, I was there as an observer and also to maybe add some helpful comments. I guess that I would say the meetings I was involved in were always in the tone of trying to help the person. But I could see that we would come out of a meeting and the person would say, 'thus and so,' and I would say, no, that isn't what they were really saying. I was sometimes a go-between and really felt nobody was my friend. But I could see that the administration was making, you know, great efforts to try to help these people and sometimes they just weren't hearing what was trying to be said to them. I feel that the administration probably did the best job that they could to try to get them to hear. I know that I did, and other people that were involved in the other union offices would sit down with these people and look at the evaluations and try to help them to see where changes need to be made. And as I say, sometimes they were just not willing to admit that there was a problem. We couldn't change their interpretation of what the situation was. I would like to think that it helped both sides. Being the one in the middle, it was one of the worst things that I had ever been through, but I think it made it a little easier for both sides.

Robert: If I could pick up on that, I think that out of the dismissals of several of our instructors came, very clearly, some guidelines for people who are in the classroom. I'm going to be very specific now: number one, some people get in trouble for not following the course syllabus. As a union president, as a faculty member, I have very little sympathy for a person who doesn't follow the course syllabus. I think that that's our job, that's our responsibility. And sometimes when you digress and so on, I think a case like this brings you back to an awareness of what you are doing and where you are going. I think that we have certain responsibilities. We have the responsibility to be up-to-date in what's happening in our field. How we do that is by going back to conferences or by going back to school or by doing something other than the normal teaching. The college has been supportive of travel. I know we appropriate monies and then we distribute them among our faculty. Another possibility would be if we have office hours. I can tell you now that we have ten office hours that are required. In addition, with the fifteen-hour load, it makes for a very full work day. Since we have them—it is a contractual number—then we have to do that. We should be available x number of hours that are on the contract. I think some of the people who were dismissed, it was involved with meeting the requirements of the job, and I think Sue would agree with that. I feel that, as a teacher, these are things as a teacher you should do. On the other side again—and what Sue said is very true—there is this chance for remediation. Dates to submit updated course outlines, or syllabus, or whatever, those are dates that you should follow, because that's in the remediation process. If they are discarded or not adhered to, you are held responsible for that, and I don't know that a union can protect you in that way for not meeting your responsibilities.

Mary Sue: Yes, I think that was a thing, that I could see, that the administration made it very clear what was expected of the people in the remediation, and they had their options to make the needed changes or not. As I said, some of the people were quite defensive and maybe didn't perceive the problems or whatever. But they, in cases I was aware of, knew clearly what was expected of them in remediation.

SUMMARY

Many people believe that teachers won't support administrative evaluation. This is not true. Faculty unions will, in fact, support remediation and, if all else fails, termination, if the process is administered fairly. Being able to remove incompetent teachers is necessary to improve the overall quality in the teaching profession.

There are four elements that are essential in getting faculty to support an administrative evaluation system: (1) trust between faculty and administrators; (2) faculty involvement in development of the evaluation system; (3) both oral and written feedback from supervisors and a chance to respond; and (4) due-process procedures and adequate time to allow one to remediate defects and deficiences.

Providing faculty a chance to participate in developing the evaluation instrument and procedures is a sound management practice. The shared ownership that evolved in one community college was presented by two former union presidents. Enlisting faculty input fosters the trust necessary to ensure the success and acceptance of the evaluation system.

SUGGESTED EXERCISES

1. Develop a team of persons representing faculty and administrators to discuss preparation of an evaluation instrument for a school district.
2. Develop questions that can be used in an open-ended evaluation form. Choose words that will cause the evaluator to carefully observe behavior of an instructor and students during a classroom observation.

4

DEFINING EFFECTIVE TEACHING AND SETTING QUALITY STANDARDS

My role is one of motivator. That role is enhanced by my knowledge of subject matter and a love for what I do. My goal is to share what I know with my students in an energetic manner. I want to touch their lives, to teach them more about the world in which they live and more about themselves as valuable participants in that world.

—*Teresa M. Griffis, Mississippi*
(Master Teacher)

If administrative evaluators are going to be effective in their efforts to appraise the performance of teachers, they must first define what *quality in teaching* is. There is no one source that captures all of the effective characteristics of teachers. They may be best defined within the specific setting where the evaluation will take place—elementary school, junior or senior high school or a community college. They should also be defined by a combination of excellent faculty and supervisors who will be involved in the evaluation process.

Conley (1988) felt that the job of the evaluator is to hold the faculty members to whatever standards they had been involved in developing and had agreed to. He also suggested that the committee that discusses and decides upon the teaching standards for a school should draw upon the research on effective instruction and effective schools. They should, however, not base their standards solely on the research but utilize the expertise of the committee within the school as well. He concluded: "Performance standards, when they are accepted as valid and fair, provide a valuable tool for adding precision to the process of determining a teacher's level of performance" (p. 82). Such behavior expectations are valuable for both the supervisor and the teacher. They provide a clear frame of reference which helps to promote *"maximum growth and improvement"* (emphasis added) for all teachers in the system.

Wheeler et al. (1993) defined *effectiveness* as "an attribute of those schools, teachers, programs, and approaches that meet the needs of students and their society" (p. 12).

GAINING FACULTY SUPPORT WITH CLEAR STANDARDS

Rosenholtz (1985) reported that in a longitudinal study, the faculty who said they were highly dissatisfied about evaluation were those who were unaware of the criteria used to evaluate them. Not knowing what the teaching standards were in their particular institution put faculty at a disadvantage: they didn't know where to direct their energies to improve their teaching.

In the study reviewed by Rosenholtz it was found that those faculty with the greatest satisfaction were often those who were most frequently evaluated. The "vital functions" he found active supervision accomplishing were as follows:

1. It furnishes teachers professional development.
2. It sends a continuous signal to the faculty, administration, and board about the priorities of the school and the importance of everyone's individual contributions toward achieving them.
3. It provides a clear basis for organizational decision making, such as on tenure, promotion, dismissal, and leadership roles.
4. It establishes criteria for knowing when goals have been attained.
5. It informs all who work within the school precisely what constitutes acceptable performance.

It seems that the main message of this study is to emphasize the importance of continuity of commitment and knowledge of standards by all faculty.

IMPROVING QUALITY AND FOSTERING GROWTH WITH EFFECTIVE EVALUATION

In another report, Duke and Stiggins (1986) stated that, done well, "teacher evaluation can lead to improved performance, personal growth, and professional esteem. Done poorly, it can produce anxiety or ennui and drive talented teachers from the profession" (p. 5). These same authors conducted an in-depth study of 30 teachers who had experienced positive growth. The study found that no small part of their success was attributable to effective evaluation. The following summarizes some of the characteristics of effective evaluation that the teachers identified as providing the "keys to growth":

- There is systemwide commitment to the evaluation process by the school board, administration, and teachers.
- Administrators and teachers are full partners in the design and monitoring of the evaluation process.
- Necessary resources—staff, materials, funds, training—are available.
- There is a clear sense of the goal or purpose of the evaluation process.
- Carefully planned procedures for feedback—which is delivered, rich in specific suggestions for change by the individual teacher— are in place.
- Recommended and required evaluation procedures are carried out to the letter.
- Teacher evaluation takes into account the individual teacher's competence, personal expectations, openness to suggestions, orientation to change, subject knowledge and experience.
- Persons responsible for teacher evaluation have credibility, patience, trustworthiness and good supervisory track records as well as the ability to persuade those being evaluated of the need to change.
- Regular review of existing procedures, improvement of the teacher evaluation environment, and upgrading of the evaluators' skills occur on an ongoing basis.

SETTING HIGH STANDARDS

Roueche (1983) said that a good teacher knows how to get students excited about learning. Successful teachers hold high expectations and motivate students to fulfill them:

> You've got to expect a lot, demand a lot, insist upon a lot, or you are likely never to be very successful, in parenting or in teaching. Those standards have to be clear; and, folks, that's not conservative. That is an absolutely essential, time-honored value. If you don't insist upon quality, you will surely achieve mediocrity. (p. 31)

He defined the two parts of the equation that add up to good teaching. The first part of the equation is to provide structure, demand the best, and use tasking. The second part is to nurture and support students as they strive to accomplish the objectives that have been set. He concluded: "the genius in teaching is in our abilities to excite students to want to learn what we have to teach. Expect a lot, demand a lot, and then help them achieve" (p. 34).

Good teachers set high standards for their students and help them to reach or exceed those goals. Good administrators and faculty should, together, set high quality standards for teachers, and use an effective evaluation system to motivate teachers to that level of excellence.

SOME DESCRIPTIONS OF TEACHER EFFECTIVENESS: ELEMENTARY

The development of a "prescription" for successful management of elementary school classrooms was presented by Evertson and Holley (1981). They observed effective teachers on their classroom organization beginning with the first days of a school year and included 16 observations during the year. The classrooms were characterized by: (1) high levels of student cooperation; (2) success; (3) task-involvement; and (4) good achievement gains during the school year.

On the basis of these observations, a manual was developed entitled *Organizing and Managing the Elementary School Classroom* (Evertson et al. 1981). It was pilot-tested and then used with 41 teachers, from grades one through six, in 14 schools. The teachers chosen had taught for two or less years, or they were in their first year at their present school. A group of 23 of these teachers were given the manual before the school year began and were given an orientation workshop. The remaining teachers received the manual later in the year. The results of this study showed the manual to be of significant help in establishing classes with higher levels of (1) student task-engagement; and (2) appropriate behavior.

The manual prescribed the following:

Prescription 1: Readying the classroom

Be certain your classroom space and materials are ready for the beginning of the school year. *Rationale:* The first days of school are crucial to the rest of the year. Advance planning can lead to avoidance of problems which result in "dead time" for students while the teacher searches for misplaced materials, or decides what to do with a late-arriving student, or try to figure out what to do next because your students have finished something in about half the time you thought it would require. (p. 18)

Prescription 2: Planning rules and procedures

Decide before the year begins what behaviors are acceptable or unacceptable in your classroom. Then think about what procedures students must follow in order to participate in class activities, to learn, and to function effectively in a school environment. Develop a list of these rules and procedures. *Rationale:* Children readily accept the idea of having a uniform set of rules and procedures. If no rules and procedures are established, the teacher and the children will waste much of their time getting organized for each activity. (p. 31)

Prescription 3: Consequences

Decide ahead of time the consequences of appropriate and inappropriate behavior in your classroom, and communicate these to your students. Then be sure to follow through consistently when a child behaves appropriately or inappropriately. *Rationale:* If the teacher plans ahead of time what rewards and punishments will be used, and when they will be used, then the teacher will have more confidence in his/her ability to control the classroom. The teacher *must* follow through consistently, using the appropriate rewards and punishments. If someone calls the teacher's bluff, credibility will be lost and forever the teacher will have problems getting adequate cooperation from the students. (pp. 61–62)

Prescription 4: Teaching rules and procedures

Include in your lesson plan the sequence in which rules or procedures will be taught on each day, when and how they will be taught, and when re-learning or practice will occur. Plan to teach those rules and procedures first that are needed first. Teach your rules and procedures systematically. Use (a) explanation; (b) rehearsal; and (c) feedback. *Rationale:* The set of rules and procedures needed to manage a classroom is complex and lengthy. Think of it as a month-long unit of instruction, in which the long range goal is learning "going-to-school" skills. (p. 70)

Prescription 5: Beginning of school activities

Develop activities for the *first few days* of school that will involve the children readily and maintain a whole group focus. *Rationale:* During the first few days of school, your children will begin to form work habits, attitudes, and behavior that will shape the rest of the year. The term "whole group focus" means presenting information and directions to everyone in class at the same time and giving all students the same assignments. (p. 76)

Prescription 6: Strategies for potential problems

Plan strategies to deal with the potential problems which could upset your classroom organization and management. Be especially aware of things which could interfere with your monitoring or otherwise teach students bad habits. *Rationale:* Unexpected problems are especially likely at the beginning of the year, when you have least time for them! The first few weeks are your best chance to establish yourself as an unflustered and competent classroom leader. If you are out of the room, uncertain about how to respond, or involved with paperwork, your students may fall idle or misbehave, and may lose some of their respect for your authority. (p. 92)

Prescription 7: Monitoring

Monitor student behavior closely. Look for:

(a) students who do not follow procedures or do not finish or even start assignments;

(b) violations of rules or other uncooperative or deviant behavior;

(c) appropriate behavior.

Rationale: Careful monitoring helps detect problems before they become critical. Early in the year this monitoring should focus on following of rules and procedures, and comprehension and completion of assignments. Look for student misunderstandings, inability to perform an assignment or procedure, and misbehavior. (p. 104)

Prescription 8: Stopping inappropriate behavior

Stop inappropriate and disruptive behavior quickly; it won't go away by itself. *Rationale:* This establishes your system of rules and procedures as well as your credibility. Inappropriate behavior thrives when ignored. Monitoring is crucial to stopping inappropriate behavior; you can't stop what you don't see. (p. 107)

Prescription 9: Organizing instruction

Organize instruction to provide learning activities at suitable levels for all students in your class. *Rationale:* One of the biggest challenges teachers face is providing instruction at appropriate levels for all their students. One characteristic of effective teachers is their ability to diagnose students' academic needs and adjust instruction accordingly, within *practical* limits. (p. *112*)

Prescription 10: Fostering responsibility

Develop procedures that keep the children responsible for their work. *Rationale:* Early in the school year, the teacher will be arranging learning activities and giving assignments requiring students to produce something. It can be assumed that if some students do not do the work, then their learning or retention will be diminished. A classroom should be *work centered.* Each of the following student accountability facets depend on the teacher for their success:

(a) clarity of overall work requirements;

(b) procedures for communicating assignments and instructions to students;

(c) teacher monitoring of work in progress;

(d) routines for turning in work;

(e) regular academic feedback to students. (pp. 127–28)

Prescription 11: Instructional Clarity

Be clear when you present information and give directions to your students. *Rationale:* Researchers have identified *clarity* as one of the more important parts of effective teaching and classroom management. Clear instruction of academic content helps students succeed and learn. This is a skill which must be acquired and practiced. (p. 132)

Knowing and using the above 11 prescriptions was shown to significantly improve instruction in the 23 out of 41 elementary school classrooms where the teachers received the manual *before* the start of the school year.

An elementary model

Mason (1993) presented some facts about an inner-city elementary school, New York's East Harlem Public School 171, which was very successful in getting its 536 African-American and Hispanic students to perform at an outstanding level. They ranked first in their district in standardized reading scores. Some 77 percent scored above grade level in mathematics, which was also first in the district. In all, they were ranked in the upper 30 percent of New York City elementary schools. The principal, Lorraine Man Skeen, has identified 10 factors that she feels have contributed to the "chemistry" of excellence in teaching at her school over the past 16 years:

- Top-notch school management;
- Excellent classroom management by teachers;
- School-wide discipline;
- Teachers' high expectations of students;
- Willingness to try new ideas, for example: reading nonfiction books, giving sustained silent reading time, allowing students to take reading books home, and focusing on problem-solving in math;
- Teachers devoted to teaching and children;
- Well prepared and detailed lessons;
- Good student-teacher relationships;

- Support from supervisors;
- Communication with parents through monthly report cards and orientation meetings.

Report cards are only required to be sent out three times during the year. This school, however, has found the monthly report to greatly improve communications with parents (pp. 1–4).

What effective teachers do

Brophy and Good (1986) found that students receiving active instruction and work supervision achieved more than students who were trying to work through curriculum materials on their own. Research of Clark and Peterson (1986) showed that much of the active learning and instruction was brought about by teachers who were planning, thinking and making decisions about the best instructional techniques to use. Clark and Peterson saw good teachers adapting their instruction to their students' needs and not following fixed scripts.

In a "synthesis of research on good teaching," Porter and Brophy (1988) described the characteristics of effective instruction:

1. Effective teachers communicate to their students what is expected and why.
2. Effective teachers provide their students with strategies for monitoring and improving their own learning efforts, and with structured opportunities for independent learning activities.
3. Effective teachers not only know the subject matter they intend their students to learn but also the misconceptions their students may bring to the classroom that will interfere with their learning of that subject matter.
4. Effective teachers often use published instructional materials, which usually contribute to instructional quality.

They also found reading to be taught in elementary schools between 30 to 45 percent of the total instructional time. This was much more time than that spent on mathematics, which was in second place (pp. 78–80).

Jantz et al. (1987) showed how professionals are struggling to identify the knowledge needed by elementary school teachers. They suggested that one of the major thrusts of the reform movement should be to "identify the nature and structure of knowledge germane to elementary education, to synthesize this knowledge base, to recognize elementary education as a legitimate field, and to support increased scholarly research within the field" (p. 41).

The impact of effective teaching practices on student achievement

A summary of the research on effective teaching strategies (Gage 1984) found evidence to support the premise behind good teacher evaluation, namely that changing a teacher's behavior and teaching methodology leads to improved instruction:

> We are beginning to have evidence that the correlations betoken casual relationships, so that changing teaching practices *causes* desirable changes in student achievement, attitude, and conduct. And the changes in achievement are substantial, not trivial. Moreover, the changes are brought about not by revolutions in teaching practice or school organization but by relatively straightforward attempts to educate more teachers to do what the more effective teachers have already been observed to be doing. (p. 91)

SOME DESCRIPTIONS OF TEACHER EFFECTIVENESS: JUNIOR HIGH

Evertson and Emmer (1982) found that it is crucial to establish good classroom management at the beginning of the year, for it to be effective. They further found that investing time in planning and decision making before the school year starts will strengthen classroom teaching. In their review of Moskowitz and Hayman's work in 1976, they found that the "best teachers" (1) had a more successful first day; (2) used that time to establish control; (3) exhibited more orienting and climate-setting behavior, and (4) experienced less off-task behavior from students than new teachers. The more effective teachers also monitored pupil behavior before it became disruptive. Evertson and Emmer studied the behaviors of "effective managers" versus "less effective managers" in Mathematics and English classes during the first three weeks of the year. They found that, in contrast to the "less effective managers", the more "effective managers":

1. Describe objectives clearly;
2. Use materials effectively to support instruction;
3. Present information clearly;
4. State desired attitudes/behaviors;
5. Have a high degree of pupil success;
6. Experience less disruptive behavior;
7. Stop disruptive behavior quickly;
8. Give rules or procedures to stop disruptive behavior;
9. Display listening skills;
10. Have a task-oriented focus in the classroom (p. 490).

In reviewing the teacher evaluation narratives of the junior high teachers in this study, it was found that the most effective teachers:

1. Understand students' entering knowledge and skills;
2. Give clear directions;
3. Give frequent academic feedback to students;
4. Command personal credibility, as behavioral and academic authority;
5. Make work requirements clear;
6. Effectively monitor student progress and completion of assignments;
7. Teach procedures and rules well
8. Are consistent with enforcement and follow-through;
9. Leave students with less dead-time;
10. Provide activities with variety, interest, involvement for many students;
11. Establish a norm of productivity and positive task orientation in class;
12. Effectively monitor at the beginning of activities;
13. Have students who successfully comply with activity-task requirements;
14. Have less student initiation of inappropriate contacts with other students;
15. Do not allow unproductive or avoidance behavior to continue more than a few seconds without intervention;
16. Challenge the more able students;
17. Have students out of seat during class less often;
18. Have fewer unsolicited call outs;
19. Do not have as much social talk among students during seatwork or lecture (p. 491).

In comparison to elementary teachers these junior high teachers placed less emphasis on teaching the rules and procedures since junior high students have more school experience. Evertson and Emmer summarize that "the junior high teacher's task is essentially one of communicating expectations clearly, monitoring subsequent behavior for compliance, and providing corrective feedback, rather than providing extensive instruction and rehearsal of correct procedures. At the junior high level, the procedures and behaviors for maintaining student responsibility for work were a more dominant feature of the landscape than in elementary school classrooms" (p. 497). Both elementary and junior high studies of faculty have concluded that the level of preparation before school starts and the early patterns of behavior established will set the tone for the school year.

SOME DESCRIPTIONS OF TEACHER EFFECTIVENESS: COLLEGE

Poole and Dellow (1983) describe the following measures of teacher effectiveness used at North County Community College:

1. Motivating students toward superior achievement within their courses;
2. Generating enthusiasm among and establishing rapport with students;
3. Presenting material in an orderly and preplanned method compatible with the stated objectives of the course. The level and intensity of the instruction should be compatible with course and curriculum objectives;
4. Making maximum use of library resources, audio-visual aids, laboratory equipment, and so on;
5. Using a variety of teaching techniques to achieve the desired objectives;
6. Evaluating student performance adequately and equitably within the framework of the defined grading policy of the college;
7. Keeping course materials, including textbook selection and reference reading lists, up to date;
8. Providing sufficient time to assist students on an individual basis and encouraging students to take advantage of such assistance;
9. Providing instruction in such a way that it is effective to the greatest possible number of people (pp. 20–21).

Centra (1979) warns about the use of persons who are not particularly effective teachers themselves being used to conduct the evaluation. He points out that not much improvement can be expected when such persons are used in the evaluation of faculty. Poor evaluators will not know what to look for in classroom instruction (p. 84).

Teaching strategies for traditional v. nontraditional (adult) students

Keller et al. (1991) surveyed 316 traditional-aged (17–19) and 278 nontraditional-aged (27–65) college students in a small southeastern university. They were asked to complete a questionnaire to identify those items that were considered most effective teaching techniques. Traditional students listed "review before an exam" and "available to students outside of class" as their top choices. Nontraditional students were more interested that the instructors teach "practical applications to real problems" and "show enthusiasm/love for the subject." Keller et al. concluded that instructors, by being aware of the behaviors that seem important to these groups, might do well to adjust their teaching to accommodate the learning needs of each group. The two groups had a number of items on which they were in agreement were similar in their responses.

Interactive teaching

Reich (1983) explained what still excites her about teaching. "I teach *with* students . . . although I am still concerned with content, I also see that if students don't understand it, I am getting through the material only for my benefit." She finds the most exciting phase of teaching to be that "gap between what the teacher teaches and what the student learns . . . that is where the unpredictable transformation takes place, the transformation that means we are human beings, creating and defining our own world, and not objects, passive and defined." She makes the practice of teaching, "the practice of what it means to be human" (p. 36).

Baker et al. (1990) found exemplary teachers to be actively involved in the teacher-learning process:

> We can say without hesitancy that effective teachers are conscious of their critical role in the learning process and their responsibilities and obligations to students. Moreover, we have demonstrated the classroom teacher's cognizance and understanding of student readiness—this factor is crucial to the ability of excellent instructors to perform as situational teachers, altering their teaching style based on student need. (p. 28)

Establishing classroom climate early

The importance of the *first class meeting* was highlighted by Wolcowitz (1982). It is here that instructors fulfill the obligation of telling students what to expect in the course, regarding content and mechanics. The first class also sets the atmosphere for the entire term. The "student-teacher contract" should be made explicit in the opening session through the written course syllabus and/or in statements by the instructor. Wolcowitz suggests that the good instructor uses the first class to:

1. Tell the students as specifically as possible what material will be covered in the course and why;
2. Provide student with a well-constructed syllabus that outlines the major and minor subdivisions, in order to serve as a framework for them in organizing their thoughts about the course;

3. Try to convey enthusiasm about the course material, as well as provide information.

4. Explain the workload (length of the reading list, number and timing of exams and papers, etc.) so students can assess the amount of time involved in the course;

5. Explain how grades will be computed;

6. Tell students how to prepare for class and whether they should come to class if they are not prepared;

7. Establish the standard operating procedures of the class (time class begins; acceptability of asking questions; amount of time to be devoted to lecture, discussion, and so forth).

Wolcowitz sees these opening session points as "defining the atmosphere that the instructor would like to create in the classroom" (pp. 11–14).

He also clearly identifies the need for instructors to learn something about their students. In order to help students learn, a good instructor will find out what prior knowledge and preconceived ideas students are bringing to the class, and what they expect to get out of it. Wolcowitz states that "at the most basic level, instructors should learn the names of their students." He suggests that faculty members should collect some basic information on each of his/her students:

1. The student's year in college.
2. The student's field of concentration.
3. Other courses taken in the field and in related fields.
4. Other courses the student is taking that term.
5. Job experience.
6. Why the student is taking the course (pp. 18–20).

Four key characteristics of "exemplary" teachers

The City Colleges of Chicago, Illinois, posed several questions to 30 of their "exemplary" teachers in a search to define those characteristics that made them effective (Guskey and Easton 1982, pp. 3–4). The following describes the characteristics shared by these teachers:

1. All of them were highly organized, planned carefully, had unambiguous objectives and high expectations for their students. Each class had a clear design:
   (a) an introduction at the beginning;
   (b) a summary at the end; and
   (c) a clear sequence of development in between.

2. All of them emphasized the importance of expressing positive regard for their students:
    (a) Most used some time during their first class session to become familiar with their students and continued to exchange personal information throughout the semester.
    (b) They generally learned their students names very early in the semester and addressed them by name.
3. They had an emphasis on encouraging student participation:
    (a) They consistently asked questions during class to stimulate involvement.
    (b) They also monitored student participation at frequent intervals to gain information as to whether the class was going well or if a change was needed.
4. In addition, they strongly emphasized the importance of providing students with regular feedback and rewarding learning successes.
    (a) Feedback was generally provided through written comments on tests or papers.
    (b) They frequently asked their students to see them after class to discuss learning problems.
    (c) Written comments were also used to praise students' efforts and to make special note of improvements.

Evertson and Holley (1981) suggest there are certain things about teaching dynamics that cannot be picked up by any other evaluation method except in-class observation: classroom climate, rapport, interaction, and functioning of the classroom (p. 90).

Classroom organization

One of the key qualities of effective teachers is that they are highly organized. They know how to plan and present a coherent, cogent lecture. The following "observational guide", which was developed for peer evaluations, describes elements of a good presentation (Diamond et al. 1978):

Organization of the content

1. Logical sequence of topics
2. Pace of the lecture, discussion topics
3. Provision of summaries and synthesis
4. Appropriate use of class time

Instructor's clarity of presentation

1. Definition of new terms, concepts, and principles
2. Relevance of examples
3. Relationship to lab and discussion group assignments

Diamond et al. list in further detail the things that effective teachers do during each of the three main parts of a lecture. This list was also designed as an evaluation tool:

Introductory portion

1. Stated the purpose of the lecture.
2. Presented a brief overview of the lecture content.
3. Stated a problem to be solved or discussed during the lecture.
4. Made explicit the relationship between today's and the previous lecture.

Body of lecture

1. Arranged and discussed the content in a systematic and organized fashion that was made explicit to the students.
2. Asked questions periodically to determine whether too much or too little information was being presented.
3. Presented information at an appropriate level of "abstractness."
4. Presented examples to clarify very abstract and difficult ideas.
5. Explicitly stated the relationships among various ideas in the lecture.
6. Periodically summarized the most important ideas in the lecture.

Conclusion of lecture

1. Summarized the main ideas in the lecture.
2. Solved or otherwise dealt with any problems deliberately raised during the lecture.
3. Related the day's lecture to upcoming presentations.
4. Restated what students were expected to gain from the lecture material.

The use of an introduction, body and conclusion to a lecture presents the evaluator with a clear picture of the instructor's organizational skills. It shows how much pre-classroom preparation time the instructor has invested. Dubrow and Wilkinson (1982) suggest that "all but the most experienced and most accomplished lecturer must come equipped with notes, a detailed outline, and with all major points and transitions between them set out legibly" (p. 29).

Testing students periodically

The testing schedule should be laid out clearly in a teacher's class syllabus when it is distributed the first day of class. Students are better prepared for such testing when they are given a review prior to a test session and a general description of the types of questions. They should also be told how many questions there are and how much each exam weighs in proportion to the total assessment of the class exams. A poor example of testing was offered by Nash (1982):

> A class, in which the professor lectures for the entire semester and evaluates student performance at the end through a paper and exam, holds the student's academic role in suspense for rather a long period of time, and offers almost no acknowledgment of the student in the classroom. Hence if the student's learning evolves, only the student knows this. (p. 79)

Nash goes on to say that "at its worst, it uncovers problems only after it is too late to correct them."

Questioning as a teaching technique

Some skillful discussion leaders are able to use questioning in such an effective manner that they seldom have to lecture, according to Kasulis (1982). The good instructor who has taken the time to find out the students' individual perspectives will be able to guide a discussion merely by calling on the right person at the right time (p. 41). Diamond et al. (1978) listed the following good questioning techniques of a teacher:

1. Asked questions to see what the students knew about the lecture topic.
2. Addressed questions to individual students as well as to the group at large.
3. Used rhetorical questions to gain student's attention.
4. Paused after all questions to allow students time to think of an answer.
5. Encouraged students to answer difficult questions by providing cues or rephrasing.
6. When necessary, asked students to clarify their questions.
7. Asked probing questions if a student's answer was incomplete or superficial.
8. Repeated answers when necessary so the entire class could hear.
9. Received student questions politely and when possible enthusiastically.
10. Refrained from answering questions when unsure of a correct response.
11. Requested that very difficult, time-consuming questions of limited interest be discussed before or after class or during office hours.

These can be used by an evaluator to check on the quality of questioning being used in a classroom presentation.

The instructor's class format, handling of the initial class, knowledge of students and their needs, classroom interaction, lecturing effectiveness, use of testing and questioning, and expectations of students inside and outside the classroom are all elements that can be assessed, and they are worthy of assessment. It is important to include faculty in setting the standards by which these instructional components will be assessed, in order to develop a system of evaluation that is acceptable and valued by administrators, governing boards and faculty.

SUMMARY

Before we can properly evaluate teachers, clear standards for quality teaching are required. Evaluators, in cooperation with faculty, should establish standards which incorporate findings from research on effective teaching. Clear and explicit standards are crucial to gaining support from teachers for the evaluation process.

A good evaluation system clearly communicates the standards to which teachers will be held. Among factors conducive to effective evaluation are: a system-wide commitment to the process; availability of necessary resources; a clear understanding of the goals of evaluation; ample provision for feedback to teachers; scrupulous adherence to evaluation procedures; and well-trained evaluators.

Good teachers set high standards for their students. A good evaluation system holds teachers to a high standard and motivates them to achieve that level of excellence. Rules that effective elementary teachers have been found to use in managing their classrooms include making sure of space and materials for the beginning of the school year; planning ahead what behaviors are unacceptable and what the consequences will be; teaching rules and procedures; encouraging a whole-group focus from the outset; monitoring student behavior and promptly stopping inappropriate behavior; developing clear, organized instruction; and keeping students responsible for their work. Other research, among both elementary and junior high schools, is consonant with these rules, though less emphasis is placed on teaching junior high school students correct procedures, with which they should already be familiar.

In identifying characteristics of effective college teaching, emphasis was placed on such matters as motivating students; establishing rapport; using a variety of techniques; and keeping materials up to date. The first class meeting is important in establishing a climate and informing students. Instructors should encourage student participation; acquire basic information about their students; give each class a clear structure; interact with students through questions; test students regularly; and give students feedback on their progress.

SUGGESTED EXERCISES

1. Break a classroom or other group down into small groups of four to seven persons. First, have them define ten to twelve teaching qualities they feel most important in providing for excellence in teaching. Second, have them prioritize these qualities.
2. Combine the teaching qualities reported by each group into a single taxonomy of *effective teaching*. Have each person discuss the one teaching quality that is considered the most important to the person presenting.

5

DEFINING EFFECTIVE EVALUATORS AND DEVELOPING THE EVALUATION PROCESS

There are several elements that must be put together if an administrative evaluation of faculty program is to be successful. Governing board involvement, chief administrator (superintendent or college president) leadership, faculty support, well trained administrative evaluators, and a well defined process are all interrelated in the success of any evaluation system. The evaluator has a key role in quality control. The quality of the institution depends upon the effectiveness of the evaluator and how well he or she carries out the evaluation process.

In their *Teacher Evaluation Glossary,* Wheeler et al. (1993) describe the evaluator as follows:

> *Evaluator:* In a system of teacher evaluation, the evaluator is the person who assembles information collected about a teacher, analyzes it, makes judgments as to whether that teacher's overall performance level meets the pre-specified standards, prepares a summary report, writes recommendations, and may or may not provide feedback to the teacher, directly or through another person. In general, the evaluator is the person who determines the *overall* merit, value, or worth of the evaluee. The term also applies more generally to those supplying sub-evaluations on particular dimensions (e.g., knowledge of subject matter) that are assembled by the overall evaluator. (p. 13)

The need for a well prepared administrative team of individuals to conduct in-class observations and evaluation of other aspects of a teacher's work is essential. The support of the court system for quality evaluation efforts is also a critical component to the overall success of evaluators. The courts have been found to support evaluation efforts when poor instruction is properly documented and legal procedural guidelines are followed.

There are any number of researchers who concur that, even though almost every school district has some form of evaluation for teachers, the carrying out of that process is "ritualistic and largely a waste of time" (McLaughlin 1990). Most teacher evaluation practices are not improving accountability or making improvements in the educational practices of teachers (p. 403).

The exceptions appear to be those which held administrators accountable for quality evaluation efforts. Moraga and Mountain View-Los Altos central office administrators review evaluation reports filed by their other administrators and hold them accountable for the quality of their observation reports. This adds reinforcement and a seriousness to the process for those school districts willing to hold their administrators accountable for quality evaluation (p. 403).

Wise et al. (1986) found several positive outcomes from evaluation. The outcomes were identified in a study of 32 secondary school districts that had faculty evaluation plans:

1. Most respondents pointed to improved teacher-administrator communication and increased teacher awareness of instructional goals and classroom practices. The researchers concluded that an evaluation reportedly "gives teachers an increased sense of pride and professionalism and motivates them to improve classroom practices.
2. Many respondents reported that evaluation had played a major role in "counseling out" tenured teachers shown to be ill-suited for teaching.
3. Other positive outcomes included improved classroom instruction, gains in student achievement, more funds allocated for staff development, and increased public confidence in the schools.

As one administrator stated, "Teacher evaluation is one of the most powerful ways to impact instruction."

SOME DESCRIPTIONS OF EVALUTOR EFFECTIVENESS

Bridges (1990) identifies the special knowledge and skills that an evaluator needs to possess if he or she is to become an effective administrator in the evaluation process:

1. The ability to describe and analyze what is happening in a teacher's classroom.
2. The ability to provide an unbiased rating of a teacher's performance.
3. The ability to diagnose the cause(s) for a teacher's poor performance.
4. The ability to prescribe remediation that is appropriate to the teacher's classroom deficiencies.
5. The ability to conduct conferences with teachers regarding their instructional performance.

6. The ability to document matters related to 1 through 5.
7. Knowledge of the legal bases for evaluating and dismissing incompetent teachers (p. 41).

He found these items seldom emphasized in the programs in the universities that are responsible for preparing administrators for their roles.

Wise, et al., (1985) believe that "the judgment of excellence in teaching . . . must be based on superior standards of practice. Thus, the evaluator must have a high level of expertise to judge excellence" (p. 93).

They also found, however, that many teacher evaluation processes focus only on assessment of the minimum criteria. They describe "a nondisruptive classroom" as the absolute minimum requirement that can be accepted in teaching (p. 93). The mastery of subject matter and a variety of teaching methods are also necessary. They point out that unless these three criteria are met, the evaluator should not certify the teacher as acceptable.

An effective evaluator can motivate teachers to change and improve their instruction. Of course, the more open to change the teacher is, the more successful the evaluator will be. In a study by Stiggins and Duke (1988) several teacher characteristics were found that could be directly linked to the receptivity teachers would have to suggestions for improvement (p. 94):

1. Strong professional expectations;
2. A positive orientation to risk taking;
3. Openness to change;
4. Willingness to experiment in class;
5. Openness to criticism;
6. Strong knowledge of technical aspects of teaching;
7. Strong knowledge of subject matter; and
8. Some positive prior experience with teacher evaluation.

They also identified those characteristics *evaluators* should possess to be successful motivators of teacher change and growth:

1. Credibility as a source of feedback;
2. A helper relationship to teacher;
3. Trustworthiness;
4. A nonthreatening interpersonal manner;
5. Patience;
6. Flexibility;
7. Strong knowledge of the technical aspects of teaching;

8. Capacity to model suggestions;
9. Familiarity with teacher's classroom students;
10. Teaching experience;
11. Useful suggestions;
12. Persuasiveness of rationale for improvement (pp. 94–95).

The faculty leaders in Chapter 2 talked about the need for high-quality, credible evaluators and for a process which provides feedback and a chance to express disagreement when necessary. They also discussed how an evaluation system can be perceived favorably, as a means of improving instruction or negatively, as a tool to "get someone." The perception of the system as a whole depends heavily on the quality of the evaluators. Stiggins and Duke cite six evaluator characteristics in a Teacher Evaluation Profile Questionnaire that were most highly correlated with teachers' ratings of an evaluation system's quality and impact:

1. *Credibility* of evaluator as a source of feedback ($r = .65$);
2. *Quality* of ideas contained in the feedback ($r = .59$);
3. *Depth* of information contained in the feedback ($r = .58$);
4. *Persuasiveness* of evaluator's rationale for improvement ($r = .58$);
5. *Usefulness* of evaluator's suggestion ($r = .57$);
6. *Trustworthiness* of evaluation ($r = .56$).

Other items relating directly to the evaluator were capacity to model suggestions, and technical knowledge of teaching (pp. 106–11).

Leas and Rodriguez (1987) hypothesized several characteristics of college deans that they felt would give good predictive measures of *ineffectiveness*. These are reverse competency traits to those documented as applying to effective managers and leaders:

1. Ineffective deans are poor communicators who are unable to listen effectively or assert themselves fairly.
2. Ineffective deans are closed, impersonal, and unattuned to the social nature of their jobs.
3. Ineffective deans are less conscientious regarding follow-up actions, are less than honest, and are often unwilling to support their faculty.
4. Ineffective deans are easily angered and are more prone to seek retribution.
5. Ineffective deans will be threatened by differences and be less objective about human situations.
6. Ineffective deans will be unsure and uncomfortable with the politics of their positions.

If these factors are turned around, Leas and Rodriguez suggest they can be used as criteria in developing a very positive performance evaluation for deans (pp. 97–101).

DEVELOPING CREDIBLE EVIDENCE

Administrators need an evaluation system that is not only fair but is the source of credible evidence, in cases where remediation or termination is sought. As a case goes forward on appeal from a principal or dean to a superintendent, college president, governing board, arbitrator or to court, it must be able to withstand close scrutiny at each level. Bridges (1990) stressed the need for such credible evidence:

> To justify its decision, the administration must be able to establish through its written records that a pattern of poor performance exists in relation to the district's criteria for evaluating teachers. Because there are no clear-cut standards or yardsticks for determining whether a teacher is meeting a particular criterion, administrators must accumulate numerous examples of the teacher's shortcomings and use these specific instances to verify that there is a pattern of unsatisfactory performances. (p. 154)

Bridges also cited the case of *Board of Education v. Ingels* in which an appellate court judge noted, "Proof of momentary lapses in discipline or a single day's lesson gone awry is not sufficient to show cause for dismissal of a tenured teacher . . . Yet, where brief instances and isolated lapses occur repeatedly, there emerges a pattern of behavior which, if deficient, will support the dismissal of a tenured teacher. Where the school board fails . . . to show the examples of conduct constitute a pattern of deficiency, then dismissal cannot be permitted." It is the pattern of behavior, properly documented, that will assist administration and governing board efforts to improve or remove poor instructors (p. 154).

Rebell (1990) found courts tending to "defer to the administrators' 'expert' judgment and to accept the results of their evaluations without undertaking any independent analysis" (p. 345).

In cases of remediation or termination, the evaluator must follow the proper procedures and collect sufficient documentation to prove incompetency or deficient behavior. Frels & Cooper (1982) and Carey (1981) outlined four tests that the evaluation process must pass:

1. The teacher received copies of the relevant documentation;
2. The documentation was delivered in a timely manner;
3. The teacher was given an opportunity to refute or comment on what the supervisor has written;

4. The persons who have filed written complaints will later testify to their authenticity.

This last item is a key one for an administrator. Administrative evaluators must be ready to stand behind their written statements. It is on this point that use of student evaluations fail. Student evaluations are written and collected to assure student anonymity. There is no way to receive testimony or to cross-examine students who have participated in the system.

Strike and Bull (1981) show that, while the Supreme Court has not listed specifically what they expect in due process formal procedures, they did refer to the procedures from *Goldberg v. Kelly* (1970) as providing a fair administrative process when a tenured teacher is terminated:

1. The right to be heard in a meaningful way;
2. Appropriate notice and a statement of the reasons for termination;
3. The right to confront and cross-examine witnesses;
4. The opportunity to present evidence and argument;
5. The right to an attorney;
6. A decision resting on legal rules and the evidence produced at the hearing;
7. A statement by the decision maker of the reasons for the decision and the evidence on which it is based;
8. A record of the hearing (p. 314).

There is a strong burden of proof on the administrators to prove incompetence in a tenured faculty member's termination.

Piele (1981) provided evidence to show that the use of expert testimony has become advantageous in winning cases in the courts. He also found that those dismissals overturned in the courts usually lack defensible data based upon administrators' evaluations of performance (p. 69).

COURT SUPPORT

It is important for administrators and governing boards to know that the courts have been very supportive of their efforts to dismiss incompetent faculty. Lovain (1983–84) found that "almost all recent challenges by tenured faculty to their dismissals for stated cause have been rejected by the courts, despite heightened legal protections of tenure" (p. 419). Court support is only possible, however, if substantial evidence has been provided as a result of the evaluation process. In *Saunders v. Reorganized School District No. 2 of Osage County* (1975) the Missouri Supreme Court upheld the dismissal of a tenured junior college professor for incompetency, inefficiency, and insubordination. They held that the college's charge of inefficiency was, indeed, supported by documented evidence of the plaintiff's manner of teaching in the college (p. 432).

Lovain found that courts support the primary authority of the administrator role on personnel decisions. He cited *New York Institute of Technology v. Commission of Human Rights of City of N.Y.* (1975):

> The management of the university is primarily the responsibility of those equipped with the special skills and sensitivities necessary for so delicate a task. One of the most sensitive functions of the university administration is the appointment, promotion, and retention of the faculty. It is for this reason that the courts, and administrative agencies as well, should only rarely assume academic oversight, except with the greatest caution and restraint, in such sensitive areas as faculty appointment, promotion, and tenure, especially in institutions of higher learning. (p. 433)

Strike and Bull (1981) describe the need for an educational institution's policies to apply to everyone included under them. This is especially true of evaluation. They show how administrators accused of capriciousness in their decision to terminate a particular faculty member can defend themselves in court by demonstrating "(1) that the grounds for this termination are contained in written school policy, (2) that all other teachers were submitted to a similar review, and (3) that other teachers have been terminated for similar evaluation-related shortcomings" (p. 313).

What is observed, recorded, and used in evidence is especially important if the school or college is to be successful in its termination cases. But at the same time, strictly following the procedures and documenting the process provides due-process rights for the teacher involved.

Rebell (1990) cited a Pennsylvania court that applauded the "model" evaluation procedures used in *Rosso v. Board* (1977):

> The evaluations occurred at two levels. At the first level is the principal; if he rates a professional employee unsatisfactory, the matter is referred to the second level, the superintendent, for further evaluation. While a teacher might object to being rated so often in a short period of time by different persons, such a procedure is clearly in the employee's best interest since it brings into the evaluation different viewpoints, thereby lessening the influence personal bias and prejudice with respect to teaching methods can have. We are particularly impressed with the ratings . . . [on] what was going on in the classroom at five minute intervals. This method of evaluation has

given us the best picture of the learning atmosphere in a classroom that we have seen to date in an anecdotal record. (p. 345)

The court, impressed with the two levels of evaluation, also liked the fact that the evaluations were conducted over a two-year period.

TRAINING FOR ADMINISTRATORS

How important is training for administrators in this sensitive area of teacher evaluation? In a study by Andrews and Licata (1990) only 28 percent of faculty leaders reported evaluation results being shared with faculty members and plans for improvement being developed. However, 61.3 percent thought that the number one purpose of evaluation should be "individual faculty development". Not surprisingly, only 27 percent felt evaluation in their college was "very effective" or "effective."

Hammons and Wallace (1977) found administrators' strongest training needs to be (pp. 62–66):

1. Evaluation of instructor (73 percent);
2. Techniques of motivating faculty/staff (72 percent);
3. Conducting performance appraisals (66 percent);
4. The law and higher education (62 percent).

Until recent years little was published to assist administrators in learning about administrative evaluation of faculty, such as what to look for during classroom observation, and how to present positive and negative outcomes. Many administrative groups this author has encountered during the past several years ask where they can gain experience and training in effective classroom observation techniques. Senior university researchers and evaluation practitioners have conspicuously failed to develop helpful models.

McLaughlin (1990) cited research that consistently points to the need for evaluators to be properly trained for the job of evaluating faculty. They must know legal procedures and be trained in: (1) observation; (2) recording classroom activities; and (3) conducting pre- and post-evaluation conferences with teachers. They must also learn to carry out follow-up evaluation activities, when called for in an evaluation, to determine if progress is being made (p. 408).

One means of enlisting faculty support in the development and administration of the evaluation process is to allow them to participate in training as well. Kauchak et al. (1985) feel that faculty involved in such joint training benefit from the symbolic purpose and gain an appreciation of evaluation as a shared responsibility. They learn that they have an important role rather than viewing evaluation as something imposed upon them.

DEVELOPING A PROCESS

Every school that wants improved instruction as an outcome must develop an effective administrative evaluation process. The following example of an evaluation process (Table 4) is presented with these assumptions:

1. An agreement upon a process has been reached among the faculty, administration, and governing board;
2. The main intended outcome is an improvement in teaching;
3. Evaluators who formerly taught or presently teach and are respected for their instructional expertise will conduct the evaluations;
4. Faculty have the opportunity to discuss the written in-class evaluations;
5. Faculty have the chance to disagree both orally and in writing;
6. The opportunity for remediation, if necessary, is available;
7. Recognition for outstanding teaching performances is another expected outcome.

Table 4 presents a flow chart of the evaluation process.

Unannounced classroom visits

This evaluation process assumes that classroom visits will take place unannounced. In many presentations this author has been involved with, this practice has raised questions and elicited different responses from both faculty and administrators. The process of evaluation in a school or college should start with the premise that *faculty will be prepared to teach for every class period.* A supervisor should, therefore, feel free to observe at any time during the year.

There may be times, on the other hand, when a scheduled visit would be appropriate, for instance, to give a faculty member an opportunity to try out a certain method of teaching or some other jointly planned teaching technique. It may be most appropriate when a prior visit has found some deficiencies in the faculty member's teaching.

Meeting with the faculty member

The classroom visit needs to be written up in narrative form. This will provide the basis for the meeting with the teacher. Faculty want and

Faculty Evaluation Flow Chart

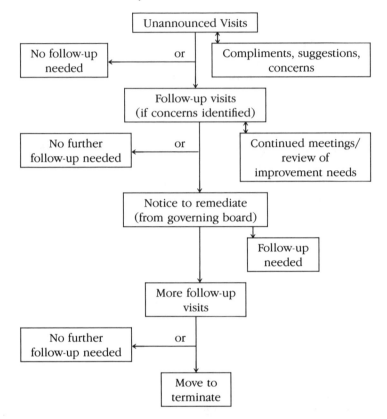

expect a meeting in a reasonably short time following the classroom visit. The anxiety level of the teacher will vary by experience, competence, emotional make-up, and so forth. This meeting might well take place immediately after the visit, later in the same day, the next day, or within a three- to five-day period. Most faculty respect evaluators who give quick feedback.

The evaluator and faculty member should review the various components of the evaluation form. The teacher should be allowed to explain how he or she felt about the visit, what was expected to be accomplished on that date, and how the faculty member felt the class went. The supervisor needs to give an overall impression of the class and go over those strengths and weaknesses that were observed. The faculty member should be encouraged to respond, agree or disagree, and clarify. There should be *compliments, suggestions,* and *concerns* verbalized where appropriate.

What is generally found in research by both union leaders and administrators is that an institution can expect that somewhere around 10 percent of all evaluations will be negative. In schools that have been carrying out effective evaluations for some time the percentage will be much smaller; those schools just beginning effective evaluation practices may find the percentage to be somewhat higher.

Most of the evaluations should be positive and should turn out to be an emotional lift for both the instructor and supervisor. It is an opportunity to give a large number of faculty their due praise for the job they are doing both in and out of the classroom. Whenever there is quality teaching, it is of utmost importance to recognize it. Praise will do as much or more to improve morale and improve instruction within a school as will suggestions for improvement. It will be very difficult for a poor instructor to sit in the faculty lounge and complain about how bad the faculty evaluation system and supervisor are when 90 percent of the faculty in the room have been evaluated positively.

Follow-up visits

It may be necessary to conduct follow-up visits to those faculty for whom recommendations for changes were made in their previous evaluation session. If the faculty member is willing to work on changing, the follow-up visits, written reports and verbal sessions become most important. If the faculty member will not change, more documentation is necessary to support remediation efforts, and the faculty member must be made aware of the serious state he or she is in. Progressive remediation will be necessary on those defects and deficiencies noted in the teaching where changes were not made. It is also necessary to document (with written reports) the meetings that are held to go over the written evaluations. These meeting notes are important in impressing on the teacher that the evaluator expects the outlined changes to be made and that both the evaluation and follow-up session were used to review and document the need for such changes.

Remediation

Remedial action may be prescribed by the supervisor(s) and involve the instructor in some of the following types of activities: (1) developing daily course outlines; (2) publishing and disseminating daily course objectives to students; (3) disseminating course requirements and grading system to students; (4) visiting other teachers' classes; (5) consulting other professionals in the field within the same school or at other elementary or secondary schools, or colleges; (6) doing course work or readings in methods of teaching or psychology of learning; (7) participating in professional workshops or meetings; (8) improving testing and grading practices; (9) providing written daily objectives and methods of instruction; (10) improving supervision of laboratory students and/or maintaining equipment and supplies; (11) keeping current on articulation matters with other faculty, schools, or colleges; (12) updating the syllabus; and (13) attending meetings as required.

The documentation from the follow-up classroom evaluations and meetings become the basis for a formal *notice to remediate,* which the procedures may require be obtained from the governing board. Evaluators must first provide a case showing "lack of improvement." It must be supported by the superintendent of the school or president of the college. These are the persons who must seek the formal remediation notice from the governing boards.

Follow-up evaluations can be carried out more frequently for those faculty who have deficiencies in their teaching. Once a pattern is reported and not improved through the series of documented follow-up evaluations and meetings, further due process action will be necessary. This action might include the above mentioned board action, arbitration and/or appeal to the court system.

Tenured or non-tenured processes

Andrews and Licata (1991) found that most faculty and administrators feel the evaluation process should be the same for both tenured and non-tenured faculty. It is expected, however, that non-tenured faculty will be evaluated several times a year during their *probationary* years. Tenured faculty, unless documented for deficiencies, need not be evaluated more than two or three times during a five-year period.

ADMINISTRATIVE STRESS AS AN OUTCOME

The system of administrative evaluation necessarily places administrators in a position that may create stress. This may be largely avoided in those school systems that do not utilize in-class observations and face-to-face conferences with faculty. Andrews (1988c) listed several situations that will, without doubt, cause anxiety and stress on the part of the administrator:

1. Writing negative reviews;
2. Meeting the teacher face-to-face to review the negative evaluation report;
3. Follow-up meetings to discuss progress or lack of progress;
4. Making the decision that not enough progress is being made to remediate the problems;
5. Going to the president (or superintendent) and board of trustees to support the need for a formal *notice to remedy* from the board;
6. Discussing the notice to remedy with the faculty member after board action is approved;
7. Continuation of several evaluations of in-class and other job responsibilities;
8. Having union and/or faculty association personnel involved in the case;
9. Feeling some negative response from other faculty members in the school who may not fully know the facts of the case;
10. Making a final determination to move toward termination of the faculty member if sufficient progress is not forthcoming (p. 63).

SUMMARY

Evaluators have a key role in the success of an evaluation system. The system's effectiveness depends on the quality of the evaluators. Many administrators, however, lack training in how to conduct evaluations and motivate their staff. Universities should take the lead in modeling and teaching these skills in educational degree programs. Teacher evaluation is one of the most powerful tools for improving instruction. Effective evaluation by high-quality evaluators will improved teacher-administrator communication, motivate teachers to improve classroom practices, assist in the counseling out of incompetent teachers, and ultimately improve student achievement.

Effective evaluators must, first of all, be well educated and experienced in the pedagogy and methodologies of teaching. This is essential if the evaluator is to gain the respect of faculty. Second, effective evaluators must have good observation skills and be able to objectively document what they observe. The evaluator's credibility and trustworthiness are dependent upon careful observation and unbiased feedback. Third, effective evaluators must be open, personable, and persuasive in order to assist those faculty who need help in developing themselves into top quality classroom teachers.

Credible evidence must be developed in cases of remediation or termination. The burden of proof is on the administration to show incompetence in the termination of tenured faculty. The courts, however, have been supportive of the administration in those cases that have been properly documented and in which due-process procedures were followed.

An effective evaluation system requires a well-defined process. The process outlined in this chapter assumes the use of unannounced classroom visits. Although some faculty and administrators are opposed to this practice, it motivates the teacher always to be prepared for every class. The evaluator should carefully document all classroom visits and follow-up meetings with the faculty member. The teacher should receive prompt feedback and have an opportunity to respond. On average, an institution can expect that only about 10 percent of evaluations will be negative. If evaluation efforts find that those faculty who are not working at a quality level will not, or cannot improve, remediation should be initiated. It is the responsibility of the school superintendent or college president to request a "notice to remediate" from the governing board. The evaluation process is an opportunity to give recognition to those teachers who are doing well in their teaching. Recognition is a major motivator and is one of the strongest tools that the evaluator can use to change teacher behavior. The administrative evaluation process necessarily puts the administrator in potentially stressful situations. However, faculty evaluation by effective administrative evaluators can do much to achieve the improved instruction and quality in teaching that everyone is clamoring for.

SUGGESTED EXERCISES

1. Discuss those characteristics that quality teachers expect from a supervisor who will conduct in-class and other job responsibility evaluations.
2. Define some ways an evaluator can gain quality experiences in evaluating faculty.

6

CONVERTING QUALITY STANDARDS INTO AN EVALUATION TOOL

If the outcomes of the evaluation process are to include improved instruction, formative development, a basis for recognition, tenure decision, remediation, and termination, there is a great deal to consider when devising the system. The quality of these outcomes depends upon the data gathered in the evaluation process. The evaluation form, therefore, is a critical component of the system. A well-designed evaluation tool will assist in the objective and informed assessment of teacher performance against the agreed upon standards of quality teaching. How does one take a description of quality teaching techniques and outcomes and convert them into an evaluation form?

FROM DEFINITION TO MEASURABLE OBSERVATION

Having faculty and supervisors agree on what is considered outstanding teaching is the first major step in developing an evaluation instrument. Faculty, administrators, and governing boards must set the highest *quality standards* for classroom teachers in their institutions. Why would a school look for less than the very best instructional techniques and outcomes that can be obtained from each teaching member of the staff? Chapter 4 described some characteristics of effective teachers, and successful teaching methodologies that were considered important identifiers of quality in teaching. This chapter focuses on how faculty and administrative groups can work together to convert quality teaching characteristics into a workable evaluation form. If it has been determined that good teaching requires a faculty member to "be prepared for every class period," then all faculty within that institution should be evaluated against that standard. If learning the names of students and their interests is considered an important motivator in the learning process, then it also should be an evaluation criterion. In short, the qualities of excellence in teaching as defined by teachers, administrators, and available research becomes the measuring stick for the evaluation process. It provides the substance from which the evaluation instrument should be developed.

The sample evaluation questions presented in this chapter are open-ended and require narrative responses by the administrator(s) making the in-class and out-of-class judgments on the quality of teaching observed. Each of the standards of teacher effectiveness listed below are converted to an evaluation question. Each question is followed by sample responses to illustrate how an evaluator might write clearly stated observations that reflect the quality or lack of quality observed.

One measure of teacher effectiveness outlined by Poole and Dellow (1983) was that of "presenting material in an orderly and preplanned method compatible with the stated objectives of the course" (p. 20). A high quality expectation is that a teacher should be totally prepared for each and every class that is taught. Converting this to an evaluation form question can be accomplished as follows:

1. What evidence is there that the instructor is or is not prepared for this class?

A *quality observation:*

The lecture was on the admission procedures for nursing homes. The topic was covered with a good blend of the instructor presenting new material and students contributing their knowledge and clinical experience to the discussion. She was prepared for this class.

A *non-quality observation:*

The instructor was not prepared for this class session. He announced the wrong date for the final exam (corrected by a student), spent the full hour attempting to review the previous exam (only reviewed 8 of 15 questions), offered no new course content, plans to repeat the same test in two days and left no time to review for the final exam two class meetings from now.

Guskey and Easton (1982) found quality teachers to be highly organized and to have high expectations for their students. Converting this into a question one might ask:

2. Is there evidence that there is appropriate homework, class participation, and other expectations of the students?

A quality observation:

The instructor's course outline includes a specific schedule of outside assignments (both reading and written exercises) and class discussions. Students ought not to have difficulty determining due dates and other responsibilities.

A non-quality observation:

There was no evidence of these things. The instructor holds absolutely no clear expectations of his students, and he has no organization.

In terms of utilizing good teaching techniques and presenting a positive learning environment the question might be stated:

3. Does the instructor use good teaching techniques and provide a good learning environment?

A quality observation:

The instructor uses the discussion method with this class, which requires extensive student participation and student-instructor inter-action. This provides an excellent learning environment.

A non-quality observation:

The instructor did not establish a good learning environment during this class period. There was little interaction or involvement of students in the learning.

Knowledge of the subject matter was mentioned in several faculty descriptions of quality teaching. It is the basis for all teaching:

4. Does the instructor demonstrate an *adequate knowledge* of the subject, activity, or skill?

A quality observation:

Yes, it is obvious that the instructor is knowledgeable about the teaching of nursing aide material. Her actual experience in the field greatly contributes to her knowledge base in the course content.

A non-quality observation:

The knowledge of the subject gets completely lost in the lack of structure, lack of checking student understanding, and almost total lack of lecture and testing.

The preparing of a logical sequence of topics in order to cover the course syllabus is most important. The following two questions deal with the course syllabus. In question 5, a quality expectation is that the instructor is on schedule or very nearly on schedule with the student course outline, syllabus, or lesson plan previously developed:

5. Is the discussion or activity germane to the course syllabus?

A quality observation:

The topics covered today—death and dying, patient care, and admission and discharge procedures at a health care facility—are definitely topics to be covered on this date in the student course outline.

A non-quality observation:

The instructor was asked by this reviewer where the topic from the exam fit into the course outline. He was unable to find it on the outline. He suggested it might be on another outline (which he was unable to produce).

In question 6, the expectation is that the teacher will complete the course material. This is essential for any class that is a prerequisite for other courses in the students' curriculum. It is also important to those high schools and community colleges which are preparing students for the next articulated level of their program.

6. What evidence is there that the course syllabus will be completed as required?

A quality observation:

The instructor is right on target to complete the content for this course. Her student course outline is an excellent guide.

A non-quality observation:

Absolutely none. The test material discussed was related closest to things which should have been covered five weeks ago at the mid-term of the class, according to the student course outline.

Nash (1982) suggested that testing should be laid out clearly in a teacher's class syllabus when it is distributed the first day of class. He also looked for testing to be used at key points throughout the course (p. 84). An expectation is that evaluation of student learning is done early in the semester or session and that student feedback is given often enough to measure learning and to adjust the teaching to meet student needs.

7. Does the instructor evaluate student progress on a regular basis?

A quality observation:

Quizzes are given periodically and unannounced. Major exams are scheduled on four dates throughout the semester.

A non-quality observation:

No. No testing took place until well into November (class started in August).

Learning students' names early (if classes are small enough) helps to facilitate student participation. Knowing the students, holding high expectations for their preparation prior to each class meeting, giving meaningful homework and checking it, and encouraging collaborative learning within the classroom, are techniques to get students to participate, which has been proven to improve student learning:

8. How has the instructor encouraged student participation in the class?

A quality observation:

In some instances the students would answer the questions as a group. This is definitely a student-oriented instructor. He has a super rapport with his students. He asks questions of both the group and individuals. He also asks for questions from the students.

A non-quality observation:

The instructor did not encourage student participation during this class. I would suggest that the instructor work through some examples of the rules discussed to see if students understand the concepts. This would increase interest, make the learning an active process, and give the instructor an opportunity to evaluate student progress.

Additional questions can be developed from the standards of quality teaching established. They can be used to evaluate both classroom and other job responsibility areas:

9. Is the person able "to get materials across" and to answer student questions clearly?
10. Does the person use appropriate audio-visual, multi-media, or other technology in the classroom?
11. Does the person attend and participate in faculty meetings, division meetings, and school committees?
12. Does the person keep current on the latest developments in his/her field of study?
13. Does the person exhibit a positive working relationship with colleagues and the administration?
14. Does the person keep course syllabi, school and state reports updated and completed on time?

Two sample evaluation forms with open-ended questions are found at the end of this chapter. The first one is suggested for elementary and middle school teachers. The second form is developed to meet the requirements for secondary school and community college evaluation.

TIPS ON DOING EVALUATIONS

Conley and Dixon (1990) suggest some "do's and don't's" in writing evaluations on faculty. These items should enhance the feedback process after the classroom observation has been made:

1. Don't try to write the report the day before the evaluation conference.
2. Don't write all your evaluations at once.
3. Don't expect evaluatees to read and react to the report in the conference.
4. Don't be afraid to change the report as a result of the conference.
5. Don't write in the third person; personalize the report.
6. Do make certain that there is nothing in evaluatees' personnel files related to the evaluation process that they have not seen and/or signed (pp. 12–13).

They also described what you might do differently if you are dealing with a candidate for dismissal from the institution: "Basically, a well-written evaluation report will provide you with the documentation you need if it becomes necessary to pursue dismissal. The act of offering help to a teacher will not be held against you in court" (p. 13). A key point they make, however, is that it will be more effective for evaluators to design the evaluation report for growth and improvement of teaching, as the percentage of incompetent faculty will be very low.

Suggestions and observations by Isenberg (1990) were made about improving ways of appraising teacher effectiveness:

1. Being objective helps make the evaluation process more consistent.
2. The principal is in a unique position to stimulate and motivate staff to achieve maximum performance.
3. An administrator who has a solid foundation in evaluation and appraisal will help his or her staff accomplish their goals.
4. A strong, fair evaluation offers the teacher the opportunity to explore personal educational philosophies and compare them with actual classroom practices (p. 17).

Utilizing fair and consistent evaluators goes a long way toward effecting support and recognition for good teaching efforts. A good evaluation form that allows for clear expression of the evaluator's observations and recommendations is essential for formative development and recognition.

SUMMARY

This chapter takes what was defined as *quality teaching*—including both successful instructional methodologies and desirable personal characteristics—and shows how they can be turned into a faculty evaluation tool. A well-designed evaluation form that measures teachers' performance against the agreed upon standards of excellent teaching should help raise the level of all faculty members, if it is objectively administered and conscientiously followed up. The evaluation form is a critical component of an effective evaluation system. The information gathered and recorded here is often the basis for decisions on merit recognition, tenure, remediation, and even termination.

The questions and sample responses presented in this chapter show what kind of expectations can and should be set for the quality of teaching in any institution. Examples are given of how observations of both high-quality teaching and substandard teaching could be written up. Two sample evaluation forms—for elementary/middle school and for secondary school/community college—are provided at the end of the chapter.

It is essential that the evaluation report be as straightforward and fair as possible. It should not be written in the third person but directly address the teacher about his or her strengths and weaknesses. An evaluator should not wait until the last minute to write up the report but should do it while the evaluation visit is still fresh in his or her mind. Discussion of the evaluation report with the faculty member will be the heart of the evaluation process. The purpose should be to help the teacher grow and improve in their teaching; the evaluator should be open and not afraid to change the report as a result of the conference with the teacher. However, it is also important to make sure that poor instruction is properly documented and its unacceptability communicated to the faculty member, should it become necessary to pursue dismissal.

SUGGESTED EXERCISES

1. Define ways you know if an instructor is prepared to teach a class. What takes place to help you verify your answer?
2. List several ways that students can become involved in active learning within a class.

EVALUATION FORM FOR FACULTY
(Community College or Secondary School)

_____ Tenured _____ Non-Tenured _____ Part-Time

Name of Person Evaluated: _____

Date: _____ Building/Room Number: _____

Class, Lab, Counseling Session Observed: _____

Name of Supervisor Making Evaluation: _____

1. What evidence is there that the person *is* or *is not* prepared for this class or lab?

   COMMENTS:

2. Is there evidence that there is appropriate homework, class participation, and other expectations of the students?

   COMMENTS:

3. Does the person use good teaching techniques and provide a good learning environment?

   COMMENTS:

4. Does the person demonstrate an *adequate knowledge* of the subject, activity, or skill?

   COMMENTS:

5. Is the discussion or activity germane to the *course syllabus?*

   COMMENTS:

6. What evidence is there that the *course syllabus* will be *completed* as required?

   COMMENTS:

7. Does the person evaluate student progress on a regular basis?

   COMMENTS:

8. Was sound use of testing and review techniques used where appropriate?

   COMMENTS:

9. Are grading standards observed to be of a level expected for college?

   COMMENTS:

10. Does the person have a meaningful interaction with students?

    COMMENTS:

11. How has the person encouraged student participation in the class?

    COMMENTS:

12. Is the person able "to get materials across" and to answer student questions clearly?

    COMMENTS:

13. Does the person use appropriate audio-visual materials in the classroom/activity?

COMMENTS:

OTHER PROFESSIONAL RESPONSIBILITIES

1. Does the person maintain attendance records as required by the college and I.C.C.B.?

COMMENTS:

2. Does the person attend and participate in faculty meetings, division meetings, and college committees?

COMMENTS:

3. Does the person maintain required office hours?

COMMENTS:

4. Does the person keep current on the latest developments in his/her field of study?

COMMENTS:

5. Does the person exhibit a positive working relationship with colleagues and the administration?

COMMENTS:

6. Does the person keep course syllabi, college and state reports updated and completed on time?

COMMENTS:

SUMMARY EVALUATION STATEMENTS AND RECOMMENDATIONS FOR IMPROVEMENT:

- -

Signatures of Appropriate Administrator(s) and Instructor

_____   _____
Dean of Instruction/Principal   Division/Department Chairperson

_____   _____
Superintendent   Instructor

86

EVALUATION FORM FOR TEACHERS
(Elementary and Middle School)

_____ Tenured   _____ Non-Tenured

Name of Teacher Evaluated: _____

Date: _____ Building/Room Number: _____

Class Evaluated: _____ Time of Day: _____

Name of Supervisor Making Evaluation: _____

Section I: Planning and Preparation

1. What evidence was there that prior planning was accomplished?

> **COMMENTS:**

2. Was the teacher knowledgable about the material being presented?

> **COMMENTS:**

3. How well did the teacher keep to pre-planned time frames for subjects or activities?

> **COMMENTS:**

4. Describe room organization for teaching effectiveness. Include use of bulletin boards, reading areas, etc.

> **COMMENTS:**

5. What range of activities were presented by the teacher during this observation?

> **COMMENTS:**

6. Describe how well the teacher maintains "time on task."

> **COMMENTS:**

Part II: Teaching Techniques

7. What evidence was there that the teacher communicates clearly with the students?

> **COMMENTS:**

8. What teaching techniques to stimulate student participation were observed?

> **COMMENTS:**

9. What feedback activities or actions to students were utilized?

> **COMMENTS:**

10. What individualized student activities and techniques were utilized?

> **COMMENTS:**

11. How does the teacher relate new ideas and materials to previous or future learning?

> **COMMENTS:**

12. What level of student active participation was observed?

> **COMMENTS:**

13. How were instructional media, audio-visual materials, or computers utilized to enhance in-class learning?

> **COMMENTS:**

Part III: Organization and Management

14. What evidence was there that the teacher has or has not achieved a level of discipline necessary for maximum learning?

> **COMMENTS:**

15. How well does the teacher accept and set goals and move toward class and overall school outcomes?

> **COMMENTS:**

16. What evidence was there that the teacher is effective in correcting inappropriate student behavior?

> **COMMENTS:**

17. How well does the teacher maintain and turn in required planning materials, grades, and other reports?

> **COMMENTS:**

Part IV: Other Responsibilities

18. Discuss how this teacher supports school policies, participates in pertinent school activities, communicates with parents (individual student concerns and parent conferences), selects appropriate books and teaching materials:

COMMENTS:

19. How does the teacher relate to other teachers, supervisors, and other school personnel?

COMMENTS:

20. How does the teacher maintain professional upgrading?

COMMENTS:

Section V: Summary

SUMMARY COMMENTS AND RECOMMENDATIONS FOR IMPROVEMENTS:

- -

Signatures of Appropriate Administrator(s) and Teacher

_____   _____
BUILDING PRINCIPAL   TEACHER

_____
ASSISTANT PRINCIPAL

_____
DISTRICT SUPERINTENDENT

7

IMPLEMENTING THE EVALUATION PROCESS: FROM FORMATIVE TO SUMMATIVE EVALUATION

Can an evaluation system be both formative and summative in nature? This has been a widely debated issue with a number of writers on evaluation. Popham (1988) and Hunter (1988b) see an inherent conflict between formative and summative functions. They argue that defensiveness and self-protective behaviors are brought out by summative evaluation activities, while it is candor, and cooperation that are necessary for staff development.

Wheeler et al. (1993) defined formative and summative evaluation as follows:

> *Formative:* An evaluation conducted primarily for the purpose of professional development, i.e., improving the teacher by identifying that teacher's strengths and weaknesses. Most often done by another teacher (or teachers) or by a supervisor. (p. 14)
>
> *Summative:* An evaluation conducted primarily for the purpose of making personnel decisions about the teacher (e.g., merit pay, reassignment, promotion, dismissal, tenure). Usually done by a senior administrator such as a principal, rather than another teacher or a supervisor. (p. 25)

Assisting teachers to improve their own teaching is the purpose of formative teacher evaluation (Barber 1990). The teacher must be able to admit that his or her teaching may be less than perfect and can be improved through the behavioral changes suggested in the formative evaluation process. Barber finds that the nature of an evaluation system is not inherently either formative or summative but depends upon how one uses the data that is obtained. If the process never deals with judgments, salary, status, tenure, or working conditions, the system can be considered to be formative. If, however, evaluations are used for any of the above stated purposes, then it is a summative system. There is no compromise in his description (pp. 216–17).

Licata and Andrews (1990) argue that both formative and summative results are necessary if an evaluation system is to be effective:

> It is our further belief that one system should be set up and both outcomes should be possible, but not until after significant efforts at formative help are attempted. Furthermore, institutions and evaluation experts must be ready to reckon with the fact that there will occasionally be negative outcomes from any evaluation system, whether it is set up to be formative or otherwise. Theorists who insist on dual systems are not dealing with the reality that those who work in the trenches and administer such evaluation systems are working toward formative evaluation outcomes. Having dual systems ignores the fact that formative attempts may, indeed, end in summative decisions that have to be made. Such evaluation outcomes are part of a continuum rather than separate systems. (p. 48)

They argue further that even the action to bring a faculty member before a governing board for a formal "notice to remedy" is part of the continuum; the remediation process is still an attempt to obtain "formative changes" without having to move for a dismissal. This argument goes against the pure separation that four-year college theorists have promoted.

Wise and Gendler (1990) suggest that an evaluation system's procedures should assume that most teachers, prior to tenure, need evaluation for improvement purposes. In this way, the system will be providing for formative results. They suggest that "management-by-exception" should be used when handling cases of candidates for dismissal (p. 393). Wise, et al. (1984) support procedures which provide for this as an *exception* and which are jointly designed and implemented by both administration and teachers (p. 111).

What follows are two sample evaluation cases: One leads to a recommendation for tenure, the other results in the teacher's resignation—at the board's request. The material for these cases is drawn from this author's files of evaluation cases accumulated over the years. The cases have been changed somewhat to protect confidentiality.

FORMATIVE ASSISTANCE FOR A NON-TENURED TEACHER: A POSITIVE CASE

The following presents the feedback given to a non-tenured faculty member. It identified some early concerns. Three evaluators were involved in assessing the teaching quality of this instructor and making suggestions for improvement, during her first three years:

First evaluation:

1. Be careful about moving through the lecture material too rapidly. Give students a chance to digest the materials and to clarify any misunderstandings.
2. Speak loudly and distinctly. Be careful about lowering your voice too much and sounding like you are mumbling.
3. Try to lessen your dependency on notes, and try not to read from them too much.
4. Spend more time checking with the students to see if they understand the material. Give examples or experiences from your personal work-related activities or readings. Take time to summarize important points after covering a specific topic.
5. Try to relax. Perhaps practicing your lecture at home may help. When you become more relaxed, your lectures will flow more freely.

   Summary: This instructor needs some good solid assistance in learning how to outline her material for a lecture class. She appeared to become as frustrated as her students as she covered a tremendous amount of material. Students were following the lecture by underlining in their textbooks.

Post-evaluation meeting with instructor:

The instructor finds herself becoming very frustrated teaching this course; too much material in a short time. We discussed her need to skim and condense important points in the material, to slow her pace somewhat in lecture, to develop overlays to help guide her lecture and note-taking, and to get the students away from underlining while she lectures. She was very open to suggestions and plans to work on her upcoming lessons in a different way. She will work with her direct supervisor and visit other related classes in order to observe and improve upon her own methodologies, audio-visual support, and lecturing.

First follow-up evaluation notes:

The instructor began the class by mentioning the objectives to be covered for today's class. The instructor appeared nervous, possibly somewhat due to my presence. There was still more dependence on notes than should be necessary.

Two students were involved in the demonstration. This is a good technique to use. The instructor appears to be gaining more confidence in her teaching. She knows her students and appears to relate well with them.

Second follow-up evaluation notes:

During this session the instructor used a brief amount of lecture, carried on discussions with students, continually asked for student responses, brought into the discussion a recent television documentary on the topic, and used transparencies that illustrated main discussion points. The students were attentive and were involved with presentations. Student interest was evident. The instructor illustrated confidence and knowledge of the topics.

Summary: This class was great. You have worked very hard on your teaching techniques, and it is paying off. Keep up this method of teaching.

Third follow-up evaluation notes:

It was a pleasure to observe the vast improvements in teaching techniques this instructor has mastered since her initial semester. The confidence in herself, material presented, and her ability to "teach" are all much stronger.

She calls on her students and expects them to be ready to respond. They take notes, listen carefully and participate. She used notes to guide the material but lectured away from the notes, used the overhead to highlight key points, and paced herself so everyone could keep up with her.

This was a well-taught and well-prepared lecture. Keep up the good work. Your contribution to this program will be felt by all your students as they move through the program.

Fourth follow-up evaluation notes:

Every time I observe this instructor I am impressed with her improvements in teaching techniques. During this session, she did all the good things of teaching:

1. Used excellent transparencies;
2. Involved students in the discussion;
3. Lectured without the direct use of notes;
4. Called upon students by name;
5. Was not "tied" to the podium;
6. Told the students what they were responsible for;
7. Related the topic to live laboratory problems.

I do not think I can help you improve much more. You have taken our suggestions and you have evolved into a good teacher. It is a pleasure working with someone who is willing to take suggestions and then watch this person effectively use those methods. Keep it up.

Last evaluation prior to tenure recommendation:

This instructor has made great strides in her teaching techniques over her non-tenured period. She has been open to suggestions, sought out assistance and turned her inexperience in classroom teaching around to where she is now very effective. Her involvement of students in the lecture has become an outstanding example of her improvement.

The lecture during this visit was well paced, clearly presented, and reviewed through questioning of the students. The positive feedback to the students reinforced their willingness to contribute.

This instructor has used her three non-tenured years to become an excellent instructor who should continue to improve and contribute to her profession and to the college.

Final observation:

The above non-tenured instructor was newly installed as a teacher for the first time immediately after obtaining a master's degree. She had been an excellent student and had not had the opportunity to teach previously. With early intervention by the three administrative evaluators she was able to turn around what may have been a very negative and tragic teaching experience. The first post-evaluation conferences brought out her concerns that she was frustrated, putting in far too many hours and not feeling successful in her lecturing. She was willing, however, to work closely with her direct supervisor over the next few weeks in areas that were targeted for improvement. With an open mind and attitude of wanting to improve, and with continued in-class follow-up evaluation, improvement was identified and reinforced after several weeks. Such positive reinforcement led to continuing improvement and the personal confidence to try out other teaching methodologies. Formative evaluation proved very useful throughout the non-tenure three year period.

FORMATIVE ASSISTANCE: FROM THE FACULTY MEMBER'S SIDE

The following is a follow-up study of the feelings and responses of the non-tenured faculty member receiving formative assistance through the evaluation system. The evaluators' report on this instructor was outlined above. The following is taken from an interview about how the evaluation system personally worked for her as she saw it:

Interviewer: How did the evaluation system assist you?

Teacher: The evaluation system assisted me by making me aware that the student is responsible for part of the teaching-learning process. I had been giving so much information in lecture that the students were not able to take notes and were frustrated.

I learned how to prioritize the material and cut down on the amount given to them. I also learned to use audio-visuals to assist me. I did not even know, prior to the evaluation process, what resources were available to assist me at the college. I also learned what was expected of me. I feel this is an important aspect of the evaluation process. As an instructor, if I don't know what is expected of me I will not be able to do the job which is expected of me.

Interviewer: What did you feel about teaching prior to receiving assistance?

Teacher: I was frustrated, exhausted, and overwhelmed. I was unhappy about the job I was doing, yet, so exhausted from the workload, I could not see the light at the end of the tunnel. I was trying to teach the students too much. As a recent graduate from an M.S. degree (in the field), I was trying to tell them everything I knew. My expectations of the students were too high. I was determined to do a good job but the more I worked the more exhausted I became. I believe this cycle could have led to failure for me without some assistance.

Interviewer: How did you feel when supervisors offered to assist you?

Teacher: I was relieved. I did not do any student teaching or have course work on how to teach in my degree program at the university. My supervisors informed me of their expectations of my work. This gave me guidelines and ideas on how to improve my teaching. I used the ideas and guidelines and now feel good about what I am doing. After recommendations were made, I knew what I needed to do to improve my teaching. I welcomed those recommendations because I was trying to do my very best but . . . I was sinking.

Interviewer: What steps do you remember about how the assistance came about? When did you feel it was starting to make a difference in your teaching?

Teacher: Two of my supervisors met with me after sitting in my classroom. They discussed what they saw as problems and suggested I talk with the director of the program. They also made recommendations on how to improve my teaching, for example, use audio-visuals and have overheads typed; move around, don't stand behind the podium; SMILE! Ask questions, and so forth. I realize most of this is common sense, but I was so exhausted from the extensive preparation I was doing I did not put this together on my own. I needed to hear it from someone else.

My program director explained I was teaching in too much depth. He told me to skim the chapters to find important subject areas and discuss what was important for students to know in class. The students were expected to read the rest. Again, this seems like such common sense now.

Interviewer: What steps did you take to change your teaching and try different strategies and teaching methods?

Teacher: After my supervisors confirmed my feelings that things were not going well I had to change what I was doing. I had lost weight and was exhausted doing it my way. I knew I was capable and decided to change my strategy. After getting some rest, I put to work what my supervisors recommended. I prioritized the main concepts of my lecture on a typed transparency. I tried to lecture on the important aspects of the content. I moved around the room more, became more relaxed as my confidence grew. I was so determined to prove to myself and my supervisors that I could do a good job as an instructor that I would have tried almost anything. My supervisors believed in me. I felt they cared enough to take time to help me and it was up to me to take it from there. I am happy the evaluation system worked for me. Without the assistance I received, I might not be teaching today.

Interviewer: Does the college's evaluation system act as a formative (assisting) system for faculty?

Teacher: I feel the college's evaluation system keeps instructors on their toes. It demands certain expectations from faculty which is important to maintain excellence in education. It is a way to inform faculty of expectations in the educational milieu.

FORMATIVE ASSISTANCE FOR A NON-TENURED TEACHER: A NEGATIVE CASE

The following describes the evaluation of another non-tenured faculty member who had some early concerns brought out through the in-class evaluation of three administrators. The reader will see that, while some improvement is noted in the instructor's work, there was a tendency to drop back in terms of preparation and student involvement.

First evaluation:

I liked your use of notes. I feel a teacher, especially a beginning teacher, is only as good as his or her preparation and organization. A well-planned lecture and one well delivered can only mean a good class, one in which learning will take place.

Suggestions: Why not use the corrected test as a learning device? I have a feeling your students missed, or did not understand, more than just the one question. Why not use prepared visuals on the overhead for both your outline and the diagrams you referred to? Keep your lecture moving and include your students more in the discussion. At times I felt you lost some; at least, they seemed to be a little bored. Examples of the various components you discussed would help.

First follow-up evaluation notes:

From what I observed there was some improvement in both the instructor's advanced preparation for the class as well as his presentation. I encourage him to:

1. Continue to specifically spell out what each student is expected to know and the skills he is expected to develop.
2. Consciously make an effort to ask specific students questions in order to check their understanding. I would suggest that you try to draw all students into the discussion.
3. Summarize as you did by asking questions and referring to the handout.

Second follow-up evaluation notes:

Get your class started on time. Five to six minutes wasted during each one-hour lecture adds up to hours during the semester.

1. Get your students, one way or another, to class on time.
2. The class moved along rather slowly.
3. You have to work at generating enthusiasm.
4. In order to check the students understanding I suggest that you make them more a part of your lecture by asking more questions.

Third follow-up evaluation notes:

Be prepared with an active lecture that takes you away from your overlays and notes. There must be ways to present this material with much more appeal and interest. Student involvement should be actively pursued to assess their learning.

What was important on the overlays? All of it? Parts? I'm not sure after observing the class.

Review of a test is a good learning device. It may have been shortened to focus on those questions that were most misunderstood.

How do the lab assignments relate to where you are in the lecture part of the class? Your assignments would indicate students have no common "lab" work they are involved with.

Based upon the division chairperson's recent complimentary evaluation, I believe we caught you on a less than fully prepared hour. I am interested in another visit in the not too distant future.

Fourth follow-up evaluation notes:

The more involvement and participation you can get from the students, the greater their interest and effort will be for the material presented.

Is time being used efficiently in lecture to cover the necessary material? The lecture only lasted for 20 to 25 minutes.

It appears to me that this instructor is not making that conscious, extra effort to do the best possible job that he can in teaching automotive mechanic courses. To be a truly fine and conscientious teacher, a person must put forth great effort to be well prepared, concerned to know everything possible about his subject, be well organized, work to involve students in the subject material, and present that material in the best possible manner so that the students can understand it.

You should make arrangements with your division chairperson to visit experienced faculty members classes.

Fifth follow-up evaluation notes:

The first part of the class was used by the instructor for review of questions on a test given in the previous week. The review was helpful in clarifying misunderstandings from various questions.

This was a definite improvement over last year's evaluation of the instructor's teaching. He has implemented some teaching techniques in his presentation that were suggested last year. As suggested on previous evaluations, I am still suggesting that the instructor make an effort to sit in on lecture classes taught by senior instructors noted for their teaching ability and effectiveness.

Sixth follow-up evaluation notes:

The instructor appears to be versed in the topic of brakes. His students took notes from the overlays projected on the screen.

The overlays were too wordy and not to the point. The instructor apologized twice that he had not updated the overlay being used and commented they were too wordy. You need to improve your lectures by bringing in some brake material to demonstrate from. Some good overlays with pictures would also clarify and supplement your lecture.

I *do not* see the improvement in your lecture that should be expected.

Seventh follow-up evaluation notes:

Needless to say, I was disappointed in your lecture. Many of my suggestions have already been made in previous evaluations:

1. Be prepared! Have transparencies prepared and ready in advance; bring tools and equipment (models, parts, mock-up, etc.).
2. The class moved too slowly. Try to "speed" things up and make them more interesting. You must motivate your students.
3. Try some new methods in your class.

I don't feel there are any changes from last year. To make improvements you must work at it.

Final observation:

This instructor tendered his resignation, effective May 30, 19XX. Much effort was put forth during the three-year period in trying to assist this instructor to make adequate improvements. He showed some improvement during the second year but relapsed during the third year. The effort necessary to prepare properly was not evident. The instructor was given the option of resigning or being terminated by the board of trustees. He elected resignation.

RECOMMENDATION FOR TENURE

The following is a recommendation prepared for a governing board to award tenure to a community college faculty member. It summarizes the strengths that were highlighted in evaluations during a three-year non-tenure period.

Recommendation from the Division Chair:

During the probationary period this instructor has taught both courses in the art history sequence, as well as studio courses in drawing, design, and visual communication, life drawing, and painting. He has taught in the extension program; the college prison program; and day, evening, and summer sessions. He has also accommodated the increasing number of art students by assuming some overload teaching.

Comments from evaluation reviews:

The following comments taken from written evaluations throughout the last three years attest to the high quality of this instructor's teaching:

1. The instructor presented the material in a clear, well-paced manner. The explanations and descriptions were understandable, and the instructor for most of the class period, interacted well with the students. The students were attentive and followed along well with the instructor in his presentation.
2. There was enough questioning to and by students to maintain an on-going communication and check on students' understanding.
3. This instructor's course in art history, as represented by this class upon this day, exists as a profitable exercise in learning. Learning constitutes the business of this class period. He does not waste his time or his students' time.
4. The instructor's studio class is not an area wherein students' creative juices flow forth in an uncontrolled stream; rather, the outside observer senses that students work carefully under the

influence of proven theories and systems relative to this particular art form.

5. New terminology and concepts are introduced and well explained. The instructor demonstrates enthusiasm in the subject matter, and it is obvious that he enjoys teaching.

6. Good study guides and vocabulary lists are prepared and distributed by the instructor to help guide student study time with the textbook. Overall, this was a well-conducted lecture hour.

Summary:

I would describe the commentary on all thirteen of the evaluation reports of this instructor as noting the continued improvement of his confidence and competence in the classroom and the studio. At this point in a relatively brief teaching career, he has taken command of the nuances of his courses, particularly in terms of organizing the material and presenting it clearly to his students. All activities go forward smoothly and with extreme efficiency. In a word, this instructor does not cheat his students; they receive from him far in excess of what they pay in terms of time and money.

Throughout his probationary period, this instructor has demonstrated a willingness to work with his students, his colleagues, and his division chair to provide strength and growth to the art program. I am confident that the attainment of tenure will allow him to develop more fully and demonstrate the leadership that the program needs to reach even higher levels of stability and success.

I remain hopeful that you, as a board of trustees, will support this recommendation for a tenure appointment.

FORMATIVE TO SUMMATIVE: A TENURED TEACHER'S "NOTICE TO REMEDY"

An administrator may be faced with a tenured faculty member whose performance of teaching and other job responsibilities are evaluated as poor or deficient. When no progress to remediate these deficiencies is observed in follow-up evaluations, the school or college may seek board action for an official "notice to remedy." This is a difficult position to be in for an instructor.

Formative evaluation, as defined by Licata and Andrews (1990), requires efforts on the part of evaluators to offer improvement suggestions and help for both non-tenured and tenured faculty. This comprises efforts up to and including a formal "notice to remedy" for a tenured faculty member by a governing board. An administrator's request to remediate current problems is, in fact, an offer to the faculty member involved to still make the improvements and changes in their teaching and other job responsibilities requested, prior to the administration seeking the formal "notice to remedy" (p. 48). The following is an example of what might be said to a teacher in summarizing the problems that may lead to a "notice to remedy":

> Our meeting in my office on June 2, 19XX, should have clarified the severity of our concerns over your teaching and overall job performance. I have subsequently received the minutes of the advisory committee from April 12, 19XX, where there were strong concerns expressed over the way you teach the particular science course in question.
>
> It should have been made clear to you that the advisory committee presented us with several major concerns regarding your teaching of the course:
>
> 1. You had no communication with these students. While you indicated that this was possibly a very poor group to work with, we have seen them being taught in the other part of the program, and they can be a very responsive group.
> 2. Your inability to produce an updated, meaningful, and completed course syllabus for this course is inexcusable after having over a two-year period in which to prepare it. This was one more vivid example of your lack of preparation and organization.
>
> In your other afternoon science course the following observations were made by the division chairperson and myself:
>
> 1. Students arrived in this class without any thought of taking notes. Note pads were not even brought to the class.
> 2. You gave no review of previous lecture material, asked for little response from the class, and completed the hour with no announced assignment for the next class period.
>
> You told us much of your testing comes from the textbook. I suggested that the students might be better taking the course by correspondence if that is the case, because they do not take notes or appear to need material from your lecture.
>
> You have some very large steps to take in order to show us that you can bring your instruction and related job functions up to the level expected and asked for in several recent evaluations. The pressure for you to dramatically improve in your organization, communications with students, responses to your chairperson's requests for organized and up-to-date materials, and overall teaching perfor-

mance will not be reduced until these performance requirements reach the level of our expectations at this institution.

We will, in the meantime, recommend that the governing board at their June 20, 19XX, meeting formally issue you a letter of remediation for the defects and deficiencies that have been cited to you over the past twelve-month period. The board has been very concerned with sub-par performances and expect faculty here to continue the tradition of high quality instruction. A vote on the "notice to remediate" will be taken in the open session of the board meeting.

The "notice to remedy" is outlined in much more detail in Chapter 11. It should be obvious to the reader that this is a severe step to take in a comprehensive evaluation process. Where does formative evaluation leave off and summative evaluation begin in a case like the one cited? Licata and Andrews (1990) argued that formative evaluation efforts should continue to be made up to a time period that is considered reasonable. If, after several months, progress is not observed and materials are not updated as requested, it becomes imperative that the administrators take a stand. The ripple effect of such a stand will be felt throughout the institution. Other faculty members who may not have taken recommendations for improvement in their own teaching seriously and doubt the effectiveness of the system will have such doubts removed. It will also be an incentive to those faculty, who had been accustomed to just getting by, to work for improvement. The message that quality is expected in all classrooms will become the banner for all of the institution's instructional programs.

There are many persons affected by both good and poor teachers. Wheeler, et al. (1993) described them as *stakeholders:*

> *Stakeholders:* Those individuals who will be significantly affected by the results of teacher evaluation. These include not only teachers and principals, but also other teachers, school and district staff, students, parents, school board members, future employers and fellow citizens, taxpayers, and community members. They are part of the audience for evaluations of teaching, but have more at stake than just potential interest. (p. 24)

The effect each teacher has can be very significant and far-reaching, to a large number of "stakeholders" within and outside of an elementary, junior high, secondary school or community college.

SUMMARY

Evaluation has traditionally been described as having either a formative or summative function. The purpose of formative evaluation is to assist teachers to improve their teaching; summative evaluation is used to make decisions about salary, status, tenure, or dismissal. Some writers argue that there is an inherent conflict between the two functions. Licata and Andrews, however, argue that they are not mutually exclusive, but rather are part of a continuum of formative attempts that may eventually lead to summative decisions.

This chapter presented two case studies that illustrate the use of formative and summative evaluation. Throughout the evaluation period of several years, evaluators observed the teachers' classes and gave suggestions for what and how to improve classroom instruction or out-of-class preparation. Each case had a different outcome. In the first case, significant progress was made by the newly-hired teacher, and she was recommended for tenure at the end of the three-year probationary period. In the second case, the teacher's chronically poor teaching proved to be irremediable, and he was asked to resign. An example of a recommendation for tenure is included in this chapter. Also included is an administrator's request for immediate remedial action, which gives the teacher one last chance to make the required improvements before a formal "notice to remedy" is sought.

SUGGESTED EXERCISES

1. Discuss and explain how defining *quality teaching* and using it as the basis for an evaluation process can improve instruction. How might it assist those faculty who are producing at an average level? What might happen to those who are poor instructors?
2. Why might an administration prefer to "coach out" a faculty member who is not making progress in his or her teaching?

8

RECOGNITION: WHO WANTS IT? WHO NEEDS IT?

As you know, I have just received a merit award which was both a surprise and an honor. What a perfect way this is for the school to say we appreciate what you are doing. Nothing can be more revitalizing for a worker than for your employer to say 'nice job.'

A Faculty Member

The practice of giving special recognition and rewards to faculty for outstanding work has long been neglected in the field of education. Few studies have been conducted to assess what practices have been carried out and to what extent. On the other hand, there is growing evidence that teachers at *all levels of education* feel neglected when it comes to recognizing outstanding teaching and other job responsibilities.

REVITALIZING TEACHERS AND AVOIDING "BURNOUT"

The key word in the above faculty member's reaction to receiving recognition for a job well done is *revitalizing*. In a questionnaire to 31 merit recognition winners in one community college Andrews (1987d) found several who used the word 'revitalize' in expressing their reaction. One teacher commented:

> I believe support from colleagues and supervisors is vital if one is to "revitalize." Encouragement from others adds to one's sense of value to an organization and its members. Often times it is the word of praise or encouragement that is more motivating than financial rewards. (p. 2)

Another response, while not using the word revitalization, does show how recognition can keep teachers motivated and stop them from becoming "burned out":

In the most self-actualized moments, one feels, 'I don't care what others think, I know this is good and I'll continue to give my all.' . . . Many of us can work with that attitude, but only for a period of time. Lack of recognition—emotional, financial, etc.—eventually evokes "burnout" from very talented and conscientious individuals. The small doses of sincere recognition along the way keeps one interested and eager to continue to improve oneself and the institution. (p.2)

This particular instructor was responding to personal merit recognition that was given for the first time after over 20 years of teaching. The college had just recently instituted a recognition system for faculty.

A review of the literature by Frase and Piland (1989) on faculty rewards pointed to the use of such rewards for motivational purposes. They cited studies and articles by Cohen and Brawer (1982), Baker and Prugh (1988), Andrews and Marzano (1983a), and Filan, Okun, and Witter (1986), as centering on the motivational value of faculty rewards (p. 25).

MONEY AS A MOTIVATOR

In his work on the study of merit pay for teachers Deci (1976) came to the conclusion that merit pay as an incentive may be unworkable. Using money as the major incentive in trying to improve teaching is likely to fail no matter how well such a program is designed by the school district. Suggestions he made from his research findings were:

1. Positive feedback can, under certain circumstances, increase intrinsic motivation (one's feeling about his/her own competence and effectiveness);
2. Schools could adopt merit praise plans. Such a plan recognizes that intrinsic satisfactions cannot be manipulated by material rewards, but can be complemented by the right kind of feedback;
3. Superior teachers should be rewarded with various types of praises and recognition. Evaluations should be descriptive and objective rather than judgmental, focusing on what teachers do rather than how one teacher's performance compares with that of another;
4. All teachers should be provided with honest, positive feedback about their accomplishments in the classroom. If this is done properly, it can increase each teacher's sense of satisfaction about the kind of job he or she is doing.

The focus of Deci's suggestions is on the "intrinsic satisfactions" that teachers want. A main sense of satisfaction comes from helping their students to learn. The recognition system he proposes can motivate teachers by appealing to their "intrinsic satisfactions" as opposed to a merit pay system that is driven by the pay increase incentives. (pp. 61–72).

Frase and Piland (1989) found that the altruistic motive "to help others learn" was prevalent at all levels of entry into the teaching profession. They summarized a large number of studies and concluded that "the intrinsic drive to help others learn has repeatedly been shown to be the primary motive" (p. 25). These researchers also pointed out how, even though research results and empirical evidence have consistently pointed to intrinsic incentives as being the most effective motivators for teachers, the 1980s reform movement turned to financial incentives to try to effect change. Career ladders and merit pay were the two largest changes sought, and as Frase and Piland pointed out, "It was predictable that both would fail."

A study by the Educational Research Service (1979) found that approximately 4 percent of the American schools in the study had some form of a merit pay plan. They found that an additional 6 percent had previously tried merit pay plans but had abandoned them.

Myths about merit pay

In a position paper by Dunwell (1986) five myths about merit pay were presented and discussed:

Myth 1: "Teachers favor merit pay."
This statement contrasts with a number of findings in other studies and surveys. Teachers have been found to favor other rewards rather than merit pay.

Myth 2: "Money is a motivator—more money produces more work."
Research studies did not support this. Money was only found to motivate some people in some circumstances, whose salaries were below market value.

Myth 3: "Merit pay will persuade highly qualified people to enter teaching."
There is no research to support this. Teachers do not enter into teaching primarily to make money. On the other hand, money is a "dissatisfier". Many people do leave teaching because of low salaries.

Myth 4: "Merit pay promotes competition, and competition promotes excellence."
The paper asserted that competition will not necessarily promote excellence but cooperation probably will.

Myth 5: "Motivating teachers is a simple matter of offering an extrinsic reward."

The researcher documented that motivational needs vary from one individual to another. Merit pay can actually depress the intrinsic motivation of some teachers.

The NEA on merit pay

In an *NASSP Bulletin* (1986) interview with Mary Futrell, who was at that time president of the National Education Association, Futrell addressed the issues of career ladder and merit pay systems:

> Teachers are rather apprehensive about differentiated staffing plans. They are opposed to merit pay systems, but are seemingly more willing to look at career ladders. Again, I think that implementing a plan like that requires working with teachers.
>
> We oppose merit pay because it has not worked and *is* discriminating. Let's face reality—the teaching profession is similar to other professions. We have some people who do an outstanding job. We have a few who are not doing a good job. The bulk are in the middle. The profession is made up of a solid core of people who are doing a good job. If I am one of those teachers doing a *good* job, are you going to say to me that I don't get a pay raise?
>
> We propose that everybody be given a pay raise so that the teaching profession can compete with other professions. Some people will say, 'What about the people who are not doing a good job?' Let's go back to our discussion of evaluation procedures that enable everyone to grow professionally. For the few who are not doing a good job, you use the summative evaluation to say either you shape up or you ship out. You protect their due-process rights, but if they don't improve, a procedure for removal should be started. (pp. 59–60)

This interview clearly articulated the NEA's stand on merit pay. It also supported the administration in the need to improve instruction and to move toward removal when necessary, as long as the due-process rights of the teachers are respected.

More important motivators than money

In a study on the motivational needs of faculty, Scherer (1983) summarized some research from Teachers College, Columbia University, on why veteran teachers had positive feelings about their teaching jobs. The items they listed, in order of importance, were as follows:

1. Receiving respect;
2. Receiving recognition;
3. Receiving reinforcement;
4. Participating in research studies;

5. Being a member of a teaching team;
6. Earning grants for curriculum development;
7. Being encouraged by principals, parents, colleagues, and students.

The research concluded that merit pay in itself was far from a means to solve problems in education.

MOTIVATIONAL THEORIES

One should be able to conclude, after several decades of developing motivational theories and testing such theories through empirical investigations, that educators would know specifically which rewards reinforce teachers' behavior and instill the desire to continue to improve and become master teachers. This does not appear to be the case in the majority of elementary, middle, or secondary schools and community college districts.

Abraham Maslow and Frederick Herzberg, theorists of the "Human Potential Movement", are often cited in educational and psychological literature. In moving from theory to practice, a major concern of educational leaders is identifying the conditions that will motivate individual teacher's to achieve excellence in instruction. Both Maslow (1954) and Herzberg (1966) perceive motivation as essentially an internally driven force in individuals. Maslow has identified the "need for self-actualization" as the internal drive that one uses to strive to be the best one might become.

Maslow describes a "hierarchy of human needs", which he sees as necessary to understanding human behavior. The basic needs of humans have to be satisfied first before the higher-level needs, such as working toward excellence and self-actualization, can be met. These basic requirements are described as survival needs, which include adequate pay to secure the essentials of living. He sees this as the most primary concern of workers. Once these first-level needs are addressed satisfactorily, the second level, which includes job security and safety can be pursued. The third level includes seeking to establish a congenial work group and having the feeling of being needed. Once satisfied on all three of the above levels, an individual is free to focus on fulfilling the higher-level needs of esteem, recognition, and self-actualization (pp. 105-7).

Herzberg developed his theory around worker motivation at two different levels. His Motivation-Hygiene Theory point to two sets of factors as being paramount in influencing workers' morale. The 'hygiene' factors within a work environment include: (1) pay, (2) working conditions, (3) relations with co-workers, (4) competence of supervisors, and (5) company policies. These can be compared to Maslow's lower-level or basic needs. These must be adequately addressed, according to Herzberg, in order to prevent worker dissatisfaction. Even if these are met, he points out, it may not be enough to unleash a worker to be highly motivated. He addresses this concern with what he refers to as "motivation" factors which also must be satisfied. These factors include: (1) achievement, (2) responsibility or autonomy, (3) recognition, (4) opportunities for advancement, and (5) enjoyable and challenging work assignments (pp. 266). One can see how these later factors relate closely to the higher-level needs in Maslow's theory.

Steinmetz (1979) showed how both theories proposed a *two-stage* approach to motivation: first, adequately satisfying basic levels of human needs which leads to the possibility of freedom; second, fulfilling the higher-level needs that can unleash greater productivity and the striving for excellence.

APPLICATION OF MOTIVATIONAL THEORIES

Moving toward a practical implementation of these two theories, first, one must see if indeed the basic needs of faculty are being met. Questions such as, "Is the salary adequate?" "Does the working environment produce a feeling of trust among teachers, and between teachers and administrators?" and "Are administrators honest and competent?" all need to be addressed and answered. An inventory needs to be taken to see if there are adequate "hygiene" factors in the institution.

Next, there needs to be a means of fostering greater individual motivation towards excellence, self-improvement, and providing a better climate for student productivity. In this case both Maslow and Herzberg identified esteem and recognition as important motivational factors. This places the burden on governing boards and administrators to provide an institutional climate and working conditions that lead teachers to desire to excel and have their higher-level needs met. Educational institutions which provide formal recognition and rewards for excellence in teaching will be creating the right condition for fostering and promoting motivation on the part of their teachers.

DEVELOPING A RECOGNITION SYSTEM

Administrators need to seek the cooperation of faculty in developing a recognition system. Both parties need to discuss and agree upon the major tenants of such a plan within each school system. McMillen (1984) suggested that if a merit recognition system is to work well, first there must be agreement on what constitutes meritorious performance in teaching. Second, there must be a mechanism to appraise what has been agreed upon. It helps if both parties understand that there are these two distinct elements to a system. Agreement needs to be reached on the desired outcomes and the theoretical base of such a plan. The emphasis can then shift to deciding on a reward system that will be acceptable to both parties, and will meet the higher-level needs of esteem and recognition of faculty. Meeting these needs should provide the motivational factors necessary for obtaining and maintaining a high level of teacher performance and student outcomes (p. 27).

Cheshire and Hagenmeyer (1981–82) suggest that a successful recognition system must have the following three elements: First, faculty and administration identification and agreement to what they consider criteria for outstanding job performances. The second component is the development of a fair, objective, and effective system of evaluating the job performances of faculty. The third component is the stipulation of the actual award.

One can see that developing a merit recognition system is no easy task and has several complex features. With such diversity in American educational systems, whether at the elementary, secondary, or community college level, it would be naive to suggest one best system for these schools and colleges. Rather, each institution should perform a close assessment of the "hygiene" factors presently at play within the school or district, adopt an appropriate theory, and apply it in developing a recognition system. It is only after these factors are sorted out that a merit recognition plan will have a chance of success.

PUTTING THE SYSTEM INTO PRACTICE

The recognition of excellence in the teaching profession is a much more complicated process than it seems it should be. Sbaratta (1983) says that encouraging teachers to strive for excellence is "maybe the most critical task," but "rewarding excellence is the trickiest" (p. 27).

Frase et al. (1982b) state that it is crucial to have "competent administrators who are capable of identifying excellent teaching" (p. 266). They also point out that principals are *legally responsible* to carry out the evaluation.

Two institutions that have put merit recognition systems into practice are the Catalina Foothills School District in Tucson, Arizona, and Illinois Valley Community College in Oglesby, Illinois (Frase et al.

1982b; Andrews 1988a). Both systems saw their programs as an alternative to merit pay, by providing a system of evaluation and positive feedback. Both systems also relied heavily on Herzberg's Motivation-Hygiene Theory outlined above.

The 'Program for Excellence' is the Catalina district's reward system for excellent teaching. It draws upon Herzberg in that it tries to identify those factors that motivate teachers to achieve high level of performance. It identifies achievement, recognition for achievement, intrinsic interest in the work, and growth and advancement as needs of its faculty. This system depends upon a reliance and trust that the administrators are competent and capable of identifying excellent teaching within the district. Catalina recognizes its principals as also being legally responsible for the evaluation of instruction (pp. 266–267).

The recognition system at Illinois Valley Community College parallels the Catalina system very closely. It provides for merit recognition of outstanding teaching and overall job responsibilities. It, too, is based upon an evaluation system that is carried out by instructional administrators and that places a strong emphasis on competence in classroom instruction.

Both of these systems, in addition to drawing much of their philosophical basis from Herzberg, also draw from Maslow in recognizing that the lower-level needs of their faculty must be met before launching into a program of recognition. Adequate base pay, professional work environment, and trust between faculty and administration are factors both schools felt had been met prior to the implementation of their recognition programs.

DOES MERIT RECOGNITION WORK? ASK THE FACULTY

Do recognition programs achieve their intended goal of satisfying the higher-level needs of the faculty? Do teachers feel that they will continue to provide quality instruction? Are they motivated to continue to excel? These were some of the questions Frase et al. asked the faculty in the 'Program for Excellence' at the Catalina Foothills School District. Andrews asked similar questions of the faculty who had received merit recognition at Illinois Valley Community College. The results of both surveys are summarized in Table 5 below.

Both groups of teachers overwhelmingly accepted their rewards as the schools had intended, that is, as special recognition for teaching excellence. Both teacher groups also over felt that receiving the rewards motivated them to continue to excel, and that they valued highly the recognition they received. There were a few

TABLE 5

Summary of Faculty Reaction to Recognition for Excellence Reward Programs at Catalina Foothills School District and Illinois Valley Community College

Faculty Responses to Objectives	Catalina Foothills N = 27		Illinois Valley C.C. N = 31	
	YES	NO	YES	NO
1. Teachers receiving awards view the recompense as special recognition for teaching excellence.	24	3	31	0
2. Faculty members who have received the rewards are motivated to continue to excel.	21	6	30	0
3. Teachers receiving awards value highly the recognition they received.	22	5	30	0
4. Faculty receiving awards believe they will continue to receive special recognition if they continue excellent teaching.	19	8	21	8
5. a. The merit recognition system is viewed as an outcome of the faculty evuation at IVCC	—	—	22	7
5. b. Faculty view the evaluation system as 'fair.'	—	—	23	5
6. Is the 'publicized' system the college uses preferred to a secret reward system?	—	—	29	1
7. The college should continue to recognize outstanding faculty performance with a merit recognition system.	—	—	31	0

more skeptics in both groups when asked if they expected the recognition to continue if they continue excellent teaching.

Several additional questions were asked only of the college faculty. Over 75 percent saw the recognition as an outcome of the college's evaluation system of faculty. An even higher percentage checked that they felt the evaluation system was 'fair.' All but one of 30 respondents preferred that the college continue to publicly announce the merit recognition winners. All 31 respondents to the last question said 'yes' to continuing formal recognition of outstanding faculty performance.

Non-monetary rewards as motivators

The Catalina district stipulates that rewards conform to Herzberg's theory. Frase et al. stated that the district expects each recognition to be an experience or reward that the teacher values highly. It should also affect the work content or the "teacher's ability to assist children in the classroom" (p. 267). Herzberg's theory holds that money is not a motivator but rather a 'hygiene' factor (or dissatisfier). It has been with this in mind that the Catalina district has focused on rewards other than merit pay as motivators. Some of the rewards given to teachers have been: (1) attendance at professional conferences held outside the state; (2) computers; and (3) classroom instructional or enrichment materials.

Responses from reward recipients and non-recipients

There was a second-stage evaluation conducted at the Catalina school district which included six of the recipients in the program and six faculty who were not recipients. The following are the five areas looked at (p. 268):

1. *Importance:* Are the rewards valued?
   "Yes," was the reply, and attendance at conferences was highly rated. Money as a reward was the least valued by both the recipients and non-recipients. They both saw it as being a non-professional reward.
2. *Flexibility:* Can the reward be individualized?
   This brought a strong positive response; both groups saw their system as giving adequate flexibility.
3. *Visibility:* Is a secret reward system preferred to a publicized one?
   This brought a mixed response. There was some feeling that the non-recipients would feel hurt, while others felt it was fine to publicize the names.
4. *Frequency:* How often can rewards be given?
   One award was provided an individual in any one school year.
5. *Cost:* How much does the program cost?
   The outlay was considered slight but very beneficial by the district.

The Catalina study concluded that the 'Program for Excellence' did indeed accomplish its goal in recognizing and motivating their best teachers. It also appeared to influence other teachers in the system, as a secondary benefit. A third conclusion was that Herzberg's Motivational-Hygiene Theory provides an adequate foundation for a program designed to reward excellence in teaching.

Faculty mandate for merit recognition

The Illinois Valley Community College rewards start out as a publicly announced award, which includes a plaque and a one time $500 check. Recipients are later selected to attend national master teacher conferences or national meetings in their field. Being honored at a meeting with the board of trustees is additional public recognition. Table 5 showed that the publicized part of the program was preferred to continue by a 29 to 1 vote. Recipients, when asked whether the college should continue to recognize outstanding faculty performance with the merit recognition program, answered with a 31 to 0 "yes" response. With such a mandate one might reasonably conclude that the recognition program was indeed meeting the motivational needs, postulated by Herzberg, of the Illinois Valley faculty.

CASES OF PEER REJECTION

In a few cases it has been reported that recognition for some teachers has resulted in negative reactions from peer teachers and administrators (McCormick 1986). This contrary behavior has been described as an attempt to reject or "punish" the teacher, especially when it comes from the principal or other supervisor. In one case an outstanding teacher who gained national recognition for her ability to encourage children to write was "stunned" by her peers' reaction to her success. She did not receive one positive reaction to her success, even though she had been in the system for 20 years. McCormick concludes: "The message is clear: Do meritorious work and you risk being misused by administrators and ignored by colleagues—or worse" (p. 14). Another teacher reported hearing from a teacher friend: "After a teacher I know was named a finalist in the New York Teacher of the Year program, her colleagues stopped speaking to her."

Another reported case involved a teacher who was asked to give two workshops by the state department of education. The teacher said, "Even the most adversarial administrator will have to be pleased about this. I mean, the state department of education! And it's only 17 miles away, so I'd be crossing no frontiers." After her request for leave was denied, she addressed her concern with the superintendent. She was granted one day of leave—if she paid for the substitute teacher. No one ever offered a "congratulations."

McCormick concluded that it is no wonder we have had mediocrity in our schools because "it is the only road to professional survival" (p. 15). Such examples, although rarely reported, do have a chilling effect on the teaching profession. Administrators must be sensitive to these possible reactions and work to provide an environment that stimulates recognition and growth for all faculty. There is much at stake. Allowing faculty to be thwarted in their growth through lack of attention and rejection by peers and supervisors will stifle the drive for excellence and cause the institution to sink into mediocrity.

THE GROWTH OF MERIT RECOGNITION PROGRAMS

The state of Virginia established $5,000 recognition awards for faculty in both public and private colleges. They are awarded to faculty based upon their "outstanding teaching, research, and public service" (*The Chronicle of Higher Education* 1987). Thirteen faculty received the awards out of 108 who were nominated during the first year. "It's a great award. I feel the many years I've put into this have paid off," stated Daisy B. Campbell, a teacher of English at Southwest Virginia Community College (p. 16).

A major finding in a 1991 study of recognition programs in two-year colleges in the Midwest (Andrews 1993) was a large increase in colleges moving to recognize outstanding faculty. The results of this study were compared to a previous study of the same two-year colleges by Andrews (1987b). A total of 166 of the 278 colleges in the 1991 study reported they had merit recognition programs for faculty. This was an increase of 111 colleges when compared to the 55 total colleges reporting recognition programs in the 1984 study. These numbers represent 60 percent of the colleges as having recognition programs compared to 20.1 percent in the earlier study. Table 6 summarizes the increases in a state-by-state analysis.

The states showing the greatest increases were Illinois (+21), Michigan and Colorado (+11), Wisconsin (+10), Arizona (+8), Minnesota (+7) and Ohio and Missouri (+6). Seventeen of the 19 states in the study reported increases in college faculty recognition programs in 1991 compared to the 1984 study.

How long have merit recognition programs been present in the above community colleges? This was one of the questions raised in the

TABLE 6

Colleges Reporting on Merit Plans
By State, 1990–91 vs. 1984–85
(19 States in North Central Region)

States	Number of Merit Plans 1990–91	Number of Merit Plans 1984–85	+ or − Over 1984–85
1. Illinois	30 of 41	9 or 52	+ 21
2. Ohio	21 of 27	15 of 29	+ 6
3. Michigan	15 of 26	4 of 23	+ 11
4. Colorado	12 of 13	1 of 16	+ 11
5. Wisconsin	12 of 24	2 of 22	+ 10
6. Minnesota	9 of 19	2 of 17	+ 7
7. Kansas	8 of 21	3 of 16	+ 5
8. New Mexico	8 of 9	5 of 11	+ 3
9. Oklahoma	8 of 13	5 of 13	+ 3
10. Arizona	8 of 12	0 of 12	+ 8
11. Indiana	7 of 11	2 of 9	+ 5
12. Missouri	7 of 17	1 of 16	+ 6
13. Wyoming	5 of 6	0 of 5	+ 5
14. Iowa	5 of 11	1 of 18	+ 4
15. Arkansas	4 of 9	0 of 8	+ 4
16. Nebraska	3 of 8	2 of 13	+ 1
17. West Virginia	2 of 4	2 of 6	0
18. South Dakota	1 of 3	0 of 2	+ 1
19. North Dakota	1 of 4	1 of 5	0
Totals:	166 of 278	55 or 273	+111

1991 survey. Table 7 shows that by far the largest number of colleges that reported had started recognition for faculty within the previous five-year period—69 colleges representing 54 percent of the total. An additional 36 colleges (28 percent) reported recognition programs being in place six to 10 years. These two groups comprised 82 percent

T A B L E   7

Number of Years Merit Recognition
Systems Administered by Colleges

Number of Years	Number of Merit Recognition Systems	
1. 0– 5	69	(54%)
2. 6–10	36	(28%)
3. 11–15	6	(4.6%)
4. 16–20	12	(9.4%)
5. 21 +	5	(3.9%)
Total	128	

of the colleges. In short, most of the recognition programs in community colleges had been in place less than 10 years.

SUMMARY

Schools and colleges have largely neglected merit recognition programs. Many teachers feel their efforts and outstanding performance have not been recognized. Teachers who have received merit recognition rewards say that the awards have had a revitalizing effect on them and rescued them from becoming "burnt out."

What motivates teachers? Contrary to popular myth, merit pay is very low on the list, if at all. Neither administrators, teachers, nor faculty unions favor merit pay as the answer to how to reward faculty. According to the motivational theorists of the Human Potential Movement, money is only a "dissatisfier." It is one of the basic-level needs that must be satisfied first. After that, what really motivates teachers are "intrinsic" things—professional recognition, esteem, challenge, and autonomy.

Before trying to develop and implement a merit recognition program, administrators must make sure that basic-level needs have been satisfied, including adequate pay, a congenial work environment, and an atmosphere of trust. The steps in developing a merit system comprise (1) agreeing on the definition of excellent teaching; (2) establishing a fair and objective system to evaluate teacher performance; and (3) deciding on what type of awards to give.

There is substantial evidence that using merit recognition to motivate teachers does work. Teachers who have received merit awards say that they value the recognition they received, and both reward recipients and non-recipients say that their merit recognition programs motivate them to excel. There have been cases, however, of some meritorious teachers who, having been recognized for their outstanding performance, find themselves being rejected by their peers. If administrators don't move quickly to strongly discourage this sort of behavior, it will surely stifle the drive for excellence and sanction mediocrity.

There has been a significant increase in the use of merit recognition programs. Most programs in the community colleges surveyed have been in place for less than 10 years. It appears that the use of merit *recognition* as a motivator for improving instruction is gaining in popularity and is becoming much better accepted as an alternative to merit pay systems.

SUGGESTED EXERCISES

1. List several recognition rewards that would be acceptable to faculty for their outstanding teaching.
2. Discuss what gives teachers a feeling of worth when they are doing a good job.

9

OBJECTIVES, OUTCOMES, AND TYPES OF MERIT RECOGNITION PLANS

Wheeler et al. (1993) defined *meritorious performance* as "a level of performance that well exceeds the standard for [what is] minimally acceptable, and that may be worthy of professional recognition, career ladder advancement, or merit pay" (p. 17). In a series of workshops on how to recognize quality instruction, Andrews (1988b) found that the majority of the participants' schools had no merit recognition program. The fact that a very large number of schools do not have programs to recognize meritorious performance was verified in a study by Stevens et al. (1991). They found that 40 percent of the faculty surveyed in three types of colleges stated that their colleges did not "reward good teaching" and a similar percentage agreed that their institution did not "provide incentives to support good teaching" (pp. 75–76).

OBJECTIVES IN IMPLEMENTING A MERIT RECOGNITION PROGRAM

One of the main objectives in implementing a merit recognition program is to encourage and reward excellence in teaching. Another objective may be to comply with mandates by the state governing board, board of trustees, president or chancellor, or the faculty contract. Andrews (1993) listed a number of influences that have led community colleges in the North Central region of the United States to initiate faculty merit recognition programs (See Table 8). The number one response listed by 45 colleges was the "desire to recognize extra efforts and excellence." The second, third, fourth, and fifth influences were far below the first one and included: (1) legislative mandate or state governing board; (2) board of trustees (local); (3) president or chancellor; and (4) a desire to improve teaching quality within the college (p. 55).

The National School Boards Association (NSBA) (1987) concluded that existing pay structures didn't give outstanding teachers any special

TABLE 8

Summary of Influences to Initiate a
Faculty Merit Recognition Program

Influence	Number of Responses
1. Desire to recognize extra efforts and excellence	45
2. Legislative mandate or state governing board	16
3. Board of trustees (local)	13
4. President or Chancellor	11
5. Desire to improve teaching quality	9
6. Faculty	7
7. Others: Faculty morale, faculty-administration-board committee, basic need for recognition, grant to college, negotiated into contract, long range plan, and consortium of local colleges	16

incentives or rewards. Those teachers working the hardest were not differentiated from those who were doing the least amount of work (p. 9). They suggested that a major challenge exists in motivating those many faculty presently in the system to become better. Boyer (1983) observed, "Whatever is wrong with America's public schools cannot be fixed without the help of those teachers already in the classrooms. Most of them will be there for years to come, and such teachers must be viewed as part of the solution, not the problem (pp. 154–55)." The NSBA summarized that school boards nationally have always supported good teaching and the good teachers. They also saw the need for boards to continue that support and offer recognition and incentive programs, based on strong evaluation processes, as ways to improve teaching and the image of teachers.

DESIRED OUTCOMES OF A MERIT RECOGNITION PROGRAM

The main idea behind implementing a merit recognition program is that rewarding excellence in teaching should produce desired outcomes, such as increased motivation and improved instruction. In the workshops on recognizing quality instruction mentioned earlier (Andrews 1988b), over 140 Central Illinois elementary and secondary school superintendents and principals were asked to identify the quality outcomes their schools might achieve from a teacher recognition program. The following are some of the outcomes these administrators listed:

1. Positive public relations for the school;
2. Faculty motivation;
3. Maintenance and reinforcement of quality teaching;
4. Increased feeling of ownership in the school;
5. Improved teacher performance and, thus, student performance;
6. Improved image of teaching profession in eyes of students;
7. Improved morale, improved instruction;
8. New and creative efforts;
9. Higher quality students entering the teaching profession;
10. Retention of talented teachers in your district;
11. Excellent instruction promoted in the school;
12. Public's attention drawn to good things happening at the school;
13. Intrinsic rewards, where extrinsic rewards are not available;
14. Decrease in marginal teaching;
15. A positive atmosphere that becomes contagious;
16. "We care attitude," improved morale;
17. Emergence of leadership and appreciation;
18. Personal satisfaction because of efforts being rewarded;
19. Healthy sense of competition;
20. Enhanced teaching climate;
21. Rewards that provide a milestone in professional growth;
22. Overall instructional improvement by students and staff.

These responses were summarized into five main categories of outcomes in order to more easily identify the main benefits of initiating a merit recognition program: (1) improvement in the quality of education; (2) promotion of a positive attitude with faculty and students; (3) improvement of the teaching environment for teachers; (4) improved public image of teaching profession and schools; (5) a caring attitude projected by administrators to faculty, because their outstanding teaching performance does not go unnoticed.

HOW TO MAKE THE PROGRAM WORK

How do administrators and faculty go about preparing an elementary or secondary school or college district to accept a faculty merit recognition program? First, someone within the school needs to understand the motivational or human potential theories, such as those of Maslow and Herzberg, outlined in the previous chapter. A governing board of a school or college needs to be apprised of how these programs can and should lead to improved instruction as well as providing an evaluation system that recognizes the most outstanding faculty within a school or college.

Importance of establishing values

Andrews (1987b) suggested that a governing board should first agree on the educational philosophy that will underlie their merit recognition program. Clarifying and developing values and placing the program within a context of faculty evaluation are the first steps. Clarifying values for an elementary or secondary school or college provides a framework for developing quality control in teaching. Some suggested values, and a plan to implement them, are listed below:

Value 1:

The Governing Board values quality in every classroom.

Plan to implement value:

A plan for evaluation will be developed to guarantee that quality instruction exists in all classrooms.

A. A plan for classroom evaluations will be developed.
B. All teachers will be evaluated on their performance.
C. Good teachers will receive appropriate praise.
D. Average teachers will be given suggestions for improving.
E. Poor teachers will be given specific directions for immediate improvement efforts.

Value 2:

The Governing Board values the individual development needs of its teachers.

Plan:

The administration, in working with the teacher organization and individual teachers, will support positive faculty growth opportunities.

A. Teachers will receive reasonable financial support to attend appropriate professional meetings and conferences.
B. Teachers will be encouraged and sometimes directed to attend specific kinds of training. "Directed" opportunities will be

developed with persons who have had a less than satisfactory job performance as cited through evaluation.

C. Sabbaticals, leaves of absence, innovative research, curriculum projects, and other well-defined job-related growth opportunities will be supported.

Value 3:

The Governing Board supports a *recognition* program for outstanding teacher and administrative accomplishments.

Plan:

The administration will recommend a merit recognition plan that will include the following:

A. Recognition for outstanding efforts by teachers in the classroom as determined through the school's in-class evaluation program.
B. Recognition for outstanding efforts by teachers in other areas of job performance, such as student outcomes, curriculum development, student club experiences, and work with business, industry, or social agencies.

Value 4:

The Governing Board values taking a strong stand on placing poor teachers into a remediation process and, if necessary, terminating them from the institution.

Plan:

The administration will recommend for board approval a "Notice to remedy" for any faculty member who has not been able, or has refused, to improve under direct supervisory assistance:

A. Poor instructors will be given adequate time to improve their performance.
B. Administrators are expected to monitor progress following formal board action on a teacher remediation notice.
C. Administrators are expected to consult the school attorney regarding possible dismissal of teachers who do not, or cannot, remove their deficiencies (pp. 29–30).

The above set of values places the recognition program within the framework of faculty evaluation, with clearly defined possible outcomes.

Importance of a fair evaluation process

In the NSBA monograph on teacher compensation and incentive plans mentioned above (NSBA 1987), one point of general agreement from all the various programs reviewed was that it is important for the evaluation process to be perceived as being fair, objective, and comprehensive by each of the participants. The items they listed as most frequently used in evaluation were: (1) classroom observations; (2) measurement of student achievement; and (3) examination of records. Classroom observation was found to be used most often (p. 24).

Savage (1983) in speaking about the Charlotte, North Carolina, school district, saw the need to have an effective evaluation system to help determine which faculty should be promoted in the career ladder program or within the district. He concluded:

> It is not hard to think of the pitfalls inherent in evaluation programs; it is also true that some teachers are outstanding and some are barely passable, and a good evaluation can help reward the first-rate and improve the mediocre. If we want to change the system, and many of us do, we must develop evaluation systems that truly identify quality teaching. We must also develop payment and promotion systems that reward outstanding performance and encourage teachers to excel. (p. 56)

Educational Research Service (1978) surveyed over 1,000 schools on their teacher evaluation systems. They found classroom observation to be used in almost all of the districts surveyed. In a later study by ERS (1983) it was found that the main reason merit incentive plans had been dropped between the years of 1978 and 1983 had to do with evaluation procedures. Such things as difficulty in sorting out teachers, difficulty in avoiding subjective evaluation, inconsistency among evaluators, and difficulty in devising a satisfactory evaluation instrument were the most significant reasons given by respondents.

The Fairfax County, Virginia teachers union voted overwhelmingly (4,275 to 748) to withdraw its support from the performance-based merit pay plan (Olson 1989). The plan had received favorable faculty support in three prior votes, and the plan had been given national recognition. The district had felt the plan needed the support and cooperation of teachers to be successful. The vote to withdraw support followed a move by the governing board to reduce the percent of pay hike that had previously been agreed upon.

MONETARY AND NON-MONETARY INCENTIVE PROGRAMS

The NSBA found six basic types of monetary incentive programs around the country and four major types of non-monetary incentive programs. They are as follows:

Monetary Incentive Programs

1. *Merit Pay.* Programs that link teachers' salaries to periodic assessments of their performance. Financial bonuses are awarded to the teachers who receive the highest ratings.
2. *Payment by Results.* Merit pay programs that base individual teacher bonuses on their students' test scores gains.
3. *Merit Schools.* Plans that reward *schools,* not individual teachers, for improved performance. In some programs, schools compete against other schools for financial bonuses. In other programs, schools compete against their own past performance or against goals that have been established within the district.
4. *Career Ladders.* Programs that establish both a hierarchy of job classifications for teachers and a differentiated salary schedule. As teachers move up the career ladder, they receive additional pay for additional responsibilities, usually outside the classroom.
5. *Incentive Bonuses.* Some districts have offered special incentives for teachers willing to teach in high-turnover (especially inner-city) schools.
6. *Enhanced Professional Responsibilities (including Master Teacher Programs).* Programs that provide increased professional opportunities and responsibilities for experienced teachers. These may include serving as "mentors" for beginning teachers, or working on special projects.

Non-Monetary Incentive Programs

1. *Teacher Recognition Programs.* Programs that provide public recognition of outstanding teachers. Teacher-of-the-Year programs are one well-known example.
2. *Non-monetary Performance by Objectives (PBO) Plans.* Programs that provide non-monetary rewards for teachers who achieve objectives that they have developed (usually in cooperation with principals) for the year. Rewards may include purchase of additional classroom equipment or attendance at a professional conference.
3. *Improved Working Conditions.* Programs to improve the physical and social conditions under which teachers work, in order to make teaching more professional and more enjoyable.
4. *Awards, Sabbaticals, and Training.* Some districts reward superior

teachers with grants allowing them to pursue special projects. Other programs offer superior teachers sabbaticals or the opportunity to participate in special training programs (p. 31).

PRAISE AND RECOGNITION PROGRAMS

The NSBA concluded, "praise and recognition are among the most powerful motivators for changing behavior" (p. 40). Such recognition efforts are inexpensive, do not require complex negotiations with faculty organizations, and do not get mixed into the salary schedules of schools.

The Arlington County, Virginia, school district recognized outstanding performances of their teachers in a number of ways: (1) sabbatical leave; (2) special project grants; (3) tuition for recertification; (4) pay for summer curriculum development; (5) stipends for "contact" teachers, (6) mentoring positions; (7) paid attendance at inservice presentations; (8) pay for training other teachers in the district; (9) opportunities to attend professional meetings; and (10) department chair positions. The school board supported the program and liked the fact the available funds were spent directly on teachers.

Andrews (1986rd) found a number of merit recognition systems in colleges. They provided for recognition of outstanding performance with cash awards, plaques, and some form of public recognition. These systems varied in how such recognition was determined. Some came through administrative evaluation while others used student, peer, or self-evaluation, or a combination of them. Some examples of these systems follow.

In a policy statement on the administrative evaluation system at the College of Southern Idaho, the college concluded that merit recognition was best conducted by the Dean of the college:

1. Merit is an administrative proclamation and should be determined by the administration.
2. Merit, by its nature, is very subjective and, therefore, cannot be quantified. We all realize how difficult it is to quantify a subjective test, like an essay, and be uniform.
3. It was the feeling of everyone on the committee that the philosophy of merit is commendable. If merit is inevitable, it was felt that the Dean should be responsible for its determination. If he does his homework, he should be the most non-biased and best-informed person to do it. His system should be given the *full* support of the faculty.
4. Merit should be based *only* on one year's performance.

At Walters State Community College in Morristown, Tennessee, one outstanding faculty member a year is recognized during the Annual Honors Day program. The president receives the recommendation from an awards committee. The faculty member is recommended primarily on classroom teaching effectiveness.

The North County Community College of Saranac Lake, New York, recognizes two to five teachers a year with merit awards ranging from $500 to $1,250. They are based upon exceptional merit in the teacher's work for the college during the year, and performance above and beyond the call of duty. The college also awards a George Hadson Merit Award to one or two persons yearly. This award is based upon the following criteria: attitude toward work, consistency in job performance, versatility, personal responsibility, and cooperation with fellow employees (pp. 46–50).

In a follow-up survey Andrews (1993) found merit recognition systems greatly expanded in the 19-state Midwest region of the country. Some examples of these recently implemented systems follow.

Columbus State Community College in Ohio uses a Distinguished Teacher Award for excellence in teaching. A luncheon and presentation of a certificate are used.

The college president at Oklahoma City Community College has awarded the President's Award for Excellence in Teaching since 1991. This includes a $1,000 cash award which is presented during the spring commencement. The four criteria used in this selection are: (1) professional competence; (2) effective teaching that demonstrates quality, creativity and resourcefulness; (3) enthusiasm for teaching and commitment to students; and (4) contribution to the teaching profession. The college uses a merit pay system which has been in effect since 1977. Merit pay is awarded based upon each teacher's individual rating. Teachers are evaluated on instructional effectiveness, professional development, instructional programs, and college and professional activities. Both supervisors and faculty profile information in each category.

An Outstanding Faculty Award program at Lake Michigan College is open to both full- and part-time faculty. The selection committee comprises the vice president for academic and student services, academic deans, and teaching faculty. One full-time and one part-time faculty member are selected as award recipients. They are recognized with a plaque, put permanently on display in the college's Hall of Pride (pp. 50–53).

What follows are three examples of nominations for merit recognition that might be written on behalf of a counselor or faculty member:

Merit Award Nomination
Counselor

1. Excellence in performance of counseling duties

This counselor provides a thorough counseling experience for all persons he works with. He is very knowledgeable, accurate, and concerned for his students.

2. Assistance in program development

He has been especially instrumental in assisting with the program to provide academic and counseling services for special needs students. In addition, he attends seminars, workshops, and meetings with regional colleges and support service organizations in order to gain information and "knowledge of the system." He has explored means of additional funding and has investigated sources by which to provide increased services to the students he works with.

3. Initiative

This counselor has never been one who simply performs his duties and goes home. Rather, he appears to demonstrate an interest in new academic programs and new approaches; indeed, he will volunteer to become a part of new initiatives, such as college honors, tech prep, testing and remediation. Further, his participation extends to sound advice on how students can succeed in such programs—both on this campus and at institutions to which they will eventually transfer.

E X A M P L E   2

Merit Award Nomination
Faculty Member

1. Excellence in teaching

This instructor prepares and teaches a variety of courses—especially in the areas of technical and business communications and journalism. She prepares her courses thoroughly and with care, updates syllabi regularly, and maintains high levels of student interest and enrollment. Her journalism students have performed well at the state universities, and at least twenty-five currently hold positions in the print and non-print media.

2. Excellence in the performance of academic assignments

This instructor has taken the lead in the Tech Prep program. She has coordinated faculty workshops and worked with faculty in other disciplines and divisions to promote Tech Prep. Further, she has addressed faculty and administrators at other community colleges on the advantages of developing such a program.

3. Contributions to the college beyond assigned responsibilities and tasks

One need only look to the stature and status of the college newspaper— the quality of its form and content, the number of awards it and its staff have earned in state and national competition—to comprehend how this instructor's contributions have enhanced the college. Further, and perhaps more important, the students whom she has trained have demonstrated abilities to secure positions with various newspapers and non-print media outlets.

E X A M P L E   3

Merit Award Nomination
Faculty Member

1. Excellence in teaching

This instructor has been evaluated as an excellent instructor by several division chairs and the academic deans. Her major responsibility is in advanced chemistry, and her students do extremely well when they transfer.

2. Excellence in the performance of academic assignments

This instructor is on several campus committees and willingly accepts new challenges. She has held several workshops in chemistry on campus for elementary and high school teachers.

3. Program development

In this area the instructor has developed several programs for elementary teachers to improve their knowledge of chemistry. She also works closely with the educational service regions in presenting these programs.

4. Contributions to the college and community beyond assigned responsibilities and tasks

In community outreach efforts this instructor was instrumental in the development of the PADS program (Public Action to Deliver Shelter) and is an active leader in this program. In addition, through her efforts the college has been awarded two NSF grants for the improvement of elementary science.

5. Initiative

The instructor has developed two NSF grants for the improvement of chemistry education in the elementary schools. These projects, and another grant to obtain equipment, involved a great deal of time outside of normal classroom and other job responsibilities.

SUMMARY

Research shows that many schools and colleges have no merit recognition programs. One of the main objectives in implementing a merit recognition program is to encourage and reward excellence in teaching. The main idea behind implementing a merit recognition program is that rewarding excellence in teaching should produce desired outcomes, such as increased motivation and improved instruction. A survey of elementary and secondary school superintendents and principals identified five main categories of desired outcomes: (1) improved quality of education, (2) promotion of positive attitudes, (3) improved teaching environment, (4) improved public image of teaching and the school, and (5) a caring attitude projected by administration to faculty.

The keys to making a merit recognition program work are first, to clarify the *values* upon which the program will be based and second, to place the program within the context of faculty evaluation. It is essential that the evaluation process be perceived as being fair, objective, and comprehensive for the recognition program to be fully supported.

The NSBA found six basic types of monetary incentive programs in use in schools: (1) merit pay; (2) payment by results; (3) merit rewards by *school;* (4) career ladders; (5) incentive bonuses; and (6) enhanced professional responsibilities. They also found four major types of non-monetary incentive programs in use: (1) teacher recognition programs; (2) non-monetary "performance by objectives" plans; (3) improved working conditions; and (4) rewards, sabbaticals, and training. The praise and recognition programs that are being used successfully at several schools and colleges are described in this chapter. Several samples of merit award nominations are also included.

SUGGESTED EXERCISES

1. What objectives do you feel should be accomplished by a merit recognition program for your school?
2. Discuss the reasons merit pay and merit recognition cause such different reactions by faculty in most schools and colleges?

10

PROGRESSIVE REMEDIATION AS
FORMATIVE EVALUATION

Faculty evaluation may be the most important means that administration and faculty have of assuring the public and the school's governing board that quality in the classroom is taken seriously. Non-tenured faculty, in elementary, middle or secondary schools and community colleges, have anywhere from two years up to seven years to prove themselves to be excellent classroom teachers. During this period administrators have a number of things they can do to help assure success.

FORMATIVE EVALUATION

Visitations to classes, written and verbal reviews of these visitations, in-service meetings, and professional meetings are a few of the most significant things that can take place. Each of these steps is taken to assist the faculty member in what is commonly known as formative evaluation. In short, it is the process of assisting the teacher to become strengthened in the teaching pedagogy and personality traits that will lead to a career of successful teaching. Once an instructor has satisfactorily served the probation period, tenure is usually awarded by official action of the governing board of the school or college.

Even after tenure is granted, faculty evaluation should continue, although not as frequent as during the probationary period. Formative evaluation should continue as a means of supporting the faculty member and encouraging changes that are deemed necessary for classroom or out-of-class job improvements.

During both the probationary and tenured evaluation periods, evaluation suggestions made by the supervisor(s) for improvement should be followed up. Progress, or lack of progress, should be documented. Positive support should be forthcoming for those areas where improvements are observed. Further suggestions for improvement may be necessary for those faculty who are not making the desired progress. In such cases the faculty member may be neglecting or may be unable to perform the suggested improvements. Licata and Andrews (1990) identifies this continuing assistance as being formative in nature and a continuation of the process of working for improvements (p. 48).

REMEDIATION

In his work as a school principal and superintendent, Kelleher (1985) used the term *incompetent teacher* to describe one "who has demonstrated his or her inability to meet minimum standards of performance *over a number of years*" (p. 362). He defines the remediation period necessary for such a person as being a year or more. In his plan for remediation there are four basic things that must take place:

1. The teacher must clearly understand what his or her teaching problems are.
2. The teacher must hear the same message about his or her problems from people at different levels and in different positions in the school system.
3. The teacher must receive a written evaluation plan.
4. The teacher must know that failure to improve will bring an escalating series of consequences.

Jentz et al. (1982) did not find administrators doing a good job of telling teachers what their shortcomings or inadequacies were when discussing classroom observations with them. He found that the administrators omitted key items, generalized rather than gave specifics, and threw in positive comments when they were not called for, thereby confusing the message that needed to be transmitted. Administrators apparently were trying to be kind by withholding negative information from the teacher. Kelleher strongly recommends that schools commit funds to in-service for administrators on learning the interpersonal skills they need to handle these sensitive but necessary personnel problems.

In Kelleher's plan (1985) an incompetent teacher hears about his or her work from several sources. He feels that several administrators should be involved. He suggested that department chairpersons, assistant principals, and principals each get involved in conducting the classroom observations. He also feels that, if necessary, the district level administrators should get involved. The alternative, as he explains, is to allow incompetent teachers to continue year after year.

Conducting these evaluations is time-consuming. Handling student, parent, and board member complaints about a poor teacher is also very time consuming if nothing is done to address the problem. Kelleher suggested that the faculty member's union should be informed. He said that union leaders had always been invited to take part in the in-service workshops that administrators received in his school district. He found the teacher union generally supportive: "The union is responsible for protecting the teacher's rights, but it is also in a position to support our efforts, if it perceives them as fair" (p. 363).

In reference to the written evaluation plan in item (3) above, the teacher should receive documentation of the specific problems, expectations for improvement, and the steps that will be followed by the administration to document improvement or lack of improvement. Kelleher also suggests that the teacher's union get a copy of the notice. This lets them know what is expected as well as showing the union that the administration is giving the teacher the opportunity to improve, within certain time limits.

In Kelleher's experience, incompetent teachers tended to leave when they saw that their work was considered unsatisfactory by a number of administrators, fellow teachers, board members, and students. Confronting incompetence is necessary, and the school should "speak to an incompetent teacher with one voice about that teacher's problems, expressing the message compassionately and sensitively but, above all, clearly; then that teacher will either change dramatically or, more likely, resign" (p. 364). Kelleher concluded that everyone who participates in the process of improving instruction or in the removal of an incompetent teacher will gain pride in the fact that quality instruction is being sought within the school.

Rapp and Ortbal (1980) pointed out that it is important to allow time for poor performance to be remediated prior to moving toward termination. They state that "if the reasons for dismissal are considered *remediable,* a board must give the teacher reasonable warning in writing stating the causes of dismissal which, if not removed, may result in charges and dismissal" (p. 39).

This starts to sound harsh when dismissal is mentioned. It is, however, part of the legal process that must be considered when a tenured faculty member is found to have 'deficiencies' or 'defects' in their teaching or other job responsibilities. The courts and laws in most states have held that due-process procedures must be granted to those faculty under tenure or with a continuing contract status. Without due-process policies and procedures being followed courts have consistently denied boards and administrators in schools and colleges support for their dismissal decisions.

The public has become much more aware of incompetence in teaching and has learned that it does not have to be tolerated. It is even more important that colleges and school systems put into place due-process procedures which will provide for proper legal support in those cases which may lead to dismissals. Teacher evaluation *legislation* has been passed in some states. In Illinois, the law provides for a one-year "probation" period and leads to termination if sufficient progress is not forthcoming by the elementary or secondary school teacher involved.

REPRIMANDS: A REMEDIATION STEP

A reprimand to an employee is a means of letting the employee know that some behavior was not carried out satisfactorily. The reprimand should be put in writing, read by the instructor involved, and placed in the personnel file of the instructor. Andrews (1987d) stated that some faculty contracts ask that the teacher sign the form to be filed. This is to indicate that it has been read but not, necessarily, that there is agreement to the contents. The faculty member may wish to write a rebuttal and have it attached to the reprimand in the personnel file. Following are some sample reprimands (p. 4):

Dear Instructor:

Your absence from the December 2 meeting, whether from forgetfulness or not, is not excusable, especially following my verbal warning to you after you missed the November 4 meeting. You are aware that important and essential business and not merely perfunctory tasks take place at the faculty meetings.

In short, this reprimand will be placed in your permanent personnel file. You must plan to be at all future faculty meetings as part of your professional obligation. Please sign this letter of reprimand and return it to my attention within one week. If you would like to discuss this matter further, please set up an appointment at any time.

Sincerely,
Dean of the Faculty

Dear Instructor:

On Thursday, September 12, at 11:30 a.m. you met in the Dean's office with the Dean and myself to discuss the circumstances that led to the need for such a meeting.

You had, earlier that morning, verbally and publicly abused a student who attempted to enter your classroom. You spoke to that student in a loud tone of voice and with some degree of profanity. The nature of your address to him was such that individuals in the classroom and in the halls outside of that room easily witnessed your anger and general loss of control.

Please know that such conduct, no matter how sincere your concern for and commitment to the student's ultimate academic success, cannot be tolerated. The profession that you serve and the discipline you represent do not tolerate such behavior; the institution in which you practice your profession cannot afford to (nor will it) tolerate such conduct. Abusive outbursts toward students accomplish little to advance the respect of the instructor or the institution.

In the future, please try to control your emotions. You can begin by setting forth (at the onset of each term) clear, specific classroom policies concerning issues like attendance and the submission of written assignments. This practice will, in the end, allow students to know exactly what you expect from them. This will go far to regulating your emotional involvement with your students.

Sincerely,
Division Chairperson

There are situations and times when such reprimands are warranted and necessary. It is responsible behavior by the administration to address behaviors that are not in line with what is expected by professional teachers.

THE "NOTICE TO REMEDY"

A "notice to remedy" is a legal step available to governing boards and administrators for letting an instructor know the serious nature of their neglect to change or improve their teaching or other job behaviors. The "notice to remedy" is a strong statement from the board that provides a list of the precise defects and deficiencies that have been brought to them by the superintendent or college president. In addition, it spells out what changes are expected to remediate such problems. It gives a time frame and makes clear that the supervisor(s) will continue to evaluate for the significant changes expected concerning the list of charges given to the faculty member. It also makes clear that if these charges are not remediated, the board will be ready to consider the teacher's termination from the institution. An example of a "notice to remedy" appears in Example 4.

E X A M P L E   4

List of Defects and Deficiencies in the
Teaching and Overall Job Performance
of_____

---

1. Lack of preparation in order to conduct an organized, logically sequenced classroom presentation.

Classroom observations indicate that you are not properly prepared to conduct your classes in a manner conducive to the learning of the complex concepts and principles in your subject matter. You must prepare yourself in such a manner that you are ready to present all of the required material contained in the course syllabus in an organized, logically sequenced way to bring about student comprehension of the concepts to be taught.

2. Lack of organization in conducting your classroom presentation.

You must organize your classroom presentation in such a manner that your students are able to understand what you are trying to accomplish. Your method of presentation is so disorganized that it is difficult to determine what objectives or goals you wish to accomplish for your classes. One minute you start on one concept and then the next minute you are off on a completely different topic which has nothing to do with the course. On occasion you leave your classroom to go get something you forgot to bring to the class. You have also been observed to discuss topics at considerable length within your classes which have nothing at all to do with the subject you are teaching. You must discipline yourself to be properly organized for teaching the required materials in your courses.

3. Failure to communicate course expectations to your students.

You need to communicate in writing the requirements and specific expectations for successfully completing your classes. Your policies and procedures for class attendance, lateness to class, grading, homework assignments, in-class participation, materials to be covered on tests, and so forth, must all be covered in your student course outlines. The students in your courses are not receiving a clear understanding of what is expected of them. This demonstrates a definite lack of preparation, organization, and consideration for the needs of your students.

4. *Failure to prepare a description of specific course objectives to hand out to your students.*

You must prepare specific goals on a daily, weekly, monthly and semester basis for each of your courses. These goals must be given out to your students at the beginning of each of your courses.

5. *Lack of preparation and planning in production of audio-visual materials to supplement lecture and discussion material.*

You must work closely with the audio-visual department in preparing this type of supplementary materials for use in your courses. The transparencies you have used are outdated, crowded, and difficult to read.

6. *Failure to adequately prepare students, to allow them to be meaningfully involved in the discussion.*

You ask such superficial questions of your students that there is no way of assessing whether they understand the basic principles of your lectures. Give your students the facts and materials they need to maximize their participation in the discussion.

7. *Insubordination.*

On two separate occasions you were requested to meet with your supervisors to discuss the classroom evaluations they had made of you during the past month. You chose to ignore these requests. This is being viewed as an act of insubordination. Future actions of this type will not be tolerated.

8. *Conclusion.*

This list of defects and deficiencies have been prepared by your supervisors after having observed these problems in your teaching and out-of-class job requirements. You should seriously evaluate how each one of these concerns can be addressed. Some of them will require a change in attitude. Others will require a great deal of work in preparation, which you have neglected for a long period of time. You will need to meet with your administrative supervisors very soon to outline a course of action for correcting these defects and deficiencies in your work. Close evaluation of your work will need to continue over the next several months.

PROOF OF INCOMPETENCE

A legal definition of incompetence is not easy to find in the literature dealing with faculty remediation or dismissal. Rosenberger and

Plimpton (1975) concluded: "There seems to have been no legal need to define competence . . . conventional wisdom and common sense, rather than precise standards, have been used in judging incompetence claims" (p. 469).

Wheeler et al. (1993) was cited in an earlier chapter describing *incompetence* as "the intentional or unintentional failure to perform the duties and professional responsibilities of the teaching job in a minimally acceptable manner as specified by the employing district" (p. 15).

Strike and Bull (1981) quoted a judge in the case of *Conley v. Board of Education of the City of New Britain* (1956) when he defined incompetence: "A grossly inefficient person would be one whose efforts were failing to an intolerable degree to produce the effect intended or desired—a manifestly incompetent or incapable person" (p. 324). Strike and Bull found that courts have accepted the following items as proof of incompetence:

1. Deficiencies in knowledge of subject matter;
2. Poor teaching methods;
3. Disorganized teaching or work habits;
4. Inability to maintain discipline or use of excessive force or other inappropriate methods;
5. Inability to motivate students;
6. Inflexibility or lack of adaptability;
7. Uncooperativeness;
8. Permitting or requiring vulgarities on the part of students;
9. Causing low morale;
10. Poor communication;
11. Poor attitude;
12. Violation of rules;
13. Mishandling of funds;
14. Low student achievement;
15. Unsatisfactory ratings;
16. Poor record-keeping;
17. Arbitrary grading; and
18. Lack of self-control (p. 324).

While the discussion in this chapter does not spell out how each of these items can be identified in proving incompetence, the above list does show the type of charges that have been reported in court cases throughout the country. The circumstances in each of them that would lead an administrator to reach the conclusion that they are serious enough to move toward termination of the faculty member involved are different for each case. "Lack of self-control" or "mishandling of funds" are clearer charges to identify as areas of incompetence than that of a "causing low morale" or "uncooperativeness." Placed in the legal context of cases involving these behaviors, each of them have been identified as incompetent behaviors.

ROLE OF ADMINISTRATOR IN "EXPERT TESTIMONY"

The role of "expert testimony and performance evaluations in making determinations about school employee competence are slowly winning approval in courts," according to Piele (1981, p. 69). In addition, he found that most of the challenges by teachers regarding their dismissals for stated causes had been rejected by the courts. He found this in spite of the "heightened legal protections of tenure." Such information is most important in giving boards and administrators confidence that there is sufficient support for their decisions to move toward remediation or dismissals for poor instructors.

Van Horn (1984) found that the most likely candidates to be called forth as witnesses were those administrators involved directly in the evaluation process. Such "expert witnesses" will have been involved in writing the observation, meeting with the faculty member, testifying during the notice to remedy and will have played a major role in the dismissal process. More courts are coming to see these persons as providing expert testimony. Van Horn quoted an Ohio court that accepted this principle:

> Teaching is an art as well as a profession and requires a large amount of preparation in order to qualify one in that profession. The ordinary layman is not versed in that art, neither is he in a position to measure the necessary qualifications required for the teacher today. In our judgment this information can be properly imparted by one who is versed and alert in the profession and aware of the qualifications required.
>
> For this reason, however, we think the principal . . . with the years of experience possessed by him can be classed properly as an expert in the teaching profession, and is in a similar position as a doctor in the medical profession. His testimony was not incompetent and certainly was an aid to the board and to the court in arriving at their respective conclusions. (p. 22).

Strike and Bull (1981) formed several conclusions from their review of judicial decisions regarding incompetence:

> 1. Courts are likely to rely on the professional judgment of administrators in the substantive aspects of evaluation.
> 2. Judicial review of dismissal decisions is likely to be more restrictive when dealing with the procedural aspects of dismissal. Courts require that legislated or contractual procedures for evaluation or due process be

rigorously followed. *They may also insist, where the defect is remediable, that opportunity for improvement be given* (emphasis added).

3. Despite the lack of an authoritative legal definition and despite jurisdictional variations in interpretation, a general and widely accepted core of meaning for teaching incompetencies can be discerned in the case law. Moreover, incompetence is to be reflected in a pervasive pattern of teacher behavior that has proven to be irremediable. (pp. 324–25)

Courts have indeed been supportive of the judgments of competent administrators. Boards should be willing to back competent administrators in their recommendations if they want quality improvements in teaching. Garber (1956) provided guidance for governing boards and administrators by suggesting that they deal with personnel in good faith, follow statutory procedures that outline steps in a dismissal, provide appropriate due-process procedures, and secure advice from an attorney.

KEY TESTS PRIOR TO ANY DISMISSAL DECISION

Van Horn (1984) suggests that there is a simple but most important test for determining whether the unsatisfactory teaching or other job behaviors are at the point where dismissal is necessary. The question, "Can it be remediated?" must be answered first before any dismissal decision is considered. He pointed out that this test is required in a number of state statutes for boards (p. 3).

When the decision time arrives to seek a formal "notice to remedy" from the governing board, the evaluators usually already will have:

1. Evaluated the instructor several times;
2. Met with the instructor in post-evaluation sessions to discuss the deficiencies or defects in the teaching;
3. Made both written and oral summaries of the weaknesses that need to be remediated;
4. Written up the discussion from these meetings;
5. Found the teaching behavior in subsequent classroom visits still to be unsatisfactory and the effort to make the required changes not being put forth.

The administrator involved needs to next notify the elementary, middle, or secondary school superintendent or the college president that the time has come to seek a board notice to remediate the problem.

The superintendent or president must review the materials presented, and if convinced that the case is well documented over a sufficient number of visits, have the school attorney review it for legal analysis. If concurrence is received from the attorney then board action should be sought. A "notice to remedy" will be prepared. Boards will usually discuss the matter in an executive session before taking formal public action in those states having a "sunshine" law for board actions.

It is important to note that supervisor ratings are the primary source of information in most cases leading to remediation or termination of a teacher. The courts usually give substantial weight to such supervisor ratings. Bonato (1987) added that having more than one supervisor involved in the evaluation of a teacher is even more persuasive than when only one supervisor has evaluated a teacher, as long as there is consistency in the findings. He quotes from *Rosso v. Board of Education of School Directors* (1977) in which the court supports the use of more than one evaluator:

> The school district's evaluation procedures are a model of how a professional employee should be rated. The evaluations occurred at two levels. At the first level is the principal; if he rates a professional employee unsatisfactory, the matter is referred to the second level, the superintendent, for further evaluation. While a teacher might object to being rated so often in a short period of time by different persons, such a procedure is clearly in the employee's best interest since it brings into the evaluation different viewpoints, thereby lessening the influence personal bias and prejudice with respect to teaching methods can have." (p. 25)

Bonato further endorses the need for multiple evaluators, if available, by citing that in almost all discharge cases involving a tenured teacher there have been bitter disputes regarding the quality of the instructor's performance of teaching. Alleging personality conflict and questioning the evaluator's competency and expertise are often used by the teacher as a defense. Bonato recommends that at least three different administrators or evaluators be used. The *Esther Fortson v. Detroit Board of Education* case was cited to support this recommendation. Fortson charged that the principal's evaluation reflected his personal animosity toward her. The Tenure Commission in Michigan rejected her argument:

> Finally, we address appellant's contention that her problem with appellee stemmed from an incident where her principal at Post Middle School, Mr. Shackelford, became angry with her after a run-in she had with him. Her initial unsatisfactory evaluation followed soon after this incident. Even if we were to completely discount Mr. Shackelford's observations, still we are left with similar observations of two other evaluators at Post—Ms. Hetes and Mr. Nash. In addition, we have the observations of two more evaluators at a different school—Mr. Kar and Mr. Tyler at Longfellow. There is no allegation that the evaluations of these four people were the result of personal bias or animosity against appellant. From these evaluations and

from the testimony presented at both hearings, we find sufficient evidence to support the action taken against appellant. (p. 32)

The stressful impact that remediation efforts and the possibility of termination can have on administrators was discussed earlier (Andrews 1988). This stress can affect department or division chairpersons, assistant principals, principals, superintendents, deans or vice presidents of instruction and others who are involved in the process at the supervisory level (p. 63). It is important that administrative personnel be able to recognize excellence in instruction, understand the due-process policies and procedures of the school or college, be familiar with court cases in the areas of remediation and dismissal, and have a firm grasp on what is meant by "improvement of instruction." This "improvement of instruction," if accomplished, will foster the learning environment for students in the months and years ahead. It is working toward this goal of instructional improvement that can bring one to perceive the evaluation process as challenging rather than stressful and lead to a feeling of satisfaction that the goal has been worth pursuing.

ARBITRATION TESTS TO KNOW

A common-law definition for "just cause", as it is developed by the American Arbitration Association in Washington, D. C., is important to know (Baer 1974). It is this common-law definition that all cases involved in arbitration are measured against. It provides a set of questions that can be applied in determining the facts in any case that an arbitrator is faced with deciding:

1. Did the agency give the employee forewarning or foreknowledge of the possible or probable disciplinary consequences of the employee's conduct?
   Note A: Forewarning or foreknowledge may properly have been given orally by management or in writing through the medium of typed or printed sheets or books of shop rules and penalties for violation thereof.
   Note B: There must have been actual oral or written communication of the rules and penalties to the employee.
2. Did the agency, before administering discipline to an employee, make an effort to discover whether the employee did in fact violate or disobey a rule or order of management?
   Note A: The agency's investigation must normally be made before its disciplinary decision.
3. Was the agency's investigation conducted fairly and objectively?

4. Has the agency applied its rules, orders, and penalties evenhandedly and without discrimination to all employees?

   Note A: A "no" answer to this question requires a finding of discrimination and warrants negation or modification of the discipline imposed.

   Note B: If the agency has been lax in enforcing its rules and orders and decides henceforth to apply them rigorously, the agency may avoid a finding of discrimination by telling all employees in advance of its intent to enforce, hereafter, all rules as written.

5. Was the degree of discipline administered by the agency in a particular case reasonably related to: (a) the seriousness of the employee's proven offense, and (b) the record of the employee in his or her service with the agency? (p. 88)

These tests should put elementary, middle and secondary school and college administrators on alert whenever they feel they need to administer disciplinary or negative evaluation action. The common-law questions above point out the necessity of having written rules of evaluation. Such rules need to be applied even-handedly to all persons involved.

The "notice to remedy" becomes a most important material item in the determination of whether the individual was given clear remediation directions. It also answers the first question above in regard to giving forewarning of possible disciplinary consequences.

SUMMARY

The process of remediation is one of the most important tools available for assuring quality teaching in the classroom. It is really a continuation of formative efforts to improve instruction. It allows for both the teacher and the school or college to know precisely what is being asked in the way of needed improvements.

Remediation must take place or incompetent teachers. In implementing a remediation plan, the administration must ensure that the teacher (1) clearly understands what his or her teaching problems are; (2) hears the same message about his or her performance from several different evaluators; (3) receives a written evaluation plan; and (4) knows that failure to improve may eventually lead to termination.

A written reprimand is one of the first steps to be taken in a remediation plan. Several sample letters are included in this chapter. If improvements still are not being made, the next step is the "notice to remedy." This serious step, taken by board action, notifies the teacher that the changes they have so far been unable or unwilling to make need to be made *now* to remedy the listed defects and deficiencies in their teaching and overall job performance. As a formal step, it also sets the stage for removal of a tenured teacher if the teacher continues to refuse or be unable to make the required changes.

When all remediation efforts have been exhausted and the teacher's performance has still not been brought up to an acceptable level, the administration should move to termination. In order for this decision to be legally defensible, administrators must be able to answer "yes" to the following test questions: (1) Was the instructor evaluated several times?; (2) Were post-evaluation session held with the instructor to discuss the teaching deficiencies?; (3) Were both written and oral summaries of the weaknesses given to the instructor?; (4) Were the discussions from these meetings documented?; (5) Was the teaching behavior still found to be unsatisfactory in follow-up classroom visits?; and most importantly, (6) Has the behavior proven to be irremediable?

Although there is no authoritative legal definition of incompetence, courts have regularly accepted as proof of incompetence certain types of charges, which are listed this chapter. Administrators have become more widely viewed by courts as "expert witnesses" in providing evidence for incompetence. The courts, however, have also placed high importance on how well due process and the legislated or contractual procedures for evaluation have been followed. In order to satisfy the common-law definition of "just cause" in termination cases, it is vital to have written rules of evaluation and to apply them even-handedly to all persons involved.

SUGGESTED EXERCISES

1. Discuss the necessity of remediation. How does it provide accountability in evaluation?
2. What happens to administrative evaluation if a governing board decides not to accept a recommendation for supporting a "notice to remedy"?

11

MOVING BEYOND 'LIP SERVICE' IN POST-TENURE EVALUATION

I would first fire all administrators who knew little or nothing or cared less about evaluation and quality education and replace [them] with competent people. Then I would create an evaluation system which did the following: Distinguished those minimally competent from those below minimal competence. Provide remediation for the latter group with an outcome that would either (a) make them competent, or (b) permit their legal dismissal. Provide enrichment and improvement for all staff according to their needs and desires. Provide adequate funding and resources for this.

A Faculty Leader
(Andrews and Licata 1990)

This startling revelation was one of many from faculty leaders around the country expressing their disgust with the state of faculty evaluation in their community colleges. Andrews and Licata (1988–89) conducted a 19-state research study to find out what both faculty and administrative instructional leaders felt about the present role evaluation played in their colleges. They were also asked what "should" be the role of evaluation. A total of 357 instructional leaders responded, which represented 58.5 percent of the population to which the questionnaire was sent. The findings of this study were quite different than expected.

As represented by the above quotation, respondents did not have a negative response to faculty evaluation, but were supportive of the need for a competent evaluation system aimed at improving teaching. However, they emphasized the need for competent persons to be involved in carrying out evaluation. They called for remediation, enrichment, and improvement efforts to change incompetent faculty prior to asking for a legal dismissal (p. 7).

The National Commission on Higher Education Issues (1982) saw post-tenure evaluation as one of the most pressing issues that would need to be addressed by higher education in the decade ahead (p. 10). Licata (1984) found the majority of faculty and administrators in seven community college campuses to be supportive of post-tenure evaluation. The effectiveness of such evaluation was, however, called into question in regard to the stated purpose of faculty development and improvement (p. 36).

DEFINING EXISTING AND IDEAL POST-TENURE EVALUATION PRACTICES

Both faculty leaders and administrators in the study were asked to respond to what they felt were the existing reasons as well as to identify the ideal reasons for post-tenure evaluation in their colleges. The responses, which included 173 from faculty leaders and 225 from instructional administrators, were similar when identifying existing reasons for evaluation. The total of 398 responses by the 357 respondents indicates that some chose more than one reason.

The results of both groups showed "individual faculty development" to be the primary stated purpose for post-tenure evaluation in their colleges. The other two major responses were: "for making decisions on promotion, retention and dismissal," and for "making merit compensation or merit recognition decisions." These responses can be seen in Table 9 below (p. 9).

Both groups were also asked what the *ideal* purpose for evaluation should be. "Individual faculty development" was selected by 61.3 percent of the faculty leaders and by 49.1 percent of the administrators (see Table 10). There is a strong consistency on the part of both groups when looking at existing as well as ideal purposes for evaluation (p. 10).

In identifying what they felt should be other ideal reasons for evaluation, faculty leaders rated "making merit compensation or merit recognition decisions" as their second choice and administrators rated it third. Comments from faculty make it clear that some felt much more needed to be done in recognition efforts:

- I'd provide funds to give bonuses or other rewards to outstanding faculty *without* reducing funds to pay all competitive salaries.
- . . . reward the effective faculty member, not the sloucher; not enough distinction exists.
- There is a need for a significant reward system for effective educators.
- If you are planning to use these evaluations tie it to excellence and

TABLE 9

What Are the Stated Purposes
for Faculty Evaluations?

Primary Purpose	Faculty Responses N = 173		Administrative Responses N = 225	
	Responses	Percent	Responses	Percent
1. Basis for individual faculty development	102	59.0	140	54.9
2. Making decisions on promotion, retention and dismissal	42	24.3	75	29.4
3. Making merit compensation or merit recognition decision	16	9.2	29	11.3
4. Other	13	7.5	11	4.3

pay for that excellence. You'd be surprised how quickly the 'sluggards' will come around and without much being said.

Similar comments were offered by a number of the administrators:

- Fund a reward system for outstanding performance.
- More specific final ratings with recognition for our outstanding faculty.
- Provide greater positive recognition of high achievers so as to encourage others to 'stretch' themselves.
- Add something to reward outstanding performance above and beyond a salary increase (pp. 24–25).

CRITERIA USED FOR POST-TENURE EVALUATION

Faculty and administrators were also asked to rank the criteria their college used to evaluate post-tenure faculty. "Classroom effectiveness" was selected first by both faculty and administrators. Faculty checked

TABLE   10

What Should be the Purpose for
Faculty Evaluation?

Primary Purpose	Faculty Responses N = 181		Administrative Responses N = 287	
	Responses	Percent	Responses	Percent
1. Basis for individual faculty development	111	61.3	141	49.1
2. Making decisions on promotion, retention and dismissal	30	16.6	78	27.2
3. Making merit compensation or merit recognition decisions	35	19.4	59	20.5
4. Other	5	2.8	9	3.2

"contribution to department" second and "campus committee work" third. The administrative group selected "course or curriculum development" second and "contribution to the department" third among the criteria utilized (p. 11). This was not unexpected since classroom teaching is by far the main job of a faculty member in a community college. This differs greatly in four-year colleges and universities where the areas of research and publications have, in recent years, far outweighed teaching in the reward or merit system (Sykes 1988, pp. 257–59).

PROBLEMS WITH POST-TENURE EVALUATION

Both faculty and administrators in this study agreed in similar proportions that the following two items were the major problems with their post-tenure evaluation systems:

1. Ineffective implementation of faculty development plans;
2. Lack of reward system.

The third item checked by a significant number of faculty was "evaluators not adequately trained." "Faculty resistance" was the third choice item checked by administrators followed closely by "evaluators not adequately trained" (p. 15).

When the faculty leaders and administrators were asked, "What happens to post-tenure evaluation in your college?," there was a major discrepancy between faculty and administrators. Faculty indicated that the results are "shared with the faculty member and they are left to their own devices to improve." A total of 62 percent checked this option while 33.8 percent of the administrators checked it. The second choice, "shared with faculty member and a plan is made for improvement" was checked by 28 percent of the faculty leaders and by 61 percent of the administrators. Evidently, administrators felt they were doing a much better job at working to improve the performance of their faculty members than was apparent from the low response of the faculty leaders (p. 13).

The effectiveness of existing post-tenure evaluation in a number of community colleges was left much in doubt by the responses found in Table 11. The reader will see another major discrepancy between the faculty leaders and administrators. Some 56 percent of the administrators rated their evaluation system as "effective" while only 25.6 percent of the faculty leaders saw it that way. "Uncertain about effectiveness" was chosen by 49.6 percent of the faculty but only 33 percent of the administrators. Notice in particular that the "ineffective" choice was selected by 23.1 percent of faculty and only 7.7 percent of administrators.

WHY SUCH DOUBTS ABOUT EFFECTIVENESS?

The two main reasons given for the doubt and uncertainty about the effectiveness of evaluation at the colleges by the respondents were:

1. Pays only 'lip service' to faculty development;
2. No mechanism to measure competence or incompetence.

These two criteria were selected by 34 and 29 percent of faculty and administrators respectively on the 'lip service' issue and 24 and 27 percent respectively on the competence/incompetence issue (p. 17).

THE QUESTION OF 'WEEDING OUT'

The question of what action is taken when a faculty member is evaluated as unsatisfactory left some gaps in terms of response.

TABLE   11

Effectiveness of
Post-Tenure Evaluation?

Criteria selected	Faculty Responses N = 121			Administrative Responses N = 144		
	Number	**Rank**	**Percent**	**Number**	**Rank**	**Percent**
1. Very Effective	2	4	1.7	4	4	2.8
2. Effective	31	2	25.6	81	1	56.2
3. Uncertain About Effectiveness	60	1	49.6	48	2	33.3
4. Ineffective	28	3	23.1	11	3	7.7

Creating a development plan was listed by 75 percent of the administrators. "Dismissal" was checked by only 3 for a total of 2.5 percent. In the section above dealing with the perceived uncertain effectiveness or ineffectiveness of their evaluation system, 8.8 percent of the faculty and 10.2 percent of the administrators felt that their doubts centered on "poor instructors not being placed on warning."

Some comments received from faculty regarding poor instructors were:

- Put some 'teeth' into the plan so incompetent staff could be dismissed.
- Give consequences to the results, both pro and con.

Administrative responses included:

- Develop a comprehensive plan . . . correlate results to merit pay, promotion, staff development and also demotion, termination, etc.
- I would implement a probation and dismissal system for those who do not perform adequately (pp. 24–25).

Table 12 shows the opinions of both administrators and faculty leaders on the question of post-tenure evaluation procedures leading to "weeding out" of incompetent faculty.

TABLE   12

Administrators and Faculty
Responses to Question on Weeding Out
Incompetent Teachers

	Administrative Responses	Faculty Responses
1. Post-tenure evaluation *leads* to the weeding out of incompetent faculty. **(Disagree/Strongly Disagree)**	57.6%	77.4%
2. Post-tenure evaluation *should lead* to the weeding out of incompetent faculty. **(Agree/Strongly Agree)**	83.1%	81.1%

The largest percentage of administrators (57.6 percent) "disagree" or "strongly disagree" with the statement, "post-tenure evaluation leads to the weeding out of incompetent faculty. The percentage of faculty disagreeing with the statement was even more dramatic with a total of 77.4 percent checking "disagree" or "strongly disagree."

The responses received to the next comment, "post-tenure evaluation *should* lead to the weeding out of incompetent faculty," are also listed in Table 12. Responses produced very high percentages of 81 and 83 for faculty and administrators, respectively, in the "strongly agree" and "agree" columns. This clearly showed the strong feelings of both groups that, "weeding out of incompetent faculty" is, indeed, a most important change to be sought in future evaluation practices (pp. 28–29).

RECOMMENDATIONS FOR CHANGE

Recommended changes to the post-tenure evaluation systems in the colleges in the above study were solicited from both administrative and faculty leaders. They were given the opportunity to respond to the open-ended question: "If you could change post-tenure evaluation plans at your institution, what changes would you make?" The changes recommended fell into three general categories: (1) evaluation system design, (2) system implementation, and (3) system outcomes. The following is a summary of the items checked under each of these categories, listed in rank order:

Evaluation design recommendations

1. Tie evaluation system to faculty development and to a formative purpose.
2. Increase peer involvement; explore classroom visitation as a technique.
3. Enhance student involvement in review through student evaluation of teaching; improve student evaluation instrumentation.
4. Involve faculty in design and establishment of individual professional goals.
5. Lessen importance of student evaluation.
6. Ensure plan is consistent and systematic, decreasing possibility for subjective assessment.
7. Include multiple resources of evaluation input.

Evaluation implementation recommendations

1. Provide opportunities for training of evaluators.
2. Decrease frequency of evaluation from yearly to a two- to three-year cycle.
3. Establish a non-threatening climate for evaluation.

Evaluation outcomes recommendations

1. Provide incentives for excellent performers.
2. Provide adequate resources for faculty development.
3. Make evaluation more effective in retention/dismissal/reward.
4. Monitor results of development plans established as a consequence of the evaluation (p. 21).

Both faculty and administrators put forth a number of recommendations that should lead to improvements in faculty evaluation systems in most schools and colleges.

SECONDARY SCHOOL LEADERSHIP FUNCTIONS

Mangieri and Arnn (1985) presented those job dimensions that led principals to have the most outstanding secondary school in America as judged by the U. S. Department of Education. The following is a list of those job dimensions mentioned most in their jobs:

1. Instructional supervision,
2. Evaluation of teacher performance,
3. Curriculum development,
4. Staffing,
5. Community involvement and support.

It can be seen that if a school is to gain recognition for being outstanding, instructional supervision and evaluation of teacher performance are key administrative functions.

The research summarized by Thomas in 1986 and 1991 shows that if administrators and governing boards move beyond lip service in carrying out action against incompetent teachers, there is support in the court system. In 1986 there were twelve incompetence cases reported. Employees were not successful in defending themselves against the charges of incompetency in any of them (p. 20). In 1991 all four cases on incompetency were upheld in the courts (p. 20).

SUMMARY

Faculty leaders and instructional administrators were both found to support the need for post-tenure evaluation. This 19-state study supported and replicated an earlier study by Licata. The number one reason stated for evaluation was "individual faculty development." The same reason was stated by these leaders when asked "what *should* be the main purpose of post-tenure evaluation?"

The need for merit pay and/or merit recognition was highlighted by faculty leaders, as their second preferred purpose for faculty evaluation was to make merit reward decisions. Both faculty and administrators indicated that their evaluations systems paid only "lip service" when it came to supporting faculty development. Recognition for excellent performers and consequences for poor instructors were both listed as needing to be addressed and improved.

Given the high level of support for post-tenure evaluation among faculty leaders, instructional administrators, and students, it should be possible for governing boards and other decision makers to take advantage of this support and move toward strengthening evaluation processes. The high level of frustration revealed in the above studies should be addressed. The recommendations received in the Licata and Andrews study included making evaluation more effective in faculty development, dismissal, and rewards. The need to monitor the results of developmental plans was also recommended. It is important to move beyond "lip service" if evaluation practices are to produce results and gain the necessary respect from faculty, administrators and students.

SUGGESTED EXERCISES

1. Discuss those things that a faculty evaluation system should do for your college, elementary, middle, or secondary school. Should they include both formative and summative results?
2. How can you solicit honest responses from students about how they feel about the teaching they are receiving? Develop a short survey form.

$$=====$$

$$=====$$

12

NON-TENURED AND TENURED FACULTY
TERMINATIONS

One of the most difficult personnel actions that a college or university can take is to terminate the employment of a tenured faculty member for cause. The emotional repercussions of such actions often extend far beyond the terminated faculty member.

Lovain (1984, p. 419)

The process involved in the dismissal of a tenured faculty member is often misunderstood by those very persons who have the legal responsibility to carry out proper evaluation techniques from which a decision for dismissal can be made. Dismissals have strict legal requirements, create much emotional stress, and are seldom carried out without a significant financial burden on the elementary, middle, or secondary school or college.

Jenkins et al. (1979) address the concern of many persons in the educational reform movement of the 1980s and 1990s:

Guaranteed lifetime employment has more often come about because administrators and boards of education have been unsure of the *process* of discharging the unsatisfactory teachers. Or they have had an inadequate system of evaluating the teacher—particularly of recording such evaluations —and therefore have been hesitant to move against the teacher. *Boards and administrators frequently blame tenure for what in fact are their own failures in evaluating teachers and in securing qualified teaching staffs* (emphasis added). This is widely reflected in the small amounts of time and money allocated to the evaluation of personnel performance in our schools. (p. 11)

"DANCE OF THE LEMONS"

School districts have been found to have done little to devise effective evaluation systems during those periods when there was a shortage of qualified teachers (Bridges 1990). A lack of clearly defined criteria, poor preparation of administrative personnel, and a lack of accountability for principals to do this task exacerbated the problem (p. 147).

The school districts used what Bridges saw as a complaint-driven approach to teacher evaluation. In short, when a parent complained, principals would go into the classroom and come out with favorable ratings so as to avoid the dirty job of having to deal honestly with such poor instruction. Bridges found that principals either overlooked such poor performances, inflated performance ratings hoping this would encourage the persons to improve through positive reinforcement, or they would send the person packing to another school within the district (p. 148). This moving around of poor teachers was defined by Wheeler et al. (1993) as the "dance of the lemons" (p. 11). Some schools do not face the need to move toward dismissal of their incompetent teachers, but rather move them around. Usually the poorer schools ended up with a disproportionate number of these persons because administrators found these schools to be the path of least resistance. In the poorer school there were likely to be fewer complaints from the parents. Middle class parents were known to be more vocal and were much more willing to come forth to express their displeasure and expect action when poor instruction was found.

Small schools did not have these escape hatches according to Bridges. He found these schools having to deal more directly with the teachers, and using two courses of action: (1) seek improvement of the teacher's performance and (2) find a way to get rid of the teacher if this failed. Some encouragement to resign or retire early was also tried. The record shows that remediation efforts did little to improve those poor teachers.

The causes of ineffectiveness are usually a very complex mix rather than evolving from one discreetly identifiable problem. These causes can be insufficient ability, lack of motivation, occasionally some type of personality disorder or pathology such as emotional stress, health problems or alcoholism. Remediation, if aimed at a single problem, may miss the mark because a single teacher may have a combination of these causes or factors listed above.

The 1990s may produce another teacher shortage, and Bridges warns that history may repeat itself and allow poor teachers to slip into tenured positions due to a lack of evaluation efforts by administrators. He cites the 1950s, 1960s, and 1970s as periods where large numbers of teachers were hired and had little supervision during their non-tenure probationary periods (pp. 147–50).

THE CRITICAL DECISION TO AWARD TENURE

The courts and hearing officers in arbitration assume that once a person has achieved tenure they are, indeed, competent teachers. Bridges (1990) stated that "incompetence, not competence, becomes the standard by which the teacher's continued employment is judged." The burden is placed upon the school district to prove incompetence otherwise the instructor will be considered to have the right to continued employment within the school district. Bridges went on to clarify what incompetence is in terms of the law: "Incompetence does not mean marginal or mediocre; rather, it means that the person is a blatant failure in the classroom—so poor that no reasonable person would doubt that the teacher is inept in the classroom (pp. 150–51). With this in mind it is imperative that future tenure decisions be made with the utmost care and agreement as to a teacher's ability to teach at the standard of performance expected by the school or college. Valente (1987) reinforces the presumption that those teachers receiving tenure are, indeed, competent employees and that there is a need to establish strong justification for considering removal of a teacher (pp. 210–216).

The real losers in the tenuring of a poor teacher are often those who can least afford to be subjected to low quality instruction. Bridges says "the students most vulnerable in the system are the ones who are most often victimized by the complaint-driven approach to teacher evaluation—the poor, the minorities, and the low achieving" (p. 147). These are the individuals and families least likely to complain when the students involved receive poor instruction. More affluent upper-middle-class persons' complaints are likely to receive the services of better teachers within the school district.

ROLE OF THE BOARD: POWER AND RESPONSIBILITIES

The governing boards of schools or colleges are only as successful as those persons hired by them to perform at a quality level. An effective evaluation system gives them a much better means of determining who is performing at the levels expected. It also offers them a means of removing those teachers who for reason of inability or refusal, are not performing at the level expected by the school for its students and taxpayers.

A review of board powers on a legal basis find that such powers are usually granted by state laws. Piele (1980) found, "It is a well-settled rule of law that boards of education have only those powers that are expressly granted or reasonably inferred to them by the legislature of the state or that have been granted to the board of education through the state board of education by rule or regulation" (p. 8). He suggested that boards should not, and cannot, delegate such powers. He concluded that board members knew little about their powers as established by law or in courts, based upon case study.

Policies of boards carry a great deal of power if properly conceived and judiciously carried out. Piele (1979) saw them as "carrying the same weight of authority as state law within the confines of the school district. Policies that are unreasonable, arbitrary, or capricious must be found so by the courts" (p. 14).

The Tenth Amendment to the Constitution places educational issues in the realm of state responsibility. Rebell (1990) determined that most issues of faculty evaluation that come before the court system center on "questions of interpretation of the specific requirements of state statutes or state board regulations" (p. 341). The specific procedural requirements are most important when dealing with faculty dismissal cases. Procedural requirements are usually spelled out clearly by state-law, common-law, or due-process rules.

Nason (1982) found that, "only the courts or the legislature can legally challenge a board's decisions" (p. 14). Such decisions are normally considered as carrying final legal authority for the policies developed for a school district. If such policies are reasonable and within the statutes, the decisions made are held as final unless challenged through the court process and found to violate the letter of the law. Piele (1980) stated that boards, in most states, are "the only bodies that can hire or fire employees" (p. 12).

NON-TENURE DISMISSALS: THE BOARD'S ULTIMATE AUTHORITY

Boards and administrators have an excellent opportunity to strengthen their teaching faculties over the coming years through (1) "open" faculty searches for new teachers which are free from political and nepotism pressures, and (2) early evaluation and formative assistance for all new persons hired. There should be no pressure on the boards or administrators that they must tenure all faculty hired. The courts have, indeed, considered the wisdom of the probationary period, prior to a tenure decision being made, and have given boards almost unlimited power to decide either pro or con on the decision of tenure being awarded.

It was not until 1972 that a major supreme court decision reaffirmed this power of local educational boards. In *Board of Regents v. Roth,* it was determined by the court that *no property interest rights* exist for non-tenured teachers. In short, the court told boards, administrators, and teachers that there was no need to provide *cause* or to provide formal dismissal proceedings when they were involved in dismissing non-tenured teachers.

Since the Roth decision, courts have used it in any number of challenges to local governing boards by faculty members and local unions. Knowles and Wedlock (1973) presented the New Jersey case of *Katz v. Board of Trustees of Gloucester County College* (1972) in which a faculty member challenged his dismissal. The instructor claimed that his non-retention was based upon his exercise of lawful union activities and thus violated his First Amendment rights. The court, in holding against the instructor, felt that to hold otherwise would be tantamount to abolishing the tenure system.

The court further stated that:

> inherent in our legislatively enacted tenure policy is the existence of a probationary period during which the board will have a chance to evaluate a teacher with no commitments to re-employ him. . . . we hold that it is the prerogative of the board of trustees to discontinue the employment of a non-tenured teacher at the end of his teaching contract with or without reason. (p. 205)

A Michigan case, *Lipka v. Brown City Community Schools* (1978), raising the issue of *reasons* and *cause* for a non-tenured dismissal, was decided by the state supreme court. In this case the court stated, "There can be no dilution of the board's authority whether the evaluation of teachers is mandated by contract or by statute." This decision supported the Roth case and concluded that there was no entitlement for tenure under the state tenure act.

In *Irby v. McGowan* (1974) the federal district court found no proof of deprivation of liberty or attachment of stigma. The court made a major statement in terms of clarifying boards' rights in evaluation:

> School authorities should have some right to make subjective evaluations of a work record of a person. The court simply cannot, and should not, sit in judgment on, and supervise every remark made concerning the employment or non-employment of persons in a school system and require that every person not re-employed be entitled to a due-process hearing.

The Third District Appellate Court of Illinois supported the power that is vested with governing boards in *Board of Trustees of Community College District No. 513 v. Krizek and the American Federation of Teachers, Local 1810* (1983). The court cited the supreme court's earlier decision:

> The supreme court has made unmistakably clear that when a governing board is vested with the power to grant tenure, or to not renew, then the

governing board cannot delegate, modify or condition its final authority to make such decisions.

The key element in this case, as in previous cases, was the clarifying of the governing board's ultimate authority on tenure questions: *"There can be no dilution of the board's authority whether the evaluation of teachers is mandated by contract or by statute"* (emphasis added). The Illinois court also stated:

> It follows then that the power to grant tenure cannot be conditioned upon the decision of an administrator to make a recommendation or hold a consultation, nor can the power be limited by the preponderance of opinion of evaluators, even though their evaluations may be conducted at the behest of the board. So long as a procedure for evaluation has been implemented, and the results of those evaluations are available to the board, we believe that compliance with the statute has been achieved, and any subsequent decisions to terminate ordered by the board are statutorily sound.

This statement clearly places the board in the front seat of the decision-making process for retention or dismissal of instructors.

This case also presented a reminder that faculty members have little to no due-process issues or rights as probationary faculty. It becomes important that as board policies and procedures are written, hints of property interest should be avoided, as such language may well mislead faculty and administrators into believing such interests may exist. This last case and the previously presented non-tenure dismissal cases make it clear that governing boards are, indeed, the final authority on tenure-granting decisions.

TENURED FACULTY DISMISSALS: THE DUE-PROCESS AND PROCEDURAL BURDENS

Lovain (1984) showed that, when proper procedures are followed by a college or university, a tenured teacher can be dismissed for adequate cause. He found that most recent challenges of tenured teacher terminations were dismissed by the courts. This was a finding that went *counter* to the beliefs of administrators and boards, namely that courts support a reversal of such terminations and that tenured faculty firings cannot be carried out successfully (p. 419).

The dismissal of non-tenured faculty members by board action without the need for formal procedures or presentation of cause was described above and came about in the 1972 landmark supreme court decision in *Board of Regents v. Roth*. A second landmark supreme court decision was also decided in 1972 in *Perry v. Sinderman*. In this case long-term and tenured faculty were found to have a *property interest* in their positions which meant that they could have assurance of continuing in their teaching position and could not be dismissed at the whim of the board or administration. It also provided faculty with the right to have due-process proceedings if the administration and board wished to move toward dismissing them. Both decisions have been cited repeatedly in dismissal cases since 1972.

In *Perry v. Sinderman* the court found:

> The contract renewal practice in effect in the college system (Texas) implicitly conferred upon long-term employees a legitimate expectation of future employment, which constituted a property interest sufficient to require formal procedures.

This case in no way was meant to deter boards and administrators from dismissing faculty for incompetence or for *cause* through other legitimate legal reasons. It did, however, provide a framework for administrators to develop a well-documented case and strictly adhere to proper due-process policies and procedures. Such policies and procedures may be developed from state law and through local board action.

Wise et al. (1984) stated that when a tenured faculty member is considered for possible dismissal it is imperative that the school district have exceptional evaluation procedures (p. 93).

TEACHERS *CAN* BE FIRED!

Tenure is often pointed to as the reason that school districts do not move to dismiss poor tenured faculty. In an interesting study by Kvenvold (1989) a survey of the Minnesota school districts presented some convincing statistics to show that tenured faculty do indeed get terminated. Approximately 70 percent of the 433 school districts in the state responded to this survey. Out of the 303 schools that responded an average of two teachers per school were removed for incompetence between 1983 and 1986.

The frustrations of administrators were vividly presented. Obstacles mentioned in the removal of faculty for incompetence were: (1) difficult legal process involving lengthy documentation; (2) strict tenure laws; (3) powerful teacher unions; and (4) an inordinate amount of time needed to pursue even one suspected incompetent teacher. Even with these obstacles the results appear outstanding compared to any other materials available relating to removing incompetent teachers.

Kvenvold found 97.7 percent of the reporting districts having formal evaluations of the teachers within their schools—both elementary and secondary. The evaluation processes included formal letters of deficiency to inform faculty that their performance was substandard and warn of future action against them. Staff development and improvement programs were used. Dismissals took an average of 12 months in order to satisfy due-process requirements. The administrators in the study considered this a major commitment in time. The following are results of their efforts. Of the 602 tenured teachers removed between 1983 and 1986:

1. Seventy were fired for incompetence. Seventeen of these faculty pursued the grievance procedure as far as the school board for a hearing. Five took legal action, and not one was successful in overturning the school board's dismissal decision.
2. Another 341 teachers were "counseled out" or asked to resign and did so. Mounting evidence of their incompetence greatly assisted in these cases.
3. In addition, 191 were induced to leave with severance pay, early retirement benefits, contract buy-offs, extended medical coverage, and encouragement to retire under the "Rule of 85."

In total, 602 incompetent tenured teachers left teaching and an additional 436 were salvaged through intensive formative evaluation efforts through the same period.

Vander Wheele's report (1992) on Chicago's public schools found that principals would fire approximately 2,000 teachers if it were not for the lengthy dismissal process that the law and the union contract requires. A total of 457 city principals participated in the study. The school system has over 26,000 teachers, so the number considered incompetent equals 7.7 percent.

A counter approach to firing incompetent teachers was discussed by Stoner (1986) which he refers to as "less visible means" than termination procedures. He quoted figures from a Stanford University School of Education study showing that within a two-year period nearly every administrator in their study had forced a resignation from an incompetent tenured faculty member.

Tenured faculty dismissal: a community college case

Petty (1986) dedicated the front page of a trustee newsletter to a court decision that upheld a tenured faculty dismissal in a community college. His effort was to show evidence for the opposite of a strongly held opinion among Illinois community college trustees, that tenured teacher terminations do not get the support necessary from the court system. He argued the following:

> While administrators and boards may often have a substantive case against an incompetent faculty member, documentation sufficient for judicial review often fails to meet established court standards. In addition, the procedural process used by the board may neglect important constitutional rights of notice, due process, a right to a hearing, etc. Frequently, the "good case" in fact turns out to be a weak one in law. Given this trend, many boards have been reluctant to move against the incompetent faculty member out of fear that the cost and perceived odds of success are not worth the risk.

He went on to show that the case being discussed followed both board policies and administrative procedures that were already established. In addition, an evaluation system was clearly laid out and was being followed. He saw adherence to these practices as building "a credible case which passes judicial scrutiny" (p. 1). He discussed some of the details in the case:

> Previous records of staff evaluations revealed little detailed documentation on the strengths or weaknesses of many faculty members. By way of example, the file on the dismissed tenured teacher revealed this statement: "Good teacher, recommend for tenure," with no supporting evidence to document such a conclusion.
>
> In the course of the administration's evaluation of the teacher in question, a number of defects and deficiencies were uncovered. These were documented and discussed with the teacher. She was given the opportunity to address the problems with her own plan of remediation. She submitted a plan but apparently failed to follow it. The board allowed her two semesters to correct the problems. She again failed to take corrective action; indeed, it was disclosed that she had not taken a professional development course in her field in over 12 years. During the evaluation process, the administration even went so far as to allow a representative from the faculty union to sit in on some of the performance review sessions with the teacher. In short, the board met and exceeded all legal requirements of notice, hearing, due process, etc. in establishing its case against the teacher. (p. 1)

Petty showed how, when the college's decision was given an arbitrator's "trial," the arbitrator found in favor of the board. This was done even with strong pressure from the instructor and faculty union bringing forth testimonial support for the instructor from fellow teachers and students. In the decision, both were given little weight. The circuit court upheld the college board and administration upon appeal.

Petty went on to point out that, "court backing of a tenured faculty member's dismissal is certainly not in itself the occasion for celebration" but he saw it as necessary if the nature of the case warrants no other decision except that of termination. He ended his editorial by stating that this case should be used as an "inspiration for boards willing, when necessary, to do the same" (p. 1).

Tenured faculty dismissal: a secondary school case

The Appellate Court in *DeBernard v. State Board of Education* (1988) found a tenured high school teacher to be incompetent in complying with the official notices to remedy her deficiencies in teaching. They found significant evidence to show that she did have consistent negative evaluations on her classroom performances. The court cited the findings of the hearing officer, which were extensive:

1. In seventeen evaluations, plaintiff did not state objectives of the lesson at the beginning of the lesson.
2. In five observations she did not outline for the students at the beginning of the lesson the activities of the lesson.
3. In ten of the observations she did not clearly and accurately sequence and present the subject matter of the lesson.
4. In seven of the observations she did not properly, clearly and accurately respond to student questions and errors.
5. In eight of the observations she did not respond to and dispel student confusion over the subject matter of the lesson.
6. In eight of the observations she did not reinforce student learning through summary or reteaching at appropriate times during the lesson.
7. In thirteen observations she did not pace the lesson to maintain organized instruction, activity and student involvement for the full class period.
8. In nine of the observations she did not require broad student involvement during lessons.
9. In eight of the observations she did not provide sufficient time to do and actually give clear directions for homework.
10. In nine of the observations she did not require homework with appropriate frequency.
11. In eleven of the observations she did not assess student readiness to proceed with each major segment of the lesson.

In the area of creating an atmosphere that was conducive to student achievement in the class, the hearing officer found:

1. In ten of the observations her classroom was too noisy, too often, for too lengthy periods.
2. In nine of the observations too many students, too frequently did not pay attention to the lesson.
3. In seven of the observations too many students, too frequently did not bring to class and/or use appropriate instructional materials

It should be noted that the teacher was evaluated by the principal, the assistant principal for instruction and by the department chair. Each observation was followed by a conference with the evaluator going over the observation and discussing any deficiencies that were noted. The number of observations make it clear that once a teacher has been placed on official notice evaluation continues. The areas of deficiency must be charted as either improving or continuing. This case documented the pattern of incompetency continuing in a number of key instructional areas needed for quality of instruction.

SOME PRACTICAL CONSIDERATIONS IN TENURE TERMINATIONS

Allhouse (1974) and Carr (1972) found that historically the removal of tenured faculty for cause had been rare. They also found that the academic community will tolerate removal for cause once it moves beyond just being a theory.

Hollander (1992) sent out an alert to educators who are faced with poor faculty who do not voluntarily retire when they become eligible. Mandatory retirement is out. The Age Discrimination in Employment Act will only allow removal of a tenured faculty member for just cause reasons. Hollander called for colleges to plan to have both criteria and methodology in place to evaluate these faculty members. Realizing that peers will have little desire to evaluate their own colleagues, administrators are asked to pay attention on how to become classroom evaluators. She also asked that procedures be honest and carefully developed so that poor teachers can be first encouraged to retire rather than removed via full-blown faculty hearings.

Andrews and Wisgoski (1987) drew up some guidelines for administrators and boards to consider when they are in the process of deciding whether to terminate a tenured faculty member:

1. *Do so reluctantly.* Keep in mind that a life and a career are at stake.
2. *Do so as a last resort.* From both a legal and moral standpoint, there is much to do before dismissal is considered. There is a need to have

a division chairperson, associate dean of instruction, and the dean of instruction, by independent evaluation, decide that the individual's classroom instruction is inadequate.

3. *Do so after the individual has been given a detailed explanation* of the nature of his or her inadequacies.

4. *Do so after the individual has been given adequate time*—typically one to two years—to enlist the expertise of peers, supervisors, and other resources of the college to improve instruction.

5. *Do so when, at the end of the period of remediation, the individual has still failed* to raise the level of his or her performance to acceptable college standards, in the opinion of the college supervisors.

6. *Do so after the president and the board of trustees have agreed* with the assessment.

7. *Do so when a law firm specializing in school law has reviewed the case* in detail and issued an opinion that dismissal of the instructor has a strong likelihood of being upheld in court.

8. *Do so when the instructor has declined to accept early retirement,* voluntary transfer to a college assignment that does not involve classroom teaching, or resignation.

9. *Then,* notify the person of his or her dismissal and the reasons for the action, being careful to observe the correct form and the deadlines imposed by the laws of your particular state (p. 164).

These guidelines offer both legally and morally responsible steps for the process of termination. They include all efforts to try to remediate a teacher's performance defects prior to a termination decision. They require specific time elements to allow changes to take place. They include bringing the governing board along throughout the process so that they do not have a surprise when they are given a recommendation to terminate by the administration and board attorney. Bridges (1990) suggested, "there is a presumption that teachers who have achieved tenure are competent employees and, therefore, school officials should not be permitted to dismiss them without establishing a strong justification for doing so" (p. 343).

FOUR DEFENSIBLE CAUSES OF TENURED TEACHER DISMISSAL

Valente (1987) described the causes, which vary from state to state, for which a tenured teacher may be dismissed: (1) *incompetence,* encompassing lack of knowledge, failure to adapt to new teaching methods, failure to maintain discipline, and excessive absence; (2)

neglect of duty or incapability, including physical and emotional illness; (3) *insubordination* and unprofessional conduct, including use of offensive language, use of corporal punishment, or involvement in shoplifting incidents; and (4) *immorality,* including dishonesty, sexual misconduct, or criminal action (pp. 210–216). Courts have been very supportive of dismissals of tenured teachers in these four main areas under cause. The following is a summary of several court-tested and board-supported cased for dismissal for the four areas listed:

Incompetence

A court found a school board being able to dismiss a tenured teacher for failure to maintain discipline in her home economics classes and not needing to transfer the teacher to a different position which she had satisfactorily taught in for a number of years previously. It was also found in this case that a tenured teacher may be asked to resign before initiation of dismissal proceedings. The hearing officer's decision to dismiss the teacher was upheld (*Stamper v. Board of Education of Elementary School District 143* 1986).

Poor relations with students and poor preparation led to the dismissal of a faculty member in *Jawa v. Fayetteville State University* (1976).

In *Mims v. West Baton Rouge* (1975) a number of factors were involved in the dismissal. Repeated violations of rules, lack of control of students and failure to follow administrators' instructions was held by the court to constitute incompetence. Bridges (1990) finds most dismissals for incompetency to follow this pattern of establishing a number of factors rather than being caused by a single isolated incident (pp. 154–55). An exception can be found in a case such as *Mott v. Endicott* (1986), where an incident may be considered by the court as constituting reasonable cause without any prior warning. In this case the teacher was dismissed for striking a student in the genitals.

The opposite was true in *Aulwurm v. Board* (1977), where the court invalidated the dismissal on the part of the board because the teacher had not received adequate notice of what needed to be improved, as was required by state law. Such is the case when the courts deem the cause as something that can be reasonably remediated.

A tenured faculty member was dismissed on grounds of intransigence in dealing with his supervisors in *Chung v. Park* (1974). The main concern was centered on poor teaching. The federal district court held that there was substantial evidence for this.

Neglect of Duty

Two faculty were found to violate terms of their teaching contract in *Shaw v. Board of Trustees of Frederick Community College* (1976). One was tenured and the other worked under a continuing appointment. Both boycotted a faculty workshop and commencement exercises in their protest of the college's plan to abolish tenure at the college.

A tenured professor in *Bates v. Sponberg* (1976) was dismissed in part for failing to submit required reports for a project he directed.

Insubordination

Challenges under the insubordination area by teachers are usually centered on their feeling that they have been dismissed against their right to "academic freedom" or "free speech," which they see as constitutionally guaranteed and being denied. The courts, however, have found such charges to be unfounded in a number of cases in which dismissal has been upheld.

The court found that by taking an unapproved leave of absence, the faculty member was out of line as "academic freedom is not a license for activity at variance with job related procedures and requirements" (*Stasny v. Board of Trustees* 1982).

A vocational instructor in Kentucky from a state school was dismissed for "friction" between her and her supervisor (*Wagner v. Department of Education State Personnel Board* 1977). The supreme court rejected her claim of statutory and constitutional violations. It also observed that sufficient evidence was presented to find her uncooperative and insubordinate to her superiors.

Immorality

In *Lehman v. Board of Trustees of Whitman College* (1978) the court found sexual advances toward female students, faculty, and others to be sexual harassment and adequate cause for dismissal.

The court found swearing at students as a way "to motivate them" was not protected under first amendment rights or freedom of speech. It led to the firing of a faculty member at Midland College (Martin v. Parrish 1986). The court described the teacher's behavior as a "superfluous attack on a captive audience." In this case it was a class of students who had paid to be in the instructor's subject area.

A tenured male faculty member was removed on grounds of sexual harassment for making sexual advances and offering grades for sexual favors to male students. Using established institutional procedures, the charges were investigated, plaintiff was notified, a hearing was held, and the president decided to dismiss the plaintiff. The relationship with a male student was admitted to by the plaintiff, but he denied that grades were involved. The plaintiff challenged and argued that his constitutional rights of substantive and procedural due process, equal protection, free speech, freedom of association, and privacy had been violated. Most of his arguments hinged on the claim that the relationship being questioned was a private consensual sexual activity outside the institution's purview. The board was supported by the Seventh Circuit and found the plaintiff's arguments lacking in merit. They found the facts supporting the institution in dismissing the plaintiff for unethical behavior. They found that he had, indeed, exploited students for his own private advantage. The court made note that this teacher was not like any ordinary person on the street, but rather found him to have a special relationship with the students which he had violated (*Korf v. Ball State University,* 1984).

In *Board of Education of Argo-Summit School District 104 v. Hunt* (1985), a tenured, male physical education teacher who pinched three second grade female students on the buttocks during class was guilty of "irremediable" conduct. In this case the teacher was dismissed without first having been given a notice to remedy by the board of education. The court found that the conduct was irremediable and focused on the damage done to the students rather than on the traditional analysis of whether or not a warning might have prevented such conduct.

OUTSIDE INTERVENTION

Knight (1986), in his essay about the need to "clean up our act in tenure and evaluation," referred to the National Commission on Higher Education Issues report (1982) which noted that "campus academic administrators, working closely with appropriate faculty committees, should develop a system of post-tenure evaluation" (p. 10). He saw the reason for the commission report coming out was because educators had failed to clean up their own houses. Knight went on to say, "refusing to support administrative and public measures to develop evaluation methods, to remediate unacceptable teaching performance, or, that failing, to remove such teachers from the profession, we have invited outside intervention, and we are now receiving it" (pp. 3–4). He quoted from the National Commission's report relating to incompetency which stated, "incompetent faculty must not be protected at the expense of the student or the maintenance of quality" (p. 10). Knight's concerns can be summarized as saying that if educators do not clean up their own problems in quality education, they will find outside forces moving in to do it.

SUMMARY

Tenure is often used as the excuse for being saddled with incompetent teachers. In fact, boards have frequently failed to take action against incompetent teachers for one or both of the following reasons: (1) many board members are unsure of the process of discharging unsatisfactory teachers, or (2) the evaluation system is inadequate to provide the necessary documentation. This failure to take action results in poor teachers—rather than being removed—being passed around within the school system. Wheeler refers to this as the "dance of the lemons." It is therefore imperative that future tenure decisions be made with the utmost care and that boards do *not* award tenure to poor teachers in the first place. Awarding tenure implies competence; once tenure is awarded the burden is on the school district to prove incompetence.

In most states, boards are the only bodies that have the power and responsibility to hire or fire employees. For non-tenured faculty, courts have found that boards have ultimate authority on decisions of tenure or termination. Non-tenured teachers have little or no due-process rights. In contrast, tenured faculty are recognized by courts as having *property interest* in their positions. To prove incompetence, administrators must develop a well-documented case and strictly adhere to proper due-process policies and procedures.

Although firing tenured teachers is rare, it can and does happen. Administrators stated that the main obstacles to terminating incompetent teachers are (1) the large amount of documentation needed, (2) strict tenure laws, (3) powerful teacher unions, and (4) the inordinate amount of time needed for the evaluation and remediation process. Two cases—from a community college and a secondary school—describe tenured faculty terminations that were challenged by the faculty members involved but were upheld by the courts.

Administrators should follow both legal and moral guidelines in the termination process. Termination should be pursued reluctantly, as a last resort. The teacher should have been clearly told what deficiencies needed to be remedied and given adequate time to try to make improvements. Termination should only be sought if, at the end of the period of remediation, the individual has still failed to raise the level of his or her performance. The president and board of trustees and the school's lawyer must agree that the administrator's assessment is valid and that the case is legally defensible before moving ahead.

Courts have been very supportive of dismissals of tenured teacher on four main areas under cause: (1) incompetence, (2) neglect of duty, (3) insubordination, and (4) immorality. Examples of cases in each of these areas have been presented in this chapter.

SUGGESTED EXERCISES

1. Identify those behaviors that you have observed in teachers that might be judged as signs of incompetency.
2. Discuss how a school district might go about setting up procedures that would support their efforts to document incompetence in a faculty member.

13

THE DISMISSAL OF A TENURED INSTRUCTOR

Incompetence: *The intentional or unintentional failure to perform the duties and professional responsibilities of the teaching job in a minimally acceptable manner as specified by the employing district. Incompetence usually results in remediation, reassignment, or dismissal.*

Wheeler et al. (1993 p. 15)

The dismissal of tenured faculty is very seldom found in the research literature in education. In a study by Licata and Andrews (1990) there were 27 percent of the reporting colleges with no formal evaluation system for tenured faculty. This helps explain, in part, why little is documented relative to tenured faculty dismissal. In this same study, 41 percent of the deans and vice presidents in community colleges that reported having evaluation systems thought that the effectiveness of such evaluation was highly questionable (pp. 44–46). Andrews (1992) suggested that, "it is quite obvious to any serious observer of faculty evaluation practices that the absence of and low effectiveness of evaluation procedures and practices provides a sanctuary for incompetent or prematurely retired faculty" (p. 1).

The process of not adequately dealing with incompetent faculty has been defined by Wheeler et al. (1993) as the "dance of the lemons." This is "the practice of reassigning teachers who are incompetent or who are performing below acceptable levels to other positions in the school or the district (rather than proceeding against them)." Other terms they use to describe this practice are, "pass the turkey" or "turkey trot" (p. 11).

COMPONENTS FOR A FAIR HEARING

Bridges and Groves (1984) listed 12 components that they found necessary from state statutes in order to assure the faculty member's rights in a due-process termination hearing:

1. A statement of charges and the materials upon which they are based;
2. A hearing before the school board, a hearing panel, or a hearing officer if requested;
3. A timely written notice of the date, time, and place of the hearing;
4. A hearing in public or private;
5. An opportunity to be represented by counsel;
6. An opportunity to call witnesses on his own behalf;
7. An opportunity to subpoena a person who has made allegations that are used as a basis for the decision of the employer;
8. An opportunity to cross-examine witnesses;
9. Witness testimony under oath or affirmation;
10. A shorthand reporting or tape recording of the hearing upon request;
11. A written decision that contains the specific findings or grounds on which it is based;
12. A written statement of his or her rights to appeal (p. 63).

Bridges and Groves show that if any of these hearings rights mandated by state statutes are neglected, it may lead to setting aside the dismissal decision. Legal counsel is important for consulting on the procedural rights of the teacher so that mistakes are not made.

Morris (1992) summarized the case of *Cleveland Board of Education v. Loudermill* (1985) in which the Supreme Court rules that three conditions must be satisfied before a school district has a fully complete hearing on the termination of a teacher:

> The essential requirements of due process . . . are notice and an opportunity to respond. The opportunity to present reasons, either in person or in writing, why proposed action should not be taken is a fundamental due-process requirement. "The tenured public employee is entitled to oral or written notice of the charges against him, an explanation of the employer's evidence, and an opportunity to present his side of the story." . . . To require more than this prior to termination would intrude to an unwarranted extent on the government's interest in quickly removing an unsatisfactory employee. We conclude that all the process that is due is provided by a pre-termination opportunity to respond, coupled with post-termination administrative procedures as provided by the Ohio statute. (p. 22)

CASE STUDY

The following is a fully developed case study that this author was involved with, concerning the dismissal of a tenured teacher for incompetence. The instructor was evaluated for both in-class and out-of-class professional teaching responsibilities. The case has been changed somewhat to protect confidentiality.

First meeting

The instructional dean apprised the instructor of the college's concern over low enrollments in his classes and let him know that the college was having trouble providing him with a full teaching load. Low enrollments, while a problem, were not cited as a charge against the instructor. They did, however, lead the instructional administrators to start some in-classroom evaluations in the months that followed this 1988 assessment.

The dean of the campus followed up the original meeting with the instructor with a memorandum notifying him that he was, in part, accountable for lack of enrollments in his classes. The memorandum included the following points:

1. The instructor had not been engaging in professional activities for several years;
2. His appearance was poor and there was a personal hygiene concern;
3. His part-time work might be a problem (drawing time away from his professional duties);
4. Brief week-by-week outlines showing where he was in his course syllabus for each course would be needed; and,
5. He should prepare a plan for self-improvement to provide to the division chairperson.

Movement to in-class evaluations

In the months following the original meeting with the instructor, the division chairperson and dean of instruction conducted several in-class evaluations to better assess classroom techniques and effectiveness. The content of these evaluations were very critical of what was taking place:

Dear Instructor:

We are sorry to have to tell you that your in-class preparation and performance was much worse than we could have imagined.

You have spent eight weeks of the spring semester teaching American Literature after 1865 in your Literature 201 course when it should have been taught in the Literature 200 course. This is inexcusable! These courses are both articulated to several four-year colleges in the state. Our agreement with these colleges is that we must teach the same course content as they do in terms of course description and syllabus.

Handouts, tests, and other materials that we have reviewed from this class show an almost complete lack of effort to update, revise, and keep a current preparation effort for this class.

We highly suggest that you start immediately to put the type of preparation, time, and effort into your full-time job at this college that we expect from all other faculty. If the outside job you hold draws you away from the time you need to do the kind of quality work necessary to retain your job at this college, you should give utmost consideration to making a change.

Your neglect of all major aspects of your job, preparation, audio-visual, proper presentation of material (both content and proper placing of material), conferences, courses and testing, put you in a very critical position.

Your division chairperson and I will plan to discuss these concerns with you in the near future.

> Sincerely,
> Dean of Instruction

Moving to a "notice to remedy"

A "notice to remedy" was decided to be necessary by the instructional administrators and the college president. This was an official notification from the board of trustees of the need to remediate the deficiencies and defects that the administrators outlined in their evaluation reports. A list of these deficiencies is given in Example 5.

E X A M P L E   5
Notice to Remedy

You are being notified by the Board of Trustees action in passing a formal notice of remediation. The following is a list of deficiencies that you must address in the very near future.

1. Lack of preparation for class lecture, determining of daily objectives, and sharing of these with your students.

The steps required in the resolution of this deficiency are to prepare daily, weekly, and semester outlines so you can adequately cover the material necessary for your courses; and to update and pass out course outlines that tell students what to expect for daily lectures, readings, test reviews, tests, and the dates they will review tests, etc. You must properly plan.

2. Disregard of the course syllabus in teaching of your courses and use of poorly prepared course outlines.

You must teach the material that is outlined for the Literature 200 and 201 courses during the proper semester. These are transfer courses to other colleges, and you are under obligation to guarantee teaching of the courses as they are articulated for transfer to four-year colleges and universities. Course outlines need to be improved and reflect better objectives for these Literature courses.

3. Poor, outdated audio-visual support for lectures.

Your complete use of audio-visuals needs to be reviewed. Overlays on the overhead projector have been evaluated as very poor and almost non-functional. Much improvement needs to be made immediately in this area.

4. Tests and handouts are dated.

Your tests have been evaluated to be old, updated by hand, and with markings by students who have previously used them. Some of your handouts are considered so old they are difficult to copy and are now most difficult to read. This is one more area in which lack of planning and effort is very evident. Future materials should show marked improvements.

5. Lack of professional upgrading.

By your own admission in a recent communication to the administration, you have not even applied for a professional conference in your field for over 12 years. This is almost unheard of in any level of education. You were unable to list any professional journal in your field of American Literature to which you subscribe, read, or have used. Not one professional activity initiated by yourself was listed after 1981. You must take your professional responsibilities in this area much more seriously starting now.

6. Conclusion.

In our judgment, the defects and deficiencies set forth above are both clearly stated, easy to understand, and reasonable to ask you to correct. The defects and deficiencies cited can only be removed, however, with a much stronger commitment to your full-time job at this college than your performance suggests you have been giving it for some time. There is no question that such a performance in your job would not be conducive to students enrolling in or being counseled by college staff to enroll in your classes. The continuing low enrollments in your classes appear to be somewhat explained by this evaluation of your performance.

Remediation efforts

The board of trustees voted 7–0 to support the administration in their efforts to remediate the deficiencies in teaching and other job responsibilities of the instructor.

A meeting was set up with the instructor following board action in order for the division chairperson and dean of instruction to review the charges and to make any clarifications that were necessary. The dean, in the follow-up memorandum to the meeting, made clear that the instructor continued to deny the allegations in his letter of deficiencies from the board of trustees. The dean concluded that he felt the meeting to be less than productive based upon the instructor's attitude.

This meeting was followed with further in-class evaluations, verbal and written reports documenting both positive and negative progress on the deficiencies cited in the "notice to remedy." The daily objectives and handouts prepared for the students were returned to the instructor after being evaluated as being "too general" and not answering the specific board remediation demands.

The administration asked the instructor to spend some of the upcoming summer months updating his course materials and to not teach during that summer. These items were to have been completed and turned in by the start of classes in the fall semester, but outlines were not received. The list of deficiencies from the board were monitored into the fall semester. This was done by both in-class visits and through written memos that continued to press the instructor to provide the written materials that were now long overdue. Some seven months following the board of trustees "notice to remedy," the administration had still not received the updated course outlines. These were finally produced after a face-to-face meeting late into the fall semester. They were deemed unsatisfactory in content and not in a weekly format as had been requested. The instructor was now given until the start of the winter semester in January to make changes to conform to the required format asked for in previous correspondence.

The following deficiencies were documented as still existing during the fall semester:

1. Lack of planning and preparation for each class;
2. Wandering from topic to topic and dealing with minute and relatively unimportant details;

3. Becoming bogged down in organization in the last half of each class visited;
4. Presenting material in a haphazard manner.

The dean's report also stated:

> You are once again directed to read and re-read these comments and make some effort to properly plan for these classes. The students are still the losers with your half-hearted efforts to date. It has been noted that you still work many outside hours on another job while your work at the college continues to show much neglect.

In a late-fall-semester evaluation of the instructor's class in the college's off-campus program some six weeks later, the dean and division chairperson once again noted in their report that he was observed providing a lecture that was "well behind the course schedule outline, disorganized, hurried, and tantamount to useless." The division chairperson's written report further stated:

> My observations today come on the heels of a recent fairly good evaluation. I can only conclude that he is not willing to devote the consistent time and energy that it takes to be a professional. Our close scrutiny this semester has forced some instances of competent teaching upon him, but when the evaluation was unexpected, he reverted to a slipshod performance.
>
> I do not know where to go from here. The instructor was notified by the Board Resolution to remove these and other deficiencies nine months ago and I find many of them are still in existence.

Recommendation for dismissal

The question of termination now became a real issue with the dean of instruction and division chairperson. All of the evaluative evidence gathered since the official board of trustees "notice to remedy" was put together and shared with the college president and the college attorney. The board of trustees, based upon recommendation of the board attorney, ordered the administration to prepare proper legal documents to present to the board at their next meeting.

The board of trustees, 10 months after their action to deliver the "notice to remedy", voted 7–0 to dismiss the instructor. They presented him with a "Notice of Charges and Bill of Particulars" listing the following six charges:

I. You have disregarded the official college course syllabus in teaching your courses.
II. You have failed to prepare for and properly manage your lectures.

III. You have failed to use effective evaluation and testing procedures for student learning.
IV. You have refused to follow administrative and Board directives to improve the quality of the audio-visual materials used in your classes.
V. You have failed to engage in any significant attempts to upgrade your competence as a professional.
VI. You have been persistently negligent in carrying out your duties as a faculty member.

Proving just cause

In this case the state statute allows for a hearing officer (arbitrator) to hear evidence from both the faculty member and representatives of the board of trustees if the instructor in question decides to seek an appeal of the board's decision. Such a hearing helps to provide a forum for a final and binding decision based upon the evidence presented. Such evidence must provide *substantial* grounds for the dismissal decision, before the hearing officer will rule in the board's favor. The state statute in this case says that the board must prove its charges by a *preponderance* of evidence. The faculty member did choose to appeal the board decision and to seek an arbitrator and hearing procedure.

Outcomes on the formal charges

The two-day hearing with the arbitrator brought about the following findings by the hearing officer:

1. Concerning Charge I, it would have been possible subsequent to the board's "notice to remedy" to reallocate the time allotted to each topic as requested by the administration; the instructor did not correct the situation in the following fall semester.
2. Concerning Charge II, the arbitrator saw the evaluations by administrators for the off-campus class as a significant indication that the instructor failed to properly prepare for and manage his lectures.
3. The arbitrator found the evidence for Charge III consisted of what was observed primarily during the class sessions the evaluators visited. He did not, therefore, believe that this charge had been proven, although this did not mean that he believed the instructor did prepare the students adequately and did cover tests properly. He just failed to find conclusive evidence in support of the board's charge.
4. The arbitrator, upon close review of materials presented, concluded that he had not been supplied with sufficient evidence to support a finding to uphold Charge IV.
5. Concerning Charge V, the arbitrator was convinced from testimony from

both the instructor and the board that the instructor had not made a significant effort to maintain his professional competence. He pointed out that despite the warning from the board in the previous spring, the instructor did not remedy the situation.

6. Charge VI centered on the failure of the instructor to meet board requests in a timely manner and the persistence of being late in holding office hours. The arbitrator referred to this last as a "catch-all" charge and did not see it as adding much to the board's other charges.

The arbitrator's decision

In addition to reviewing the six charges in light of the evidence provided, the arbitrator read letters from five students and heard favorable testimony on the instructor's behalf by three teachers and two students. While he indicated that he was impressed with this show of support on behalf of the instructor, he did not give as much weight to this evidence as he did to the negative findings in the administrative evaluations. He noted, "It seems normal for teachers to support another teacher with whom they have been associated for some time even though the teacher may be guilty of the charges made against him by the employer."

The arbitrator also noted that some student evaluation forms submitted by the faculty member in his support were given in small classes where the anonymity of students was not fully protected.

On the issue of holding a conference with the instructor after each evaluation, the board was reprimanded. They had omitted holding one such conference. The arbitrator, however, did not feel that this procedural error was of sufficient importance to serve as grounds to set aside the dismissal of the instructor.

In summary, the arbitrator concluded that the instructor did not remedy the deficiencies that he was given over 10 months earlier by the board of trustees. These were restated as Charges I, II, and V accompanying the dismissal resolution of the board which was sent to the instructor. The arbitrator further concluded that the board did indeed have *just cause* to dismiss the instructor. The decision of the board of trustees was upheld and the appeal of the instructor denied.

The circuit court also denied the appeal of the instructor at the next level and the case was not appealed any further.

SUMMARY

There were several key points learned during the processing of this case:

1. Tenure does not guarantee a life-time position to a faculty member if competence in one's job becomes eroded.
2. Proving incompetence is a lengthy and tedious process. In-class evaluation by administrative supervisors carries a high degree of weight in such cases.
3. Student evaluations are unlikely to carry the same weight in arbitration and in the courts as carefully conducted supervisory evaluations. The formalized weight given to student evaluations, by colleges using both administrative and student evaluations, should be assigned much lower weight in board policies than that given to *administrative* evaluations.
4. The formal "notice to remedy" is a most important legal step to be taken in trying to improve an instructor. It also provides an excellent baseline with which to judge improvements and in which to conduct subsequent evaluations.
5. In-class observations, course syllabus, semester course outlines, grade books, copies of examinations, and records of individual faculty development efforts are all documents important in determining a faculty member's competence to provide the expected tenure-level quality instruction.

SUGGESTED EXERCISES

1. Discuss and list the key points made by the arbitrator in the above case that led to the dismissal.
2. Review the strengths and weaknesses found by the arbitrator in the formal evaluation process and how the process was administered.

PART-TIME FACULTY: MAJOR GROWTH AND MAJOR NEGLECT

There are approximately 40 percent of all higher education faculty working as part-time faculty members according to Mangan (1991). In the community college system this number goes over 50 percent. As startling as these numbers may appear, they may not yet have peaked out.

In a report on campus trends (El-Khawas 1990), it was found that 56 percent of administrators in the institutions surveyed were concerned about the effects such a large number of part-time faculty was having upon their institutions. The growth of part-time faculty was seen as causing additional strains and increased burdens upon the institutions' support service systems.

TREATING PART-TIME FACULTY LIKE FULL-TIME FACULTY

Some of the recommendations for improving this support system was discussed by Norman (1984). He proposed fringe benefits on a proportional basis, title changes to "adjunct" or "associate" instructors, office space and clerical assistance. Other recommendations include parking privileges, names of part-time faculty placed on mailing and telephone lists, attendance at social as well as departmental functions, mentoring with a full-time faculty member, and an invitation to attend all developmental programs offered on the campus.

In the California community colleges, Spinetta (1990) has suggested that part-time faculty be given pro-rata pay, that is, a proportion of the salary that is given to full-time faculty. He cites the Joint Committee for Review of the Master Plan for Higher Education, 1989, who recommended this as "the only long-term solution to the part-time faculty issue in the California community colleges." Spinetta believes such a pay increase would increase part-time faculty's feelings of professionalization and job satisfaction, and possibly the college's effectiveness.

This move would, however, put an undue burden on an already financially strained system of education. Spinetta doesn't deal with the fact that economic savings is one of the main reasons that colleges have moved toward more part-time faculty.

The large Maricopa Community College system in Arizona has made some moves to improve part-time faculty effectiveness (Lampignano 1990). They present their part-time faculty with an orientation program. This includes workshops and seminars taught by content professionals and setting up some mentoring arrangements. Miami-Dade Community College District in Florida has incentives that are given to full-time faculty to participate in staff development activities. Little has been done, however, to grant similar inducements to the part-time faculty.

EFFECTIVE EVALUATION OF PART-TIME FACULTY

Andrews (1987c) listed four areas which would lead to an effective evaluation system for part-time faculty: (1) establishing minimum qualifications for instruction; (2) providing teaching orientation, (3) conducting in-class observation and evaluation, and (4) performing follow-up action as a result of evaluation. In-class observations are necessary to provide these faculty with helpful insights into the improvement of their teaching and also to assist in the retention of these faculty members. Such assistance should improve the image part-time faculty have of their work and also show that the college does care about their teaching contributions. Evaluation is a way to provide the part-time faculty with suggestions for improvement and to share the teaching expectations of the college with them.

There are some problems that are inherent in hiring a large number of part-time faculty. In order to establish quality instruction in these teachers' classrooms, administrators must be prepared to deal with the following:

1. Deans, division chairpersons, and others may have to become the "teacher education" trainers for many of these faculty members, who have little to no teaching methodology, orientation, or training.
2. Part-time faculty may not come to the job with any previous teaching experiences. Some will come with poor experiences, which have never been assessed or evaluated.
3. This influx of part-time faculty presently and in the future means that more students will judge the colleges by the quality of work of

the part-time faculty. Students will relate their positive or negative experiences to relatives and friends at home and in the workplace. Poor instruction can damage the college's reputation through this grapevine.

I have seen first-time adult students "lost forever", because they felt insulted by poor and ineffectual instruction at the college. While a full-time faculty member can positively or negatively affect from 100 to 175 or more homes each semester, one part-time faculty member can affect from 15 to 80 homes each semester.

RESEARCH ON PART-TIME FACULTY

Erwin and Andrews (1994) conducted a study in 353 community, technical and junior colleges to find out how effective, comprehensive, and well-planned services for part-time faculty were. A return of 283 responses (80 percent) provided a significant snapshot of the state of the services to part-time faculty in these colleges. The instructional vice president or dean was the person responding in each of these colleges.

Services provided for part-time faculty

The largest number of colleges (94) reported 50 or less part-time faculty. This was followed by 47 colleges having 51 to 100 and 44 colleges having between 101 and 150. Another 33 colleges had over 300 and 21 reported over 400. Six of the colleges reported having over 600 part-time faculty.

The services being offered most often were:

1. Course syllabus;
2. Meetings with full-time faculty;
3. Orientation by department;
4. Review of materials by supervisor; and
5. Meetings during the semester.

The number of respondents checking these as well as other services is summarized in Table 13, in rank order.

Evaluation

In the service area of evaluation and in looking to improve services in the future, several questions were asked. A total of 226 (88.6%) of the

TABLE 13

Services Provided to Part-Time Faculty

Service (rank order by responses)	Number of Responses (N = 283)	Percentage
1. Course Syllabus Assistance	236	92.5%
2. Meetings With Full-Time Faculty	223	87.5%
3. Orientation by Department	214	83.9%
4. Review of Materials by Supervisor	168	65.9%
5. Meetings During the Semester	156	61.2%
6. Assistance in Teaching Methodology	135	52.9%
7. Assistance in Test Preparation	109	42.7%
8. In-Class Assistance by Supervisor	104	40.8%
9. In-Class Assistance by Faculty (FT)	98	38.4%

respondents indicated "yes" they did have a faculty evaluation program for their part-time faculty. The number saying they were "not satisfied" with the faculty evaluation was 103 (41.2%). In asking which type of evaluation components were utilized the responses were:

(1) Evaluation by students	204
(2) Evaluation by supervisor	160
(3) Evaluation by faculty	50
Total	414

The 414 figure from the 283 respondent colleges would indicate that a combination of these methods are utilized in a number of the colleges.

Recognition

Only 33 out of the colleges reported any type of merit recognition programs for their part-time faculty. This represented only 13.2 percent. On the other hand, 166 (60%) reported they now had recognition programs for their full-time faculty.

The type of recognition programs reported were "recognition and small stipend," "associate faculty member of the year award," "part-time of the year award by the president," "'extra mile' award," and "similar (awards) to those for full-time faculty." This was an area found to be very under-developed. It, no doubt, reflected the lack of or weakly developed evaluation programs.

Concerns regarding evaluation

There were several areas of concern specified regarding the implementation of part-time faculty evaluation (see Table 14). Thirty-six respondents in the study said that systematic improvements were needed to address the following problems:

1. Poor implementation;
2. No consistency;
3. Too cumbersome;
4. Inadequate follow-up;
5. Done too late in semester;
6. Done too sporadically;
7. Doesn't distinguish 'good' from 'bad' teachers.

The second area of concern checked by 22 colleges centered on either having no evaluation system in existence or having one they considered as being too weak or incomplete to be effective. The third area of concern in 16 colleges found, "too many part-time faculty and not enough administrative help," available to administer a system of evaluation effectively.

Improvements planned

Many of the colleges responded positively to the question, "Do you have plans for the future to improve services to part-time faculty?"

TABLE   14

The State of Part-Time
Faculty Evaluation: Concerns

Concerns	Number of Responses
1. Systematic Improvements Needed	36
2. Evaluation is Non-Existent	22
3. Large Part-Time Faculty and Limited Administrative Help	16
4. Evaluation System Just Implemented	5

Expanding orientation services and adding in-service and faculty development days were reported by 38 and 37 colleges respectively. Other plans included improving benefits such as merit recognition, office space, assistance in tuition for further coursework, and access to computers. The need for improved and/or addition of a part-time faculty evaluation system was also identified (see Table 15).

EVALUATING PART-TIME FACULTY

Colleges in the above study ranged in part-time faculty from less than 50 to several reporting over 600 on their campuses. Each college needs to consider a practical method of analyzing how these faculty might be evaluated by supervisory personnel.

In some colleges the number will be small enough for a dean or vice president and division chairpersons to conduct classroom visitations of all of these faculty. In colleges with large staffs it will take more creative thinking to conduct effective evaluation practices. Hiring of master teachers in the subject matter may assist the administration in getting to all of these faculty. In those cases where the teaching appears to be of high enough quality, further follow-up visitations may not be needed. In those classes that may be identified as having significant problems or

TABLE 15

Future Plans to Improve Services
to Part-Time Faculty

Services Planned	Number of Responses
1. Orientation (Expanded, Improved, etc.)	38
2. Provide In-Service and Faculty Development Days	37
3. Add Mentoring	31
4. Improved Benefits (Recognition, Offices, Tuition Waivers, Access to Computers, etc.)	30
5. Improved Evaluation	24
6. Provide for Center for Teaching/Learning/Teaching Methodologies	17
7. Invite to Deparment Meetings With Full-Time Faculty	15
8. Provide Professional Growth Opportunities	13

concerns the administrative personnel could be sent in to conduct further evaluation of the class. In few cases should this be more than 8 to 15 percent of the classes. In short, if master teachers in a large college with 650 part-time faculty found 50 to 60 concerns, it would not be unreasonable for supervisory personnel to be available to follow-up this number of part-time instructors.

Once a review of these part-time faculty has been made, it is not necessary to continue to be in their classrooms on a semester-to-semester or even an every-year basis. A number of those persons found to need assistance can be helped and will respond. They will need follow-up supervision. Some will simply not come up to the standards demanded or be unable to make the adjustments necessary; these persons should be removed and replaced. This may cause some problems when a poor instructor who was hired a number of years ago now is removed. It is during these decisions, however, that administrators must remember that the students are their number one concern.

Another approach might be to plan to visit 20 percent of the part-time faculty each year. All would be visited within a five-year period. Supervisory personnel usually can identify some of their problem areas for the first-year review. Student complaints and generally knowing the personal habits of part-time faculty will allow one to make some assessments of those persons who need to be reviewed early in the process.

Once all part-time staff have been evaluated and appropriate staff changes made, administrators can better focus on those new faculty being hired. Early visits and suggestions for improvement can be made before poor practices become ingrained in the faculty member's approach to teaching. It is not improbable that such visits will lead to an occasional removal and replacement of an incompetent part-time faculty member during the semester.

Behrendt and Parsons (1983) recommended the following strategies to help improve the use of part-time faculty:

1. There must be a general institutional commitment to *overall* staff evaluation for adjunct faculty evaluations to be effective.
2. The institution must possess a base of expertise to conduct the evaluation system properly.
3. Adequate support services similar to those available to full-time faculty members must be provided to adjunct faculty.
4. While trying to integrate adjunct faculty into the college community through such techniques as evaluation, we must remember that the needs of these people are different from those of the full-time faculty members (p. 42).

SUMMARY

The role of part-time faculty members is increasing in both community colleges and secondary schools. As this population of teaching personnel increases it becomes more important that they be looked at closely in terms of evaluating the quality of their teaching.

The use of student evaluation is a weak method at best for determining whether quality teaching exists in the classrooms of part-time faculty. Yet many of the schools in the Erwin and Andrews study (204 out of 414) reported using evaluation by students. Less than half (160) reported using evaluation by supervisors. Only 58.8% of the colleges in the study felt satisfied with their part-time evaluation system.

The recognition of good part-time faculty was one of the major weaknesses identified in the study. The total number of colleges reporting some form of merit recognition for their outstanding full-time faculty was 60% but dropped to 13.2% for their part-time faculty.

Overall, there are severe gaps and a lack of systematic methods being utilized to integrating part-time faculty into the mainstream of teaching in community, technical, and junior colleges. Many of the services offered to full-time faculty are neglected when looking at part-time faculty.

Whether a faculty member teaches five courses or one course in a given semester of work, he or she must remain accountable to those students who come prepared to receive quality instruction in each of their classes. The areas of neglect discussed in this chapter make it evident that part-time faculty are treated as second-class in many institutions. Students should expect better on behalf of their college administrators and governing boards.

SUGGESTED EXERCISES

1. Determine a plan to integrate part-time faculty into a higher level of quality teaching at a secondary school or community college.
2. Outline an approach to assuring competent supervisory evaluation of all part-time faculty in a secondary school or community college.

THE GOVERNING BOARDS: WHERE DO THEY FIT IN?

How do governing boards or boards of education fit into the process of faculty evaluation? Do they have rights in hiring and dismissal of faculty? What is the legal basis for such rights? These are a few of the questions that need to be addressed when setting up a faculty evaluation system. It is necessary to establish both a moral and a legal base for the governing board as they deal with personnel policies, procedures, and decision making.

MORAL BASE

Board members will achieve prestige from good policies which are properly administered. Solid personnel policies demanding quality in hiring, evaluation, and tenure decisions will likely outweigh all other responsibilities that boards have. Boards must learn the laws that govern educational institutions and avoid capricious action when making personnel decisions. Policies and procedures that remove all doubt about politically motivated appointments, nepotism, and patronage and allow for open searches for personnel will be significant in a board's quest for quality and respect.

Woodruff (1976) suggested seven basic rules for board members that deal openly and honestly with personnel matters:

1. Avoid precipitous action. Do not lose your self-control.
2. Make sure you have all the facts. Do not rely on only one side's version of a disputed issue. Demand sufficient information before voting.
3. Remember your duty is to the institution you serve, not to any one member of the administration.
4. Follow the rules—the board or college policies and procedures that have been written down.

5. Make an effort to attend every board meeting. By being chronically absent, you may incur liability.
6. When in doubt, use your paid professionals. Consult your president, chancellor, and counsel.
7. Avoid conflicts of interest by disclosing any potential ones up front. Refuse to debate, discuss, or vote on any matter in which you or your family have an interest.

Woodruff suggested that these "rules" should be taught at in-service training with governing boards (pp. 11–18).

LEGAL BASE AND AUTHORITY

State laws determine most of the powers and duties that board members have. Piele (1980) states that "it is a well-settled rule of law that boards of education have only those powers that are expressly granted or reasonably inferred to them by the legislature of the state or that have been granted to the board of education through the state board of education by rule or regulation" (p. 8).

Piele also finds that such power or authority cannot be delegated. He has found that the powers of boards are better known in the law and the courts than they are known by many individual board members. It is imperative that such knowledge become part of the in-service training of all new board members, since personnel matters are the ones that cause the greatest concern in college or secondary schools.

In addition to state laws and board of education rules and regulations, individual boards also have the power to establish policies for their own school district. Such policies have been found by Piele (1979) to carry the same weight of authority as the state laws when applied to the confines of the school district. Local policies and procedures that are unreasonable, arbitrary, or capricious, however, will be so found in the court system (p. 14).

Board decisions are considered as final in terms of legal authority according to Nason (1982) as long as they are within their established policies. Only the courts or legislature can legally challenge such board decisions (p. 15). Decisions by boards are not always well accepted or pleasing to faculty members or other personnel but they stand up legally unless challenged and overturned through the court system.

Piele (1975) reported a court decision in *Irby v. McGowan* (1974) on the rights of administrators and governing boards in making personnel decisions. The court stated that school authorities should have some right to make subjective evaluations of a work record of a person. They did not think that it was the court's job to judge every remark made concerning the employment or non-employment of non-tenured teachers and require that the ones not re-employed be entitled to a due-process hearing (p. 10).

Morris (1992) reported that the South Dakota Supreme Court found unlawful encroachment upon boards' rights concerning dismissal of a tenured faculty member in *Worzella v. Board of Regents* (1958). The tenure policy that had been locally developed would not allow for board dismissal without first gaining approval of both the president of the college and the faculty tenure committee. The court ruled that "such delegation of authority to subordinates is an unlawful encroachment upon the board of regents' constitutional and statutory power of control over such college" (p. 7).

The sensitivity of board decisions in hiring and firing was described by Jasiek et al. (1985): "There is no greater responsibility of a board of trustees than personnel management. The board's role in hiring and firing is an issue that is so sensitive and misunderstood that no one wants to mention it." They went on to list what they deemed the most important ingredients for effective personnel management, dealing with hiring, retaining, or dismissal of college personnel: (1) a strong governing board, (2) a strong president and staff, (3) mutual support, and (4) clearly defined personnel policies and procedures. They predicted that the effectiveness of any personnel system would be doomed if it lacked any one of these four ingredients (p. 87).

Kauffman (1983) states that the quality of relationship between the board and college president is also a determinant in the effectiveness of how board policies are carried out. He finds the authority of the college president enhanced when a board assumes responsibility and insists on approving major policy and fiscal matters, including tenure (p. 19).

Rebell (1990) found no explicit right to education in the federal Constitution. The Tenth Amendment to the Constitution reserves the right to educational issues for the states. His review of cases found courts specifically interested in how closely *procedural requirements* were carried out from state law, common-law, or due-process requirements. Most of the court cases he reviewed involved questions of interpretation of the specific requirements of the state statutes or state board regulations (p. 341).

TENURE AND BOARD MEMBERS

Possibly nothing is more misunderstood by governing board members than the concept of *tenure*. In the business and industrial world there is nothing equivalent to tenure in education. The way that many administrators treat tenure has added to the confusion and has led many board members, students, and lay persons to believe that tenure is a guarantee of employment until retirement or death. The literature written on tenure usually has only served to help perpetuate this belief. The example of universities has especially contributed to this, where ineffective faculty have seldom been removed.

The literature and legal review of cases at community colleges and secondary schools show that tenure is not necessarily a *sinecure* for faculty who are not performing competently. A number of these cases were presented in Chapter 12. Appendix A also presents a significant number of cases to show board members, administrators, faculty, and lay persons that dismissal of incompetent faculty does happen. The *Board of Regents v. Roth* (1972) case was the landmark court case establishing that a non-tenured faculty member could be dismissed without the need for formal dismissal proceedings. The court found non-tenured faculty to not have a property interest in the job.

Tenured faculty have also been removed and such action has been upheld through the courts for the following four reasons: (1) incompetence, (2) immorality, (3) neglect of duty, and (4) insubordination. This was dealt with in detail in Chapter 12.

Tenure is recognition that is granted after a specified number of years (usually three to seven) to those faculty who have achieved a high enough degree of competence in instruction and other job responsibilities. The governing board is the final authority on the rewarding or denial of tenure.

Olswang and Lee (1984) support the important protections of "academic freedom" that tenure has provided instructors. They do, however, point out that protections for such faculty are not "unlimited." They went on to say that "evaluating the continued competence of faculty does not infringe on faculty freedoms as competence is a condition of tenure" (p. 3).

Olswang and Lee presented the court's balance on individual professional freedom of faculty and the need for society to gain from research and learning in the *Browzin v. Catholic University* (1975) case:

> "Tenure's real concern is with arbitrary or retaliatory dismissals based on an administrator's or a trustee's distaste for the content of a professor's teaching or research, or even for positions taken completely outside the campus setting. It is designed to foster our society's interest in the unfettered progress of research and learning by protecting the profession's freedom of inquiry and instruction . . ." (p. 3)

The AAUP developed its statement on academic freedom in 1916 and tried to make special efforts to disassociate academic freedom from the protection of incompetence. Olswang and Lee quote the statement they formulated:

> If the profession should prove itself unwilling to purge its ranks of the incompetent and the unworthy, or to prevent the freedom which it claims in the name of science from being used as a shelter for inefficiency, for superficiality, or for uncritical and intemperate partisanship, it is certain that the task will be performed by others. (p. 3)

The concern about neglect in dealing with incompetent or unworthy faculty was clearly stated. This statement in 1916 shows that the education profession has for a long time had cause for concern about the profession housing incompetent personnel.

POLICIES FOR EVALUATION

With the legal right and authority to develop policies and practices that assure quality in instruction, it is most important that appropriate board policies be put in place that reflect the desire to improve instruction. Andrews (1985, pp. 53–54) outlined several possible policies that would establish a framework for quality evaluation practices. Example 6 can be viewed as an "overall" policy as it relates to evaluation:

E X A M P L E   6

Board Policy—Evaluation of Faculty Assistant to Instruction, and Counselors: Tenured, Non-Tenured, and Part-Time

It is the policy of the Board of Trustees that all faculty of the college shall be evaluated by their supervisors in order to assure that quality in instruction and other professional conduct is maintained.

Persons to be covered by the above mentioned evaluation procedures will be: (1) tenured faculty; (2) non-tenured faculty; (3) part-time faculty; (4) counselors; and (5) assistants to instruction.

Example 7 helps boards to assure that proper hiring will take place and that quality personnel will be hired:

EXAMPLE 7
Board Policy—Hiring of Professional Staff

The Board of Trustees will hire a professional staff, educated and prepared in accordance with generally accepted standards and practices for teaching in the discipline and subject fields to which they are assigned. These include collegiate study and/or professional experience. As a general rule, graduate work to the Master's Degree or beyond in the subjects or fields taught is expected except in such subjects and fields in which college programs are not normally available or in which the work experience and related training is the principal teaching medium.

Example 8 acknowledges the responsibility of the governing board in a decision to not rehire non-tenured faculty and other instructional support personnel:

EXAMPLE 8
Board Policy—Decision Not to Rehire
Non-Tenured, Full-Time and
Instructional Support Personnel

A decision to not rehire (dismiss) a non-tenured faculty member for the ensuing school year or term will be made by the Board of Trustees reviewing the President's recommendation.

The above sample policies bring to the forefront governing boards' authorities and responsibilities as they relate to the teaching and instructional support staff.

IMPLEMENTATION OF POLICIES

How well the above policies are administered will greatly depend upon the quality of the administrative staff that is hired to implement them. Administrators need to be oriented to the importance of in-class evaluation procedures, and the law as it relates to evaluation, tenure, and dismissals. Administrative evaluators must be well versed and experienced in quality classroom instructional methods. It enhances the process with faculty a great deal if such evaluators were excellent classroom teachers themselves. One of the major concerns I have heard expressed by faculty throughout the United States and Canada is, "Who is evaluating the evaluator?" This concern is legitimate in many elementary, middle and secondary schools and colleges where administrators are promoted and given responsibilities for evaluation, knowing little about the dynamic processes involved in teaching and learning.

POOR IMPLEMENTATION OF BOARD POLICIES

The carrying out of board policies, if poorly done by administrators, can lead to litigation, public criticism, and court appearances. Brown (1977) found very little court involvement with instruction prior to the 1970s. Most of the disputes were decided within the school system. He describes the action since 1970 as an "explosion of litigation in the areas of tenure and employment contracts" (p. 279).

The Grand Rapids board of education in Michigan paid a heavy public relations price for the decision they made to quietly remove incompetent teachers and any evidence of such incompetence from their records. *The Grand Rapids Press* harshly criticized the board's action in preparing special agreements with the faculty members involved. The paper's editorial, which argued the inappropriateness of the board's action, was replied to by the board of education. The third response was from a taxpayer in the district, who reacted very angrily to the board's attempt to justify their actions. The following is a shortened version of each of these essays on the matter:

Expedite Over Principle

"The end doesn't justify the means" is an adage old enough to be stenciled on the consciences of all nine members of the Grand Rapids Board of Education. They ought to recall it the next time they dismiss a teacher for incompetence.

In each of three contested cases last year in which tenured teachers were permanently removed from city classrooms, the board agreed to cooperate with the teacher in hiding the whole matter from other employers. In one instance, the board went so far as to provide the ousted teacher with a letter of recommendation.

The arrangement is worked out in varying language in each settlement agreement. In all three cases, the board agrees to withdraw charges against the teacher and erase all mention of them from the teacher's personnel file. One settlement restricts the board from releasing evaluations of the teacher to any prospective employer; another requires that evaluations "and all negative materials" be removed from the personnel file. The letter of recommendation given to one teacher noted "she was a

hard working and conscientious employee during her years of
employment in Grand Rapids."

Con men would take pride in such flim-flam. School trustees
should be ashamed. The effect of sanitized files and misleading
recommendations is to pass the Grand Rapids problem along to
some other school district—and some other set of children . . .
No school board, moreover, can define its moral responsibilities
so narrowly as to include only children inside its own school
buildings; a board is answerable for actions, which put children at
risk, regardless of where they are.

The schools will be seeking removal of more teachers this
spring. The cases might well go longer and cost more if the board
refuses to set the teachers up for new jobs elsewhere.

There is at least an equal chance, however, that a policy of
firmness and honesty over time will strengthen the board's hand
in improving the faculty. At the least, such a commitment would
assure that no child is made a victim of expedience. (*Grand
Rapids Press* 1988a)

The board of education response was printed on the editorial page on
February 2, 1988:

Dissent! School Personnel Practices

As trustees of public monies, were officials of the Grand Rapids
Public Schools correct to negotiate a settlement with teachers
who were being dismissed for alleged incompetence? During the
proceedings, the teachers in question agreed to resign, but the
district had to agree to remove any information pertaining to the
tenure proceedings from their files.

After lengthy debate, the board made a very tough decision to
accept those settlements in three out of four tenure cases that
were heard in 1987, because we were concerned about the
exorbitant legal cost to continue the hearings. As it was, this
school district spent more than $100,000 to terminate three
teachers who were allegedly incompetent. Continuing those
cases could have cost an additional $100,000 to $300,000.

Even if we had fought these cases to the very end, and were
upheld, would we have been able to tell potential employers that
these people had been dismissed for incompetency? Without
written notice to a former employee, a former employer cannot
reveal the content of an employee's personnel file. If a district

were to take this course, they would be subject to further financial liability.

You also severely criticized the district for agreeing to give one of the employees in question a letter of recommendation. The letter in question was agreed to only after long and intense negotiations with counsel representing the plaintiff. The letter does not recommend, but simply states that the individual was hard working and conscientious, which was true. We can't speak for your hiring practices, but that letter would certainly demand more scrutiny by personnel officials in receiving school districts.

What position would *The Grand Rapids Press* have taken editorially if this school district had to lay off up to a dozen highly qualified teachers to pay the legal cost to protect out-state and out-of-state school districts from incompetent teachers? After all, they too have highly qualified personnel departments to thoroughly examine and interview prospective new employees to measure their skills.

> Board of Education,
> Grand Rapids Public Schools
> (*Grand Rapids Press* 1988b)

The third in this series was a response by John Douglas, a local taxpayer, who was most upset with the attempted justification by the board. Douglas's editorial is shortened but contains the gist of his comments:

Why pay so much, hide so much to fire teachers?

I was going to keep my mouth shut about the situation in which the Grand Rapids Board of Education spent more than $100,000 to fire three teachers because of their inability to teach. But when I read the letter sent to the *Press* by the members of the Board of Education which was printed in "Dissent!" last Tuesday, I just had to leap into the fray.

In the first place, it is absolutely ridiculous for it to cost that much to do some weeding. Something is wrong. Perhaps we need to take a look at the tenure system and scrap it in favor of a less costly one. I've always felt that the combination of tenure and a union is a bit much, anyway.

I don't care what the school board said in its letter to the *Press*—giving an incompetent teacher a letter of recommendation is the pits. I'm willing to admit that a person can be a hard worker and a bad teacher. People often find themselves in the wrong field of endeavor. The least that could have been done was to see to it that the letter of recommendation not be used in obtaining another teaching position.

Our school system's personnel department was unable to spot problems with these people—why should other school systems be expected to do what we couldn't?

I also find it offensive that there seems to be some kind of extortion going on which forces the school board to give in lest it has to lay off teachers so it can afford to carry on the tenure hearings to their proper conclusions.

Is the world going mad? What is all this?

John Douglas
(*Grand Rapids Press* 1988c)

The above scenario only reinforces the public image that governing boards and administrators are afraid to challenge faculty members who are not performing. It clearly shows how incompetence can be perpetuated through poor board procedures and poor execution. There is also the possibility of board or personal liability in this type of decision which resulted in letters of recommendation when the board knew full well that the teacher in question was indeed incompetent.

COLLECTIVE BARGAINING AND EVALUATION

Another concern for boards is that area of contract negotiations that relate to the evaluation process. A caution was given by Strike and Bull (1981) that boards be careful not to negotiate away their legislated prerogatives. Boards must be aware that such agreements can end up violating a statute or a strong public policy. They concluded that "the substantial criteria of evaluation are usually not negotiable" (p. 328).

In the case of *Foleno v. Board of Education of the Township of Bedminster* (1978) the court found: "the board has the duty, in furnishing a thorough and efficient education, to evaluate the performances of its employees and to staff its classrooms with skillful and effective teachers" (Piele 1979, p. 11). Piele found another court decision, *Teacneck Board of Education v. Teacneck Teachers Association* (1978), against bargaining teacher evaluation practices: "Nevertheless, negotiation of evaluation criteria is against public policy because retention or promotion of teachers is a management prerogative" (p. 147).

Orze (1977) did not find faculty power to be limitless when it comes to the faculty contractual negotiations. He sees some boundaries coming out of legislative acts in some states. He stated that the "legal powers of the union extend only to the mandatory subjects for collective bargaining that the administration must negotiate with it." He finds that management sometimes goes beyond its legal rights in negotiating away some of its legal prerogatives:

> The union has no legal right to bargain for authority beyond those mandatory subjects. Whatever additional powers the union may gain at the bargaining table can only be achieved if the administration is willing to share one or more of its managerial rights with the union. The administration controls the scope of negotiations, and, in so doing, it determines the actual limits of the legal powers of the union. Unions will attempt to expand the scope of bargaining as broadly as employers will allow them to, but the employer always has the right to say "no" to any nonmandatory demand for negotiations. (pp. 507–08)

In contrast to the cases above, the supreme courts in North Dakota and Indiana both allowed for teacher evaluation policies to be permitted in negotiations. In the Indiana case of *Evansville-Vanderburgh School Corp. v. Roberts* (1979) it was upheld that the school board should have held discussions with the union before implementing its new teacher evaluation plan. The term "discussible" was used to describe evaluation as a working condition. Orze warned boards that once they negotiate a subject in the faculty contract it becomes almost impossible for the employer to negotiate it back out if the union wishes to retain it. Hornbeck (1977) found the Public Employee Relations Act of Pennsylvania (ACT 195) to pave the way for statewide negotiations. It involved the commonwealth and their more than 4,500 faculty in the 13 state colleges.

Piele (1979) points out that negotiated procedures on evaluation does *not negate* management's rights (p. 163). This includes the management's exclusive right to hire and to fire personnel. Negotiated procedures might include administrative, student, peer, or self-evaluation procedures. The Michigan Supreme Court in 1978 concluded that "adoption of student evaluations of faculty was within the mandatory scope of bargaining since it would affect reappointment, tenure, and promotion" (p. 146).

In Iowa the negotiated contract in one school was found to be contrary to public policy. The Iowa Supreme Court found the Davenport Community School District was in violation of what they could negotiate into the faculty contract (*Moravek v. Davenport Community*

School District 1978). In this case they had negotiated language to allow an arbitrator to decide on the non-renewal of faculty members. The court ruled that this was not an item that could be negotiated away from the responsibility of the governing board of the school.

The faculty contract in the Rio Hondo Community College District in California clearly spelled out that *administrative evaluation* was the system that had been selected by the board of trustees. They did, however, allow for the procedures to be negotiated into its faculty contract language.

Andrews (1991), in his study of community colleges in the North Central region of the country, found that 87 colleges out of the 283 responding had negotiated faculty evaluation systems. Eleven of the 19 states covered in the study reported no negotiated evaluation systems. An additional 45 colleges reported that they had negotiated faculty contracts that did not include any language about faculty evaluation at all. Table 16 below shows that 42.5% of the instructional leaders who responded that they had negotiated evaluation language were not satisfied with the language. Some 26 percent indicated that they had been hindered as a supervisor by the restrictive language included (p. 4).

The areas that the instructional leaders found to be of greatest concern were (1) the language imposing restrictions on their role as administrators with responsibilities for evaluation; (2) poor language written into the contract; (3) deficiencies in procedures to develop criteria and (4) use of student evaluation. Table 17 shows the number of responses received for each of these restrictions (p. 5).

TABLE 16

Instructional Leaders Responses to
Evaluation Systems Negotiated
into Faculty Contracts
N = 87

Questions on Negotiated Language	Yes	No
1. Are you satisfied with the negotiated contract language?	50	37
2. Has evaluation, in your opinion, been hindered for you as a supervisor since the language is negotiated?	23	64

TABLE   17

Unsatisfactory or Incomplete Language
Negotiated into Faculty Contracts—
Categories of Written Responses
by Instructional Leaders

Restrictions/Deficiencies in Contract Language	Number of Responses
1. Restrictions Imposed on Administrators	9
2. Poor or Incompete Language in Content	11
3. Deficiences in Criteria and Procedures	8
4. Student Evaluation Concerns	4
Total Written Responses	32

The specific restrictions on administrators were identified
as follows:

1. Tenured teachers are no longer evaluated by administrators.
2. The system is now too confining; more avenues for evaluation are
   needed.
3. Department chairpersons are not allowed sufficient responsibility.
4. There is not enough language regarding supervisory evaluation.
5. It is now faculty controlled. Administrators are only used when a
   bona fide problem has been acknowledged.
6. The system does not include tenured faculty.
7. Evaluation needs to be more frequent.
8. Division chairs should be involved, as they are closest to
   faculty.
9. The language is too restrictive and not really formative.

The deficiencies in "criteria and procedures" were:

1. No provision is made for improvement of instruction.
2. It is not precise enough.
3. It doesn't focus on curriculum outcomes.
4. The system identifies strengths and concerns but does not provide
   for rewards or corrections.
5. No specifics and no consequences are given.

6. It does not take into account the individual's goals.
7. Plans of action are not clear enough (pp. 5–6).

One Wisconsin college response indicated that the contract requires student evaluation but does not make it a requirement to have supervisory evaluation. It was indicated, however, that movement was underway to improve the condition. In another case, a large metropolitan college instructional leader submitted contract pages showing faculty evaluation to be restricted to student review. She pointed out that she was unable to visit a classroom *unless invited.* She stated that administrative evaluation should be a requirement.

In a Michigan college the contract was written to let the faculty member decide if he or she wished to have supervisor evaluation. A second respondent from Michigan mentioned that supervisory evaluation was almost non-existent except when the "department recognizes areas of deficiency" (p. 8). In an even more frustrating stipulation, the request for evaluation by the immediate supervisors must be made by no later than January 1 of any given year. The contract also stated that "such a request shall not become a part of the faculty member's personnel file, nor shall it serve as cause for dismissal." One other college contract made clear that any documents produced through supervisory review are "the property of the reviewed faculty member, and such documents or copies shall not be kept by the department members involved in the review, or become a permanent part of the faculty member's record without the faculty member's permission" (pp. 8–9).

Is it any wonder that evaluation which produces any substantial improvement in instruction is difficult to find in very many elementary, middle or secondary schools or community colleges? There were a total of 50 colleges in this study that did not respond negatively to the negotiated language on evaluation that existed in their faculty contracts. In some cases the language was developed to support good evaluation practices. In some other contracts the student evaluation was the major system outlined, but this was not presented by those in the study to be a problem.

Licata (1986) questioned how a faculty union on campus might affect the viability of a post-tenure evaluation plan. Kleingartner (1984) had found that all aspects of evaluation and how it is implemented came under the scope of negotiations, and administrators must take their guidance from the negotiated collective bargaining agreement. Cohen and Brawer (1982) found that evaluation procedures became so elaborate and complex that they gained "labyrinthine complexity" (p. 75).

Arreola (1983) cited the importance of faculty evaluation being carried out effectively: "Only when the administration realizes that well-constructed faculty evaluation and development programs do not diminish their ability to direct the course and quality of their institutions, but rather enhance and strengthen it, will a truly successful faculty evaluation and development program have been established" (p. 92).

Andrews (1985) described the several check points in the total evaluation process that require involvement by governing boards. He listed, "hiring, granting of tenure, dismissal of non-tenured staff, formal notices to remediate, merit recognition programs, and firing of tenured staff as both the prerogatives and/or legal responsibilities of governing boards" (p. 56).

STATUTES INTRODUCED

There are any number of statutes that have been introduced by legislative bodies in a number of states that have done damage to the role previously given to governing boards of colleges, elementary, middle, and secondary schools. Providing a statement of reason in the non-renewal of non-tenured faculty member's contract is one such change. The requirement of a predetermination hearing before an independent hearing office has also appeared.

Piele (1981) found a statute that requires, on request, a written statement of the grounds for dismissal of non-tenured faculty members in Kentucky. He found similar requirements added in Alaska and Vermont (p. 89).

In a parallel case in Michigan (Piele 1980), the question of whether a reason needed to be given for denial of tenure was addressed by the supreme court. After being evenly divided in a previous hearing of the case, one justice changed his mind, and the court concluded that it was not necessary to state reasons for such a dismissal. The decision cited the 1970 *Roth* case and concluded that the Michigan state tenure act did not give entitlement to such notice (p. 84). This case, while not succeeding in reversing the previously established practice, presents another in a line of court challenges and legislative attempts to challenge the power of governing boards in educational matters.

An Illinois case, *Board of Trustees of Community College District Number 513 v. Dale Krizek and the American Federation of Teachers, Local 1810* (1983), summarized the power that is vested in the governing board. Citing several previous state cases, the Third District Appellate Court concluded:

The supreme court has made it unmistakably clear that when a governing board is vested with the power to grant tenure, or to not renew, then the governing board cannot delegate, modify or condition its final authority to make such decisions. Although the statute here in question differs slightly from the one at issue in the prior cases, there is no variation from the essential factor relied on in those cases, i.e., *the governing board's ultimate authority on tenure questions. There can be no dilution of the board's authority whether the evaluation of teachers is mandated by contract or by statute* (emphasis added).

They went on to describe the fine balance necessary to maintain quality in the schools and the question of job security:

> We are mindful that the tenure laws represent an elaborate balance between the need to maintain the quality of schools and the opposing interest in job security. (*Board of Education of Chicago v. Chicago Teachers Union, Local 1, 1981*). In striking that balance, the legislature has crafted a system where there appears to be unlimited power in boards to dismiss probationary teachers at the board's discretion while the power to dismiss tenured teachers is considerably restricted. (*Lockport Area Special Education Cooperative v. Lockport Area Special Education Cooperative Association* 1975). We perceive Krizek's position as an attempt to erode the area of the board's discretion by injecting elements of cause into the board's decision to terminate. Inasmuch as this is repugnant to the policy embodied in the statute, we decline to adopt the statutory construction proffered by Krizek.
>
> Finally, in her brief Krizek raises a constitutional issue concerning infringement of her right to due process. Although the Board seeks to have those portions of the brief stricken as representing theories not pursued in the court below, we hereby deny the motion to strike, but dismiss the substantive issue raised by Krizek as without merit, relying on the authority of *Board of Trustees v. Cook County College Teachers Union (1987)* which presented the same question for review in a factually indistinguishable setting.
>
> We conclude, then, that the decision of the circuit court of LaSalle County was correct, and its judgment should be affirmed for the reasons we have set forth.

Lewis (1980), as a board member, stated some of the frustration faced by board members in their most important role in the delivery of excellence in programs. He directed his plea to college presidents when he said, "If you decide to help us, be expansive and generous, and give us a little more instruction. Tell us that our primary duty is to determine and, if necessary, redetermine the mission and purpose of our college, and that only in that context do we really involve ourselves with 'policy'—policy related to the delivery of excellent education services at the classroom (or equivalent) level, is above all, else, our *raison d'etre"* (p. 20).

SUMMARY

The role of a board member is most important in assuring that there will be quality instruction in every classroom in the elementary, middle, or secondary school or higher education campus. It is a role that needs to be taught and understood early in a board member's election to a position on the board.

Quality in classroom instruction can be assured through well-thought-out board policies related to hiring, tenure, merit recognition programs and dismissal. The abilities and attitudes of administrative staff, from the college president or elementary, middle or secondary school superintendent through other key instructional leaders, will determine how well board policies are carried out. They will also determine if quality instruction in every classroom can be guaranteed to all students.

The willingness of board members to make both the easy and the tough decisions will help assure the students of a school district or college that they will attend a quality institution. Good decision-making on tenure, recognition, and dismissals will also send a strong message to all outstanding faculty that they are indeed the models of the institution to be emulated by all faculty.

SUGGESTED EXERCISES

1. Develop two or three board policies that will allow the administration and faculty union to ensure that evaluation will be conducted in the spirit of improving instruction.
2. Identify some of concerns that both administrators and faculty will have when dealing with boards when it comes to decision time on evaluation recommendations. For example, what if the teacher or chief administrator has a social relationship with a board member? Or what happens within the institution if the board rejects the administration's recommendation for remediation or dismissal?

16

CONCLUSION: QUALITY TEACHING IN EVERY CLASSROOM

The next several decades will see a continuation, and even an intensification, of the TQM movement, by whatever name, in every branch of American industry. NAFTA and the next phase of the GATT merely recognize the reality of worldwide competition. Japan and other Pacific Rim countries, the European Community, and the rise of new competitors in Latin America, India, China, and Russia will not permit Americans to settle into a comfortable stagnation.

Competition, in the new world order of rapidly rising standards of life, means, above all, ceaseless pursuit of the highest quality. And quality can only be defined by consumers: the customer is always right. Chief among the education system's customers are students, parents, taxpayers, and prospective employers.

Total Quality Management has already moved into education, but there has been hesitation about applying TQM principles to the central mission of the schools and colleges: *instruction*. It is as if an army command were to impose stringent efficiency measures upon the organization of entertainment, kitchens, uniforms, and latrines, and ignore the way in which front-line combat was planned and executed. Teachers are our front-line troops, and we should never forget it.

Ancillary or support functions in the schools, like purchasing, book-keeping, maintenance, and secretarial services, are easily identified and dealt with in the small groups which are often used in the TQM process. But there has also been, in varying degrees, an uneasiness about consciously bringing the pursuit of quality into the classroom. As I have tried to show in this book, any such uneasiness or hesitation is largely unjustified. Most teachers will embrace evaluation if it is comprehensible, fair, objective, and effective.

I have called this book *Teachers Can Be Fired!* I did so partly in order to shake up people's preconceptions and prejudices. It is, as a matter of fact, almost always feasible, as well as beneficial, to fire teachers who have repeatedly failed to change their performance to conform to an acceptable standard. If dismissal is handled correctly, it will be legally defensible and will win applause from conscientious and competent teachers. But dismissal is a last resort. For maximum effectiveness, dismissal has to be seen as part of an ongoing process of evaluation and improvement.

Faculty evaluation—quality control of instruction—is often relegated to students or 'peers'. I have shown that these methods are of very limited effectiveness and are frequently not taken very seriously. I have argued that supervisory/administrative evaluation is crucial. Students and peers have been absent in legal cases involving dismissal of incompetent faculty; on the other hand, there have been numerous cases where administrative evaluation has been employed to document incompetence. Similarly, research suggests that input from students or peers rarely leads to improvement of teaching or to disciplinary measures, whereas administrative evaluation often does.

Involvement of faculty in the design of a supervisory evaluation system is both possible and necessary. It is one of the best means of gaining faculty support. Determining what is quality teaching is a good first step in the process. Once quality teaching methodologies and techniques have been identified, they can become the standard for all teachers in the system. The evaluation form should reflect the quality standards that have been identified. Faculty have usually given preference to an open-ended evaluation form that allows for written responses from the evaluator who comes into the classroom and also encompasses out-of-class job responsibilities.

Faculty are further involved in one-on-one meetings with supervisors to discuss strengths and weaknesses in their teaching. Such conferences and written reports can clearly identify concerns and provide for a place to underscore what needs to be improved.

Faculty unions have been found to favor quality faculty evaluation if it is conceived of as a means of improving instruction. They also support movement to terminate poor instructors as long as they are first given help to improve and are then given their due-process rights if they are tenured. There is no pride in working with persons who will not carry out their teaching responsibilities. Usually such incompetence makes for very difficult instruction at the next level, an additional burden for those teachers who are depending on their colleagues to provide a quality base in the subject matter they are teaching. All of the teachers within an elementary, middle or secondary school or community college department or division suffer.

The major concern I have encountered when meeting with faculty groups to discuss supervisory evaluation is the issue of who will be doing the evaluation. The second strongest concern is raised by the question, "Who evaluates the evaluators?" It is important for governing boards and administrative leaders to make certain that evaluators possess strong and credible teaching backgrounds. They also need to be flexible and well-versed in a variety of teaching techniques and delivery systems. Each teacher has his or her own unique personality and teaching methodologies and it is important to distinguish what works for the individual teacher in the classroom presentation.

Evaluation will lead to both positive and negative outcomes. Whether a single evaluation system can accomplish both formative (assisting) and summative (decisions on tenure, remediation, promotion or dismissal) results has been debated by a number of researchers. Licata and Andrews presented their finding that one system can, indeed, be a continuum achieving both outcomes. How does a school or college divide these into separate systems? The same evaluators will be visiting classes and making formative suggestions as long as there is positive movement toward improvement. When such improvement does not happen Licata and Andrews suggested that remediation should still be considered as formative in nature. Remediation happens prior to any decision on dismissal and gives those faculty members another chance to carry out the improvements that were requested at the level of face-to-face discussion with supervisors.

Positive outcomes will emerge in the large majority of all evaluations. Nationally it has been determined that somewhere around 90 percent of the faculty are performing at an acceptable level. Union leaders have agreed with this figure. Research over the years has found many gaps in schools and states not having recognition programs for their best teachers. Recent research studies show that this has started to improve. Faculty are being better rewarded for outstanding work. There are, however, far too many schools that have still neglected this most important and significant means of improving the school climate by reinforcing the best instruction that is taking place within the elementary, middle, or secondary school, or community college.

Part-time faculty have become very prevalent in community colleges. Studies show that there is much lacking in providing good orientation, assistance in the classroom, evaluation processes, and other important support services to assure a high level of quality teaching. This same kind of neglect for the best part-time faculty was cited in a study of community colleges in the 19-state North Central region of the United States. While recognition programs were expanding for full-time faculty, this did not occur for part-time teachers. As secondary schools and community colleges come to rely on more part-time faculty, it becomes necessary to improve all phases of support to improve their chances of success in the colleges or schools.

Governing boards have been found to know little about what can be done to improve instruction through a quality evaluation system. The laws and courts in most states, however, make it very clear that the final decisions on personnel rests with the governing boards. Boards should demand that the administrators they hire know something about how to improve classroom instruction as well as about budgeting, scheduling, maintenance, and other functions of the school or college.

The governing boards, administrators, and teachers are all part of the team that is necessary to make quality improvements in the classroom. If the governing board does not support the superintendent or college president when a decision to move toward dismissal is presented, evaluation will become ineffectual in practice. Who will want to go through the many steps and stresses that are necessary to reach the decision to go after a remediation notice or a dismissal if support will not be forthcoming? If the superintendent or college president is not well-versed in quality evaluation techniques and processes, those administrators reporting to them will be frustrated if they are serious about improvements. Boards often become frustrated as well when nothing is done to handle the complaints about teachers they often hear about.

I have found evaluation of faculty to be the most stimulating part of the job of an instructional leader. It provides for many opportunities to discuss classroom instruction and what teachers are doing right. Teachers are most receptive to hearing such a message if it is sincere and if the evaluator is respected. It is also stimulating to let a poor instructor know that changes need to be made or to let that same instructor know that a notice to remedy is being sought from the governing board. The stimulation comes in these cases from knowing that such decisions *must be made* on behalf of those students who are suffering through poor instruction. The student leaders who spoke out in the chapter on student evaluation vented their high level of frustration about paying for such instruction and losing out on a significant piece of their education.

The TQM movement in education must adopt effective faculty evaluation as the "engine" to the overall goal of total quality improvement. Elementary, middle, and secondary schools and community colleges need to develop evaluation of faculty as a *priority effort* in their quest to obtain a quality education for each student they serve. Quality in every classroom is indeed attainable for those schools and colleges willing to develop meaningful and honest faculty evaluation.

APPENDIX A

LEGAL CASES IN DISMISSALS OF FACULTY

This appendix is designed to provide a variety of legal cases that have been decided in the courts as they relate to faculty terminations. They should give the evaluation practitioners, faculty, and governing boards a good sense of what is acceptable and unacceptable behavior in teaching and other professional job responsibilities.

NON-TENURED DISMISSALS

Procedural challenges

Elementary

In Missouri the state statute which governs termination of a probationary teacher was found to not prescribe a particular form for notice of termination. In *Lovan v. Dora R. Illinois School District* (1984) the court ruled that any language written or spoken that would reasonably be understood to mean that the teacher's employment will be terminated would suffice. In this case, the probationary kindergarten teacher admitted that she knew that the district had decided to terminate her employment after the superintendent talked to her. She was again told during the required statutory period and the court found the statutory notice requirement was met.

In an Indiana case *(Tishey v. Board of School Trustees* 1991) a teacher who was not tenured was given notice and reasons for nonrenewal of contract. She was alleged to have been rude to personnel and parents. She also used profanity in the presence of students. The court found she received appropriate notice under the state law.

Free Speech or Individual Disputes

College

The court found in favor of the school in *Landrum v. Eastern Kentucky University* (1984) when the faculty member in question alleged he had been denied tenure because of his speech, in violation of the first amendment:

> The plaintiff had made a number of critical statements to various groups about the dean and the vice president. His department chairman stated that the plaintiff would tend to withdraw support from endeavors if a decision was made with which he disagreed. The plaintiff alleged that these pronouncements were within the purview of free speech and could not be used as the reason to deny tenure. The district court ruled that when an employee speaks out, not on matters of public concern but rather on matters of personal interest as an employee, his pronouncements are outside the scope of the first amendment. The court stated that, "(t)he first amendment does not require a public office to be run as a roundtable for employee complaints over internal office affairs." Plaintiff's speech in this case was characterized by the court as that of "individual disputes and grievances". (Thomas 1985, p. 309)

A Pennsylvania case, *Rossi v. Pennsylvania State University* (1985), concerned the dismissal of an employee who complained about supervisors on "non-public issues." The employee plaintiff complained the way his supervisors managed the Instructional Services Division at a public institution. He defended himself by saying his pronouncements were matters of public policy and he was making recommendations on how to save the state taxpayers money.

The court found under common law that the employee could be dismissed at will and that the plaintiff's pronouncements did not concern public policy, but rather were differences of opinion on how to manage this particular division of the university. It was ruled that the defendant college may dismiss an employee who becomes troublesome or hostile to his superiors.

Denial of tenure: Poor communications skills

College

Denial of promotion to full professor was made on the basis of an evaluation process that found a teacher to have an accent in his speech that affected his teaching effectiveness. The faculty member in *Hou v. Pennsylvania Department of Education* (1983) was found to be denied tenure on valid, educationally sound reasons. The teacher, of Chinese origin, did have a distinct accent and a manner of speech which could affect communication skills in his teaching. Since communications were found to be a factor affecting teaching the court did not find the decision to be *discriminatory.*

The collective bargaining agreement cannot assume delegated power of a board in the dismissal of a non-tenured teacher in Illinois *(Board of Trustees v. Cook County College Teachers Union* 1987). The court ruled in favor of the state statutory authority of the board in the dismissal.

Part-time or full-time?

How much can a part-time faculty member be used? This is becoming an issue in the courts when it comes to determining if they can obtain tenure. In *McGuire v. Governing Board of San Diego Community College District* (1984) a part-time employee who taught a 60 percent course load for one semester and a 40 percent load during the remainder of his employment period was also employed elsewhere on the campus. He claimed he was working as a "full-time tutor" in addition to his teaching. Because of this he claimed he should have been awarded tenure since he met the minimum requirement of at least two consecutive years of employment in a 60 percent teaching assignment. In this case the state court of appeals reversed the lower court's finding that the plaintiff should have been awarded tenure. They found that the tutorial position was not a regular teaching position within the statutory scheme controlling the award of tenure.

TENURED DISMISSALS

Procedural challenges

Two different tenured faculty cases were decided, in part, from procedural due-process actions. The first one in Alabama involved a teacher who resigned prior to having a dismissal hearing. In *Swann v. Caylor* (1987) the instructor lost his right to due-process because when he resigned he lost "his property and tenure rights to that job."

The second case *(Petrella v. Siegel* 1988) found the teacher still able to have a protectable property interest and a procedural right to a due-process hearing. The state law provided that such public officers can resign only in writing and the oral resignation given by the instructor did not negate this right.

Incompetency

Elementary

In *Hamburg v. North Penn School District* (1984), the second grade teacher was dismissed for incompetency based upon the following: continual failure to maintain poise and composure in front of her students and in dealings with other professional employees and parents.

In another elementary case, Carden, a sixth-grade teacher, was ordered to be reinstated by the Appellate Court, and charges of incompetence and insufficiency were determined not proved due to lack of specificity. In *Jefferson Consolidated School District C–123 v. Carden* (1989), the court found three months of alleged deficiencies in the principal's and superintendent's notebook had not been presented in advance to Carden. The charges were determined not to be specific enough to comply with the applicable statute. Teacher was reinstated and awarded back-pay for the salary which was lost during the appeal process.

The Missouri Court of Appeals held that Hanlon (1) had adequate notice of her deficiencies and more than the statutory period to correct them; (2) there was no error in the board's refusal to grant teacher discovery of certain documents and substance of testimony of superintendent's witnesses or in its refusal to subpoena particular witness; and (3) board's finding of incompetency and inefficiency was supported by competent and substantial evidence. Deficiencies were listed in areas of organization of instruction, assignments, instruction, team teaching, supervision and control, relationship with roommothers and volunteers, communication with parents, grading, and record keeping (*Hanlon v. Board of Education of the Parkway School District 1985*).

Middle school

In *Bradshaw v. Alabama State Tenure Commission* (1988) the Alabama Court of Civil Appeals supported the board's decision to dismiss a long-time tenured teacher for behavioral change. His behavior included (1) smoking in front of students in the classroom; (2) using inappropriate language in the presence of students and fellow employees; (3) leaving his classroom unattended; (4) failing to submit proper lesson plans and class rolls; (5) using inappropriate materials in the classroom which created a danger to the health of the students; (6) making sexual remarks to female students and teachers; and (7) making harassing phone calls to the female assistant principal. The teacher tried to enter alcoholism as a cause in his case but the court did not find that such behavior was committed while he was under the influence of alcohol.

Secondary

Dismissal of a tenured counselor was upheld in Alabama's appeal's court. The counselor was repeatedly negligent in preparing referral packets on students, reporting to work on time, having numerous unexplained work absences, and failing to submit acceptable weekly and monthly plan books and yearly plans (*Alabama State Tenure Commission v. Birmingham Board of Education* 1990).

The Supreme Court of Nebraska supported the school board's decision to dismiss a tenured secondary school teacher for incompetence. The seventh grade teacher was evaluated and had been told that improvement in controlling her classes in mathematics and English was needed. A second evaluation visit to her class found her marginal in 13 areas and unsatisfactory in two areas. Some of the items listed were: (1) inability to control her classes; (2) shrillness of her voice; (3) using improper English and grammar; (4) inability to control her emotionality when correcting students; and (5) lack of ability in using demonstrative instructional materials. The Supreme Court found that the teacher had been given adequate notice, and she was found to be terminated properly by reason of incompetence (*Eshom v. Board of Education of School District No. 54* 1985).

The Supreme Court of Wyoming reversed the dismissal of a secondary school tenured teacher. The termination was based on charges that he had shown inability to establish rapport with students which was not considered by the court to be a proper ground for dismissal (*Powell v. Board of Trustees of Crook County School District No. 1* 1976).

In *Nevels v. Board of Education of School District of Maplewood-Richmond Heights* (1991) a tenured teacher's dismissal was based upon errors in attendance reports and in the midquarter and quarterly progress reports turned into the administration. The Missouri "meet and confer" requirement was considered by the appellate court to have been met through meetings with the superintendent, school counselor, and secretary. In addition, this requirement was supported with a warning letter and observation by a teaching area specialist over several weeks.

Incompetency and inefficiency

Elementary

A Missouri Court of Appeals supported the school board's decision to terminate a teacher due to her incompetency and inefficiency. The charges, including problems with spelling and grammar, complaints from parents about the teaching, and misspelling of 26 of her own students names, were documented over a two-year period *(Beck v. James, Superintendent Palmyra R–I School District* 1990).

Middle school

Wiley was a tenured middle school teacher dismissed for willful neglect of duty over a three-year period while serving two different parish school superintendents. In *Wiley v. Richland Parish School Board* (1985) the charges of repeated complaints from fellow teachers and parents, failing to follow directives, concern about grades given, not complying with written directives of the superintendent, and being unreceptive to suggestions made to her for improvement purposes were all well documented. The board decision to terminate was affirmed by a Louisiana Court of Appeal.

Secondary

In *Jackson v. Sobol* (1991) the Appellate Division of the New York Supreme Court upheld dismissal of a tenured secondary school teacher. She had entered the principal's office without authorization, ignored established procedures for disciplining students despite prior warnings, refused to meet with a troubled student's parents, failed to send a student's parents progress reports, did not have her lesson planbook available as required by school district policy on at least three occasions, and inaccurately graded students.

The board was overturned in its effort to dismiss a tenured counselor in *Selby v. North Callaway Board of Education* (1989). The Missouri Court of Appeals found the board to be deficient in its documentation of whether the previous notice had led to a remediation of the behavior in the warning document. In short, the board was found to have failed to meet this burden. The court found the list of concerns in the warning statement could have led to termination of this permanent teacher's contract had the board followed all procedures faithfully.

Inefficiency and insubordination

Middle school

The Missouri Court of Appeals found that a tenured school teacher's dismissal was supported by the evidence of both inefficiency in teaching and insubordination. Inefficiency was found in the evidence: (1) poor rapport with students; (2) insufficient communication with parents; (3) many requests for transfer out of his classes; and (4) test scores indicating poor student progress. In the area of insubordination the teacher made no effort when asked to comply with directives to (1) improve his relationship and rapport with both students and parents; (2) specifically that he provide worksheets containing assigned problems instead of having students copy them off the board, and (3) furnish each student with copies of tests and materials used to supplement textbook (*In re the Proposed Termination of James E. Johnson 1990*).

Inefficiency

Community college

A case of "inefficiency" was presented by Morris (1992). He showed in *Saunders v. Reorganized School District* (1975) that the Missouri Supreme Court sustained the board decision for dismissal of the tenured community college faculty member. The court ruled that substantial evidence was presented to prove there was both "inefficiency" and "insubordination:"

> Saunders had failed and refused to instruct the curriculum as requested; that he refused to discuss the curriculum and its teaching with his superiors; that he gave one second-year class a choice as to whether he should teach the first year material again or "teach the subject matter as he wanted to;" that he refused to participate in the preparation of the course outline; that he refused to discuss teacher evaluations with his superiors; that he had been

inefficient as shown by the evaluation reports; that he refused and failed to use the required textbooks in his teaching . . . that he had been guilty of excessive and unreasonable absence. (p. 67–68)

Insubordination

Elementary

An elementary school teacher of a preschool class was dismissed and the board was supported by the Court of Appeal in Louisiana. In *Ford v. Caldwell Parish School Board* (1989) Ford was dismissed for displaying an uncooperative attitude which caused problems between herself and her working relationships with her supervisors as well as managing her class within the policies set forth by supervisory personnel. The court found the plaintiff established a staggered attendance schedule for the students even after being told not to, leaving her class and the school without permission and abruptly leaving a meeting between herself, the principal, and the school superintendent. This was sufficient evidence in the case of a non-tenured teacher.

A New Mexico case involved dismissal of a tenured elementary teacher for insubordination, conduct unbecoming a teacher, unprofessional conduct, and open defiance of supervisory authority. Excessive tardiness, recurring absences from her classroom, inadequate supervision of her students, inadequate lesson plans and yelling or screaming at her direct supervisor within hearing distance or presence of students and parents were all cited as reasons leading to dismissal in *Kleinberg v. Board of Education of the Albuquerque Public Schools* (1988).

College

A tenured instructor with a history of unexcused absences was terminated in *Stasny v. Board of Trustees* (1982). He was denied permission to take a leave of absence by a supervisor and was threatened with disciplinary action if he defied the decision. He, nevertheless, took the leave and was dismissed for *inter alia* insubordination. In court he asserted that (1) his defiance was merely a single respectful act of disobedience, not insubordination; and (2) his dismissal violated his right to academic freedom and freedom of expression. These arguments were rejected by the appellate court which found his contention on academic freedom to be wrong. They stated "academic freedom is not a license for activity at variance with job-related procedures and requirement, nor does it encompass activities which are internally destructive to the proper function of the university or disruptive to the educational process."

Secondary

A termination was reversed by a court in *Board of Education of Chicago v. Johnson* (1991) when it was decided the alleged misconduct on the part of the teacher was remediable under state statute. In addition, the teacher had not received the appropriate notice available under the law.

Gaylord made a critical error of insubordination by calling in sick after being turned down in his request for a day off to be interviewed for another job in another school district. His principal received a call from the principal in the district to which he had applied wanting a recommendation for Gaylord. The principal was able to learn that Gaylord was indeed at an interview the morning he had called in sick. Teacher absences were not allowed during the first and last week of any semester according to the negotiated faculty contract. The Kansas Court of Appeals upheld the school district in their dismissal *(Gaylord v. Board of Education, Unified School District No. 218* 1990).

Caldwell, a continuing employment teacher, was found to be dismissed properly in *Caldwell v. Blytheville, Arkansas School District No. 5* (1988) in the Court of Appeals. He was dismissed based upon conduct at a faculty meeting, conferences with the school principal where he shouted at his supervisors, called them liars, and accused them of conspiring to have him fired. He also walked out of the meeting. The case was sufficiently documented.

Failure to prepare proper lesson plans led a court to assess an $8,000 fine payable in twenty-six biweekly payments. The appellate court upheld the fine as not being excessive and supported the need for "formal lesson plans" as being "indispensable to effective teaching" *(Meyer v. Board of Education of the Charlotte Valley Central School District* 1992).

In *Malverne Union Free School District v. Sobol* (1992) the charge of insubordination was upheld at the appellate level when a teacher was dismissed for refusing to turn over her lesson plans and grade books.

Another case was overturned through the process of statutory interpretation. In this New Hampshire case the administration's warning letter sent to an absent teacher because of illness failed to state the corrective action that was expected to be taken to avoid termination. Three other letters sent on three consecutive days did not provide adequate time for corrective action. The court found them to be so flawed that the school was ordered to reinstate the teacher with back pay (*In re* Fugere 1991).

Irremediable behavior

Elementary

In *Board of Education of City of Chicago v. Box* (1989) a tenured elementary school teacher was found by the appellate court to have had "unprofessional physical contact" with female students which was considered as irremediable behavior. His discharge was considered warranted. In this case four students had testified against the teacher as having touched them on the buttocks, breasts, and in one case he had looked inside the student's blouse. He had denied the charges originally but later admitted he had done so on some occasions. Written warnings from the board were not necessary in this case as such warnings are not necessary in a case of irremediable action.

Poor or inappropriate discipline

Elementary

An elementary school case in Connecticut found the board's decision to dismiss a tenured faculty member to be supported by the evidence: continual neglect of her overall teaching responsibilities (supported by repeated warnings and reprimands) and a pattern of failure to supervise her first grade students to the extent that safety of the students became an issue *(Cope v. Board of Education of the Town of West Hartford* 1985).

In the Michigan case of *Board of Education of Benton Harbor Area Schools v. Wolff* (1985) the Court of Appeals supported the board in their dismissal of the teacher for failure to establish and maintain discipline. This lack of discipline was found to subvert the instructional process. Wandering freely about the room, talking out of turn, frequent fighting and leaving and entering the classroom without having to obtain permission were all documented. Efforts to remediate such behavior was not forthcoming.

A tenured teacher in New York was found to be terminated for just cause for her inability to control her class and lack of planning and teaching of lessons (*Mongitore v. Regan* 1987).

Another elementary teacher in *Rolando v. School Directors of District No. 125* (1976) was found to be dismissed properly by an

Appellate Court in Illinois. He had used a cattle prod to discipline his pupils. His behavior was found to be irremediable as the damage had already been done to the students, the faculty, and to the school. The court determined that none of the damage could have been corrected even if the board had served the plaintiff a written warning.

A home economics teacher can be fired for failing to maintain discipline rather than having to be transferred back to a different position in which she had previously satisfactorily taught for a number of years, according to *Stamper v. Board of Education of Elementary School District 143* (1986). It was also found that a tenured teacher may be asked to resign before initiation of dismissal proceedings. The hearing officer's decision supporting the school in dismissing the teacher was upheld by the court.

Junior high

The appellate court of North Carolina supported the board in dismissal of a career teacher for not providing adequate discipline in her classroom. School authorities were found to have been thoughtful, patient, persistent, but unable to obtain sufficient change on the part of the teacher to properly control her classes *(Crump v. Durham County Board of Education* 1985).

Secondary

In *Hatta v. Board of Education, Union Endicott Central School District* (1977) in New York, the teacher dismissed was found to be incompetent for lack of control and discipline in the classroom. The decision was supported by the Supreme Court, Appellate Division, of the state.

A tenured teacher in Michigan was dismissed for using corporal punishment with four students in violation of the school board policy. Once he was found to have kicked and pushed a student to get her to return to his classroom. He struck another student in the face with his fist as a disciplinary measure and received a written reprimand for this incident. A third incident found him grabbing a student in a headlock and slapping or punching the student, leading to a cut on the student's face. The fourth incident was where the petitioner struck a female high school student in the face and knocked her down. The teacher sought to have these earlier incidents kept inadmissible in the present dismissal case but the Court of Appeals allowed them. The court upheld the decision in *Tomczik v. State Tenure Commission, Center Line Public Schools* (1989).

An Illinois Appellate Court upheld the dismissal of a tenured teacher for having lack of discipline in classrooms, improper use of corporal punishment and poor teaching practices. The court conducted a full and independent review of the record of the school board and found that a fair hearing and proper evidence had been provided (*Hagerstrom v. Clay City Community Unit High School* 1976).

Insubordination and irremediability

Elementary

In an elementary school district a teacher refusing a classroom assignment was dismissed for behavior unbecoming a teacher. The Appellate Court of Illinois, First District, Third Division overturned an arbitrator and Circuit Court decision in *Board of Education of Chicago v. Harris* (1991). The behavior was deemed to be irremediable. The teacher refused to accept a classroom assignment. She alleged to have notified the principal and superintendent of a medical problem, which was found to be unsubstantiated. The court found that her behavior was "irremediable and teacher could be discharged for insubordination and unbecoming conduct even without official warning from school board; teacher's conduct damaged faculty morale, parental relations, and orderly school administration, and teacher did not actually show that failure to warn her, beyond oral and written warnings by principal and district superintendent, was subterfuge to expedite dismissal or that she would have altered her conduct if officially warned by board."

Insubordination and incompetency

Elementary

The case of *Meckley v. Kanawha County Board of Education* (1989) found the teacher to have a continuing course of infractions. These included failing to return a student's report card and a permanent record when directed to do so by the principal. The Supreme Court of Appeals of West Virginia found her conduct causing concern about her obligations to the school authorities as well as to her duties as a teacher of her students.

In *Roberts v. Santa Cruz Valley Unified School District No. 35* (1989), the elementary teacher was found to have committed "unprofessional conduct" by having her elementary students hit and kick other students as part of a "game" as well as when they were asked to notice other students not following classroom rules.

Junior high

In a Missouri case, *Nevels v. Board* (1991), a physical education instructor was terminated for the type of behavior he demonstrated: (1) his teaching style was too remedial for the students he was teaching; (2) he used militaristic commands; (3) he made frequent errors in grading; (4) he used a pay phone outside his classroom after being instructed not to; (5) he inappropriately referred to the school secretary as the principal's "lap dog;" (6) and told a seventh grade student "we are going to make love" when replying to a question regarding the lesson to be covered that day. Warnings had been delivered to this instructor on several previous occasions. The dismissal, upon being upheld by the circuit court was appealed to the Missouri Court of Appeals.

The court of appeals supported the board's finding based upon the facts presented. It also found that the teacher's behavior was at the level of incompetency and insubordination necessary for termination. The teacher was found not to have remedied the concerns from the earlier written warnings. The termination was *upheld*.

Secondary

In *Dunnigan v. Ambach* (1985), the Appellate Division of the New York Supreme Court found dismissal of a tenured teacher to not be arbitrary and capricious. Petitioner's alcoholism was not viewed as having sufficient enough weight when viewed with other significant and uncontradicted evidence presented. Petitioner testified that she had deliberately chosen not to carry out the directives of her employer school. Reasons of incompetence and insubordination were supported for the dismissal.

Other incompetency charges in Illinois and Missouri in *DeBernard v. State Board* (1988) and *Atherton v. Board* (1988) centered on failure to remedy teaching deficiencies in outline objectives, sequencing subject matter, following lesson plans, and maintaining adequate and accurate grades for students.

A teacher in Florida (*Johnson v. School Board* 1991) had been previously warned not to have physical contact with students and was dismissed. The school board received numerous complaints of improper contact. The court upheld the dismissal even though the hearing officer felt a one-year suspension would have been adequate. Insubordination was the cause used by the board.

In a second Missouri case inefficiency, misconduct, and insubordination were all reasons for termination. The board found (1) use of profanity in front of students; (2) physically accosting students; (3) engaging in a physical confrontation with the parents of a student; and (4) refusal to accept duty schedules as causes leading to the termination. The teacher's suit was not upheld by the circuit court. The Missouri Court of Appeals found that the board did have documentation sufficient to justify termination. The court found that the board has the discretion and authority to dismiss for a proven, one-time violation of board regulations *(Catherine v. Board* 1991).

In a Colorado case the instructor was fired and the board upheld by the court when the instructor continued to use profanity in the presence of students after a prior directive to cease such behavior *(Ware v. Morgan County School District* 1988).

Sexual misconduct

Secondary

Sexual relations with a student led to termination of a teacher in Minnesota. In this case the student sued both the school and the teacher. The teacher asked the school to provide legal counsel on his behalf. When the school district refused he sued the district. The trial court found the school district did not owe him legal support. At the Minnesota Court of Appeals he was also found not to be eligible for legal support because of being guilty of malfeasance in his office. Normally the school district would be obligated to provide such legal defense for their teachers *(Queen v. Minneapolis Public Schools* 1992).

The Supreme Court of South Dakota affirmed the dismissal of a tenured male teacher in *Strain v. Rapid City School Board* (1989) for sexual contact with a student. The court affirmed that the school board was correct in allowing testimony of a former student who testified that the teacher had sexual contact with her five or six years prior to the current complaint.

Giving controlled substances and having sexual activity with a juvenile teaching aide led to the discharge of a teacher on grounds of conduct unbecoming a teacher. The teacher's credibility in *Hall v. Board of Education of City of Chicago* (1992) was held suspect by the hearing officer, and the students were not asked to testify.

In *Sauter v. Mount Vernon School District* (1990) a teacher was discharged for his several conversations with a student on whether they should engage in sexual intercourse. This was decided as constituting sexual exploitation of a student and the court of appeals in Washington supported the board on the basis of immoral conduct.

In Pennsylvania *(Manheim Central Education Association v. Manheim Central School District* 1990) a teacher's love letters and profession of love to students was found under state statute to constitute "immorality" and "just cause" for dismissal under the collective bargaining agreement.

Sexual harassment

University

In *Korf v. Ball State University* (1984) male students accused a tenured faculty member of making sexual advances and offering the students better grades for sexual favors. Following proper investigation of the charges, notification to the plaintiff, and a hearing, the plaintiff was dismissed by the president. While admitting to a relationship with a student (who testified at the hearing) the plaintiff denied that grades were involved. The plaintiff based his case around his constitutional rights of substantive and procedural due process, equal protection, free speech, freedom of association, and privacy having been violated. He claimed that the relationship being questioned was a private consensual sexual activity outside the institution's purview. The Seventh Circuit court found these arguments lacking in merit. They supported his dismissal for *unethical behavior* and found that he had exploited students for his own private advantage. He was found to be unlike any ordinary person on the street because he had a special relationship with the students which he had violated.

Elementary

In a second case, *Board of Education of Argo-Summit School District 104 v. Hunt* (1985), "irremediable" conduct was determined in the dismissal of a tenured male physical education teacher. He pinched three second grade female students on the buttocks during class. The teacher was dismissed without having to receive "notice to remedy" from the governing board. The court, in determining that the conduct was irremediable, focused on the damage done to the students rather than on the traditional analysis of trying to determine whether a warning might have prevented the misconduct.

Other job responsibilities: rules

Secondary

In a Michigan case *(Sutherby v. Gobles Board of Education* (1984) it was established that a tenured faculty member can be fired even though the work in the classroom may be satisfactory. In this case Sutherby was fired for other job responsibilities: "Professional competence covers more than just classroom behavior and teaching skills. The Court of Appeals of Michigan upheld a tenured teacher's dismissal for incompetence even though his classroom performance had been satisfactory. His failure to comply with reasonable administrative rules and regulations that are required for the effective operation of the school and the school system justified his dismissal for incompetence" (Thomas 1985, p. 115).

Neglect of duty

Elementary

A sixth-grade teacher was dismissed for being excessively absent from his duties. He was consuming more sick leave days than the most generous interpretation that could be given to the policy within the district. A second charge was made that he failed to call the district to report his absences which made it difficult to obtain a substitute in an orderly manner. The Commonwealth Court of Pennsylvania confirmed the board of education in their dismissal of the teacher in *Ward v. Board of Education of the School District of Philadelphia* (1985).

University

The courts have been found to be fairly consistent in upholding tenured faculty dismissals if the documented evidence is produced to show "neglect of professional duties." In *McConnel v. Howard University* (1985) the teacher became embroiled in an argument with a black student enrolled in his class. The instructor, working in a predominantly Black institution, complained about the skills of students in his class and related a story about monkeys. This generated a verbal retort from a student in the class who called him a racist. The teacher refused to teach his class until this student apologized. The student refused and the administration refused to intercede to try and resolve the matter. Charges were brought against the faculty member when he remained adamant about resuming teaching of the class.

The college grievance committee found him guilty of neglect of duty and he was subsequently removed. The dismissal was upheld by the federal district court in a summary judgment. It found no right had been violated in the institution's action against the teacher for neglect of professional duties.

Verbally abusing students

Secondary

In *Catherine v. Board of Education of City of St. Louis* (1991), a tenured teacher was terminated for using profanity, shouting and physically handling his students. He had been able to respond to each of the charges as they had occurred, and the appellate court found him to not be able to contend that he had been surprised or prejudiced by the charges.

The power of the board of education to suspend a tenured teacher without pay for a short-term basis for verbally abusing students and using profanity was upheld by the Illinois Supreme Court. In *Kamrath v. Board of Education* (1987) the Supreme Court found the board had satisfied the teacher's constitutional due-process rights. The board's teacher suspension policy was written to permit suspension of up to 30 days for misconduct which would constitute legal cause for dismissal under the state School Code. It also provided for written notice of the charges on which the suspension proceeding were carried out. The teacher was allowed a hearing before the board upon request of the teacher, permitted representation by an attorney and the right to present and cross examine witnesses at the hearing.

Summary

The above cases summarize a variety of cases that have received support in the courts. It is by no way exhaustive or includes all cases within any of the categories presented.

APPENDIX B

BOARD POLICY—EVALUATION OF FACULTY, ASSISTANTS TO
INSTRUCTION, AND COUNSELORS: TENURED, NON-TENURED,
AND PART-TIME

It is the policy of the Board of Trustees that all faculty of the college shall be evaluated by their supervisors in order to assure that quality in instruction, in other professional duties, and in professional conduct is maintained.

Procedures for evaluation will be developed and published in the Faculty Handbook which will be approved by the Board of Trustees each time the Faculty Handbook is updated.

Persons to be covered by the above mentioned evaluation procedures will be: (1) tenured faculty; (2) non-tenured faculty; (3) part-time faculty; (4) counselors; and (5) assistants to instruction.

The ultimate decision as to the granting or denying of tenure or the dismissal of a tenured teacher rests with the Board of Trustees. The evaluation procedures provide a means of obtaining information from which to make its decision.

APPENDIX C

TENURED EVALUATION PROCEDURES

Procedures for the evaluation of all full-time tenured faculty, assistants to instruction, and counselors

It is the responsibility of the college administration to implement the following procedures which will provide for the evaluation of all full-time tenured faculty, assistants to instruction, and counselors:

1. The Division Chairpersons and Dean of Instruction (or his representative) will evaluate classes or labs of each tenured instructor and/or assistant to instruction in the college and complete the faculty evaluation form.
2. The Dean of Student Development will evaluate counseling sessions, career workshops, classes or seminars of tenured counselors.
3. The Division Chairpersons, Dean of Instruction (or his representative), or Dean of Student Development (for counselors) will also evaluate all other aspects of the jobs to be performed by faculty, assistants to instruction, and counselors. The criteria that will be used in the evaluation process in addition to classroom or other formal activity (depending upon an instructor's teaching assignment and/or a counselor's assignments) will include where applicable:

(A.) Performing advisory committee work in programs.
(B.) Maintaining course curriculum updates and revisions.
(C.) Performing college committee work.
(D.) Maintaining records as required by law, college policy, and administrative regulations.
(E.) Maintaining scheduled office hours.
(F.) Attending and participating in faculty and division meetings.
(G.) Attending local, state, and regional professional meetings and/or participating in other forms of professional upgrading.

(H.) Maintaining proper controls on and maintenance of tools, equipment, and supplies under one's area of responsibility.

(I.) Performing professional job-related duties as assigned by the administration in accordance with college policies and practices.

(J.) Assisting in upholding and enforcing college rules and administrative regulations.

(K.) Providing public performances and displays in such areas as music, speech, theatre, art, and reader's theatre.

(L.) Providing students with co-curricular activities in such areas as athletics, field trips, and occupationally related clubs.

(M.) Providing timely and complete reports required for D.A.V.T.E., I.C.C.B., North Central, Special Accreditation Associations, and the Board of Higher Education.

(N.) Disseminating program information to area students through (1) high school visitations, (2) college nights, (3) college open houses, and (4) invitations to high school faculty and students to the campus.

(O.) Providing an atmosphere of cooperation with administrations; insubordination is considered a very serious offense.

4. A formal evaluation conference with the Division Chairperson, Dean of Instruction (or Dean of Student Development for counselors) and the faculty member will be held within a reasonable time period following a classroom visitation and/or evaluation filed on the other job performance criteria that are outlined above. The conference should be held within 1 to 5 working days following such evaluation.

5. A faculty member, assistant to instruction, or counselor will be apprised of any defects and/or deficiencies in his/her performance as discovered in the formal evaluation process. The person evaluated will be advised to take appropriate action to remediate the defects/deficiencies cited.

6. Remedial action may be prescribed by the administrator(s) to involve the instructor in such activities as: developing daily course outlines; publishing and disseminating daily course objectives to students; disseminating course requirements and grading system to students; visiting other instructors' classes; consulting other professionals in the same field (on-campus or at other colleges and universities); course work or readings in methods of teaching, psychology of learning; participating in professional workshops or meetings; improving testing and grading practices; providing written daily objectives and methods of instruction; improving

supervision of laboratory students and/or maintaining equipment and supplies (assistants to instruction); attending articulation meetings with an agency and/or college and university (counselors); properly preparing an orientation talk or career decision-making seminar or keeping current on articulation matters with senior colleges (counselors); updating syllabus; and attending meetings as required.

7. All tenured faculty, assistants to instruction, and counselors will be formally evaluated a minimum of twice during any five-year period following election to tenure. (Formal evaluations will be administered as often as is deemed necessary for those persons who have been found to have defects and/or deficiencies in their work that needs follow-up attention).

8. All evaluation visits will be made unannounced. (This does not preclude a faculty person from inviting an administrator into a class for an informal visit or administrators making an occasional announced visit.)

9. Faculty, assistants to instruction, and counselors who continue to display the same defects and deficiencies after several formal evaluations and conferences with appropriate administrators will be considered for more severe remediation steps. If such steps are deemed necessary, the appropriate Dean will recommend to the college president that the Board of Trustees be notified of the continuing defects and deficiencies in the person's work performance. The Dean will recommend that a formal notice to remedy said defects and deficiencies be made known to the person by the Board of Trustees.

10. A review of the defects and deficiencies cited by the Board of Trustees to the person affected will be conducted by the appropriate college Dean and other administrative persons involved. A written statement of disagreement with the evaluation may be filed by the person being evaluated.

11. Formal evaluation of the deficiencies will continue until such time as the defects and/or deficiencies are remediated to the satisfaction of the administrative personnel involved or until it is determined that a recommendation to dismiss the person involved should be made to the Board of Trustees.

12. This evaluation procedure recognizes that only the Board of Trustees has the authority by law to dismiss a tenured faculty member for cause in accordance with the Community College Tenure Act of 1980.

13. All written evaluations of tenured staff shall be kept on file.

14. If a dismissal of a tenured staff member (as named in this section)

is sought, the Board of Trustees will follow requirements in the Community College Tenure Act, Ill. Rev. Stat. Chap. 122, Paragraph 103B–4, "Dismissal of Tenured Faculty Member for Cause." Nothing in this policy, or other policies, shall be construed so as to abridge the rights of the Board of Trustees pursuant to Ill. Rev. Stat. Chap. 122, Paragraph 103B–5, "Reduction in Number of Faculty Members."

APPENDIX D

Procedures for the evaluation of all full-time non-tenured faculty, assistants to instruction, and counselors

It is the responsibility of the college administration to implement the following procedures which will provide for the evaluation of all full-time non-tenured faculty, assistants to instruction, and counselors:

1. The Division Chairpersons, Dean of Instruction (or his representative) will evaluate classes or labs of each non-tenured instructor and/or assistant to instruction in the college.
2. The Dean of Student Development will evaluate counseling sessions, career workshops, classes or seminars of non-tenured counselors.
3. The Division Chairpersons, Dean of Instruction (or his representative), or Dean of Student Development (for counselors) will also evaluate all other aspects of the jobs to be performed by faculty, assistants to instruction, and counselors. The criteria that will be used in the evaluation process in addition to classroom or other formal activity (depending upon an instructor's teaching assignment and/or a counselor's assignments) will include where applicable:

(A.) Performing advisory committee work in programs.
(B.) Maintaining course curriculum updates and revisions.
(C.) Performing college committee work.
(D.) Maintaining records as required by law, college policy, and administrative regulations.
(E.) Maintaining scheduled office hours.
(F.) Attending and participating in faculty and division meetings.
(G.) Attending local, state, and regional professional meetings and/or participating in other forms of professional upgrading.
(H.) Maintaining proper controls on and maintenance of tools, equipment, and supplies under one's area of responsibility.

(I.) Performing professional job-related duties as assigned by the administration in accordance with college policies and practices.

(J.) Assisting in upholding and enforcing college rules and administrative regulations.

(K.) Providing public performances and displays in such areas as music, speech, theatre, art, and reader's theatre.

(L.) Providing students with co-curricular activities in such areas as athletics, field trips, and occupationally related clubs.

(M.) Providing timely and complete reports required for D.A.V.T.E., I.C.C.B., North Central, Special Accreditation Associations, and the Board of Higher Education.

(N.) Disseminating program information to area students through (1) high school visitations, (2) college nights, (3) college open houses, and (4) invitations to high school faculty and students to the campus.

(O.) Providing an atmosphere of cooperation with administrations; insubordination is considered a very serious offense.

4. A formal evaluation conference with the Division Chairperson, Dean of Instruction (or Dean of Student Development for counselors) and the faculty member will be held within a reasonable time period following a classroom visitation and/or evaluation filed on the other job performance criteria that are outlined above. The conference should be held within 1 to 5 working days following such evaluation.

5. A faculty member, assistant to instruction, or counselor will be apprised of any defects and/or deficiencies in his/her performance as discovered in the formal evaluation process. The person evaluated will be advised to take appropriate action to remediate the defects/deficiencies cited.

6. Staff members hired with less than the appropriate minimum qualifications as outlined in the college's Minimum Qualifications Handbook should satisfy these requirements within a one- to three-year period as required by the supervisors and outlined to the staff members when hired. Failure to meet these standards may lead to dismissal of the non-tenured staff member.

7. Division Chairpersons will evaluate non-tenured staff a minimum of twice a semester during the first year of employment.

8. Division Chairpersons will evaluate non-tenured staff a minimum of once a semester during the second and third years of employment or until tenure is conferred.

9. The Dean of Instruction, or his representative, will evaluate non-tenured staff no less than once a year as a minimum.

10. All evaluation visits will be made unannounced to the staff member involved.

11. Any faculty member, assistant to instruction, or counselor who has been employed in the college for a period of three (3) successful consecutive school years shall be eligible for tenure. Recommendations for tenure will be made by the Division Chairperson in consultation with the Dean of Instruction to the college President. The Dean of Student Development will recommend tenure to the college President for counselors.

12. The President will review recommendations for tenure and make his recommendation to the Board of Trustees.

13. This evaluation procedure recognizes that only the Board of Trustees has the authority by law to confer tenure.

14. The Board of Trustees may, at its option, extend the non-tenure period for one additional school year by giving the faculty member notice not later than 60 days before the end of the school year, or term during the school year, or term immediately preceding the school year, or term in which tenure would otherwise be conferred. Such notice will state the corrective actions which the staff member should take to satisfactorily complete service requirements for tenure. The specific reasons for the one-year extension shall be confidential but shall be issued to the teacher upon request.

15. If the implementation of the above formal evaluation system results in a decision to dismiss a non-tenured staff member (as named in this section) for the ensuing school year or term, the Board of Trustees shall give notice thereof to the faculty member not later than 60 days before the end of the school year or term. The specific reasons for the dismissal shall be confidential but shall be issued to the teacher upon request.

16. If a decision to dismiss a non-tenured staff member is made, all requirements as outlined in the Community College Tenure Act, Section 3B-3 "Dismissal of Non-Tenured Faculty Member" will be followed.

BIBLIOGRAPHY

Allhouse, M. F. (1974). Tenure? A quest for truth and freedom. *Soundings* 57: 471–81.

Amundson, K. R. (1987). *Rewarding excellence: Teacher compensation and incentive plans.* Washington, DC: National School Board Association.

Andrews, H. A. (1994). Communicating with the governing board. In A. M. Cohen and F. B. Brawer (eds.), *Handbook of community college administration* (pp. 400–421). San Francisco: Jossey-Bass.

Andrews, H. A. (1993). Expanding merit recognition programs in community colleges. *Community College Review* 20 (5): 50–58.

Andrews, H. A. (1992). How to dismiss a tenured faculty member. *Administrative Action* 4 (6): 1–5.

Andrews, H. A. (1991). *Negative impact of faculty contract negotiations on community college faculty evaluation systems.* Oglesby IL: Illinois Valley Community College. (ERIC Document Reproduction Service No. ED 343 628).

Andrews, H. A. (1988a). Merit recognition: The acceptable alternative. *ACCT Quarterly* 12 (3): 24–27.

Andrews, H. A. (1988b). Objectives of a merit recognition system. *Administrative Action* 2 (3): 1.

Andrews, H. A. (1988c). The 'notice to remedy' in tenured faculty terminations. *Journal of Personnel Evaluation in Education 2:* 59–64.

Andrews, H. A. (1987a). A necessary road to quality in education: Evaluating part-time faculty. *Administrative Action* 2 (1): 3.

Andrews, H. A. (1987b). *Merit in education.* Stillwater, OK: New Forums Press.

Andrews, H. A. (1987c). Part-time faculty evaluation—a mirage. *The Community Services Catalyst* 17 (3): 22–25.

Andrews, H. A. (1987d). Recognition in education . . . reversing neglect. *Administrative Action* 1 (5): 1–2.

Andrews, H. A. (1987e). Reprimands: Useful when necessary. *Administrative Action* 2 (1): 4.

Andrews, H. A. (1987f). Reward merit with praise. *The School Administrator* 44 (9): 23–26.

Andrews, H. A. (1986a). *Awarding faculty merit based on higher-level needs.* Oglesby IL: Illinois Valley Community College. (ERIC Document Reproduction Service No. ED 266 840).

Andrews, H. A. (1986b). Administrative vs. student evaluation in accountability and professionalism. *Administrative Action* 1 (1): 6.

Andrews, H. A. (1986c). A proposal: Faculty evaluation bill of rights. *Administrative Action* 1 (2): 2.

Andrews, H. A. (1986d). Merit pay and merit recognition plans in community and junior colleges. *Journal of Staff, Program, and Organization Development* 4 (2): 46–50.

Andrews, H. A. (1985). *Evaluating for excellence*. Stillwater, OK: New Forums Press.

Andrews, H. A., and Knight, J. II. (1987). Administrative evaluation of teachers: Resistance and rationale. *NASSP Bulletin* 71 (503): 1–4.

Andrews, H. A., and Licata, C. M. (1991). Administrative perceptions of existing evaluation systems. *Journal of Personnel Evaluation in Education* 5: 69–76.

Andrews, H. A., and Licata, C. M. (1990). Faculty leaders' and administrators' perceptions on post-tenure faculty evaluation. *Journal of Staff, Program, & Organization Development* 8 (1): 17–21.

Andrews, H. A., and Licata, C. M. (1988–89). *The state of faculty evaluation in community, technical, and junior colleges within the North Central region, 1988–1989*. Oglesby IL: Illinois Valley Community College. (ERIC Document Reproduction Service No. ED 303 204).

Andrews, H. A., and Marzano, W. (1983a). Faculty evaluation stimulates expectations of excellence. *Community and Junior College Journal* 54 (4): 35–37.

Andrews, H. A., and Mackey, B. (1983b). Reductions in force in higher education. *The Journal of Staff, Program, & Organization Development* 1: 69–72.

Andrews, H. A., and Marzano, W. (1984). Awarding faculty merit based on higher-level needs. *The Journal of Staff, Program, & Organization Development* 1: 105–7.

Andrews, H. A., and Wisgoski, A. (1987). Assuring future quality: Systematic evaluation and reward of faculty. *The Journal of Staff, Program & Organization Development* 5 (2): 163–68.

Arreola, R. A. (1983). Establishing successful faculty evaluation and development programs. In A. Smith (ed.), *Evaluating faculty and staff: New directions for community colleges* (pp. 83–93). San Francisco: Jossey-Bass.

Baer, W. E. (1974). *Labor Arbitration Guide*. Homewood, IL: Dow Jones-Irwin, Inc.

Baker, G. A., Roueche, J. E., and Gillett-Karam, R. (1990). Teaching as leading. *AACJC Journal* 60 (5): 25–31.

Baker, G., and Prugh, S. (1988). Reward structures in unionized and nonunionized community colleges. *Community/Junior College Quarterly* 12: 121–36.

Barber, L. W. (1990). Self-assessment. In J. Millman and L. Darling-Hammond (eds.), *The new handbook of teacher evaluation* (pp. 216–28). Newbury Park, CA: Sage Publications, Inc.

Beckham, J. (1986). *Faculty/staff nonrenewal and dismissal for cause in institutions of higher education*. Asheville, NC: College Administration Publications, Inc.

Behrendt, R. L., and Parsons, M. H. (1983). Evaluation of part-time faculty. In A. Smith (ed.) *Evaluating faculty and staff: New directions for community colleges* (pp. 33–43). San Francisco: Jossey-Bass.

Bonato, D. J. (1987). *Legal and practical aspects of teacher evaluation.* Lansing: Michigan Institute for Educational Management.

Bourne, B. (1988). Making ideas work: Ralph Bedell and the NDEA Institutes. *Journal of Counseling and Development* 67: 136–42.

Boyer, E. (1983). *High School.* New York: Carnegie Foundation.

Boyles, N. L., and Vrchota, D. (1986). *Performance-based compensation models: Status and potential for implementation.* Des Moines, IA: Iowa Association of School Boards.

Bridges, E. M. (1990). Evaluation for tenure and dismissal. In J. Millman and L. Darling-Hammond, (eds.), *The new handbook of teacher evaluation: Assessing elementary and secondary school teachers* (pp. 147–57). Newbury Park, CA: Sage Publications, Inc.

Bridges, E. M. (1986). *The incompetent teacher: The challenge and the response.* Philadelphia: Falmer Press.

Bridges, E. M. (1985). How do administrators cope with teacher incompetence? *Education Week* V (20 Nov.): 24.

Bridges, E. M., and Groves, B. (1984). *Managing the incompetent teacher.* Eugene, OR: ERIC Clearinghouse on Educational Management.

Brophy, J., and Good, T. L. (1986). Teacher behavior and student achievement. In M. C. Wittrock (ed.), *Handbook of research on teaching,* 3d ed. (pp. 328–75). New York: Macmillan.

Brown, R. C. (1977). Tenure rights in contractual and constitutional contest. *Journal of Law and Education* 6: 279–318.

Carey, W. (1981). *Documenting teacher dismissal.* Salem, OR: Options Press.

Carr, R. K. (1972). The uneasy future of academic tenure. *Educational Record* 53: 119–27.

Cashin, W. E. (1988). *Student ratings of teaching: A summary of the research.* Manhattan, KS: Center for Faculty Evaluation and Development, Kansas State University.

Cashin, W. E. (1983). Concerns about using student ratings in community colleges. In A. Smith (ed.), *Evaluating faculty and staff: New directions for community colleges* (pp. 57–66). San Francisco: Jossey-Bass.

Centra, J. A. (1979). *Determining faculty effectiveness.* San Francisco: Jossey-Bass.

Centra, J. A. (1977). How universities evaluate faculty performance: A survey of department heads. GREB Research Report No. 75–5bR. Princeton, NJ: Educational Testing Service.

Centra, J. A. (1973). Self-ratings of college teachers: A comparison with student ratings. *Journal of Educational Measurement* 10 (4): 287–95.

Centra, J. A. (1972). *Two studies on the utility of student ratings for instructional improvement.* Princeton, NJ: Educational Testing Service.

Chait, R., and Ford, A. T. (1982). *Beyond traditional tenure.* San Francisco: Jossey-Bass.

Cheshire, N., and Hagenmeyer, R. H. (1981–82). Evaluating job performance. *Community and Junior College Journal* 52 (4): 34–37.

Chronicle of Higher Education, The. (1987). 'In' box. *The Chronicle of Higher Education* 33 (35): 16.

Clark, C. M., and Peterson, P. M. (1986). Teachers' thought processes. In M. C. Wittrock (ed.), *Handbook of research on teaching* (pp. 255–96). New York: Macmillan.

Clemente, J. D., Greenblatt, R. B., and Maher, R. E. (1992). Watching teachers teach. *The Executive Educator* (Apr.: 32–22).

Cohen, A. M., and Brawer, F. B. (1982). *The American community college.* San Francisco: Jossey-Bass.

Conley, D. T. (1988). District performance standards: Missing link for effective teacher evaluation. *NASSP Bulletin* 72 (511): 78–83.

Conley, D. T., and Dixon, K. (1990). The evaluation report: A tool for teacher growth. *NASSP Bulletin* 74 (527): 7–14. (ERIC Document Reproduction Service No. EJ 414 832).

DaMarto, S. (1990). Is SB 813 working? *Thrust for Educational Leadership* 20 (3): 34–35. Association of California School Administrators, Burlingame, CA.

Deci, E. L. (1976). The hidden costs of rewards. *Organizational Dynamics* 4 (3): 61–72.

Diamond, N., Sharp, G., and Ory, J. C. (1978). *Improving your lecturing.* Urbana: Office of Instructional Resources, University of Illinois.

Dubrow, H., and Wilkinson, J. (1982). The theory and practice of lectures. In M. Gullette (ed.), *The art and craft of teaching* (pp. 25–37). Cambridge: Harvard-Danforth Center for Teaching and Learning.

Duke, D. L., and Stiggins, R. J. (1990). Beyond minimum competence: Evaluation for professional development. In J. Millman and L. Darling-Hammond (eds.), *The new handbook of teacher evaluation: Assessing elementary and secondary school teachers* (pp. 116–32). Newbury Park, CA: Sage Publications, Inc.

Duke, D. L., and Stiggins, R. J. (1986). Teacher evaluation: Five keys to growth. In *Reports on public education 1986: A summary of major recommendations* (p. 5). Washington, DC: National School Boards Association.

Dunkleberger, G. E. Helping teachers to grow—classroom observations— what should principals look for? *NASSP Bulletin* 66 (458): 9–15.

Dunwell, R. R. (1986). Merit, motivation, and mythology. Paper presented at the annual meeting of the American Association of Colleges for Teacher Education, Feb., Chicago, IL.

Eble, K. E. (1984). New directions in faculty evaluation. In P. Seldin (ed.), *Changing practices in faculty evaluation: A critical assessment and recommendations for improvement.* San Francisco: Jossey-Bass.

Eble, K. E. (1973). Tenure and teaching. In B. L. Smith (ed.), *The tenure debate* (pp. 97–110). San Francisco: Jossey-Bass.

Eble, K. E. (1971). Teaching: Despite attacks on tenure, there is no evidence that it actually leads to ineffective teaching. *Chronicle of Higher Education* (26 Apr.): 8.

Education Commission of the States. (1983). *Action for excellence.* Report of the Task Force on Education for Economic Growth.

Educational Research Service (1983). *Merit pay plans for teachers: Status and descriptions.* ERS Report, Arlington, VA.

Educational Research Service (1979). *Merit pay for teachers.* ERS Report, Arlington, VA.

Educational Research Service (1978). *Evaluating teacher performance.* ERS Report. Arlington, VA.

Educational Testing Service (1975). *Comparative data guide—student instructional report.* Princeton, NJ.

El-Khawas, E. (1990). Campus Trends, 1990. Higher Education Panel Report No. 80. Washington, DC: American Council on Education.

ERIC Clearinghouse on Educational Management. (1981). Merit pay. Research Action Brief No. 15. Eugene, OR: ERIC Clearinghouse on Educational Management. (ED 199 828).

Erwin, J., and Andrews, H. A. (1994). The state of part-time faculty services at community colleges in a 19-state region. *Community/Junior College Quarterly* 17 (6): 559–62.

Evertson, C. M., and Emmer, E. T. (1982). Effective management at the beginning of the school year in junior high classes. *Journal of Educational Psychology* 74 (4): 485–98.

Evertson, C. M., Emmer, E. T., Clements, B. S., Sanford, J. P., Worsham, M. E., and Williams, E. L. (1981). *Organizing and managing the elementary school classroom.* Austin: University of Texas at Austin, Research and Development Center for Teacher Education. (ERIC Document Reproduction Service No. ED 223 570).

Evertson, C. M., and Holley, F. M. (1981). Classroom observation. In J. Millman (ed.), *Handbook of teacher evaluation: national council on measurement in education* (pp. 90–109). Beverly Hills: Sage Publications.

Filan, G. L. (1992). The trick to being a community college chair. *Leadership Abstracts* V (1): 1–2. Laguna Hills, CA: League of Innovation.

Filan, G., Okun, M., and Witter, R. (1986). Influence of ascribed and achieved social statuses, values, and rewards on job satisfaction among community college faculty. *Community/Junior College Quarterly* 10: 113–22.

Florio, D. II. (1983). Education and the political arena: Riding the train, shaping the debate. *Educational Researcher* 12 (8): 15–16.

Fraher, R. (1982). Learning a new art: Suggestions for beginning teachers. In M. Gullette (ed.), *The art and craft of teaching* (pp. 116–27). Cambridge: Harvard-Danforth Center for Teaching and Learning.

Frase, L. E., Hetzel, R. W., and Grant, R. T. (1982a). Promoting instructional excellence through a teacher reward system: Herzberg's theory applied. *Planning and Changing* 13 (2): 67–76.

Frase, L. E., Hetzel, R. W., and Grant, R. T. (1982b). Using Herzberg's Motivational-Hygiene Theory—Catalina Foothills School District . . . Reward system for excellent teaching. *Phi Delta Kappan* 64: 266–69.

Frase, L. E., and Piland, W. E. (1989). Breaking the silence about faculty rewards. *Community College Review* 17 (1): 25–33.

Frels, K., and Cooper, T. (1982). *A documentation system for teacher improvement or termination*. Topeka, KS: National Organization on Legal Problems of Education.

Futrell, M. (1986). How principals, teachers can improve relationships. *NASSP Bulletin* 70 (489): 52–65.

Gage, N. L. (1984). What do we know about teaching effectiveness? *Phi Delta Kappan* 66 (2): 87–93.

Garber, O. (1956). Causes and procedures for dismissing a tenure teacher. *Nation's Schools* 58: 73–74.

Gaynes, C. (1990). Only the best. *Thrust for Educational Leadership* 20 (3): 30–32.

Good, T. L. (1979). Teacher effectiveness in the elementary school. *Journal of Teacher Education* 30 (2): 52–64.

Grand Rapids Press. (1988a). Expedite over principle. (Editorial). *Grand Rapids Press* (22 Jan.).

Grand Rapids Press. (1988b). Dissent! School personnel practices. (Editorial reply by Board of Education). *Grand Rapids Press* (2 Feb.).

Grand Rapids Press. (1988c). Why pay so much, hide so much to fire teachers? (Editorial by J. Douglas). *Grand Rapids Press* (5 Feb.).

Greenwood, G. E., and Ramagli, H. J., Jr. (1980). Alternatives to student ratings of college teaching. *Journal of Higher Education* 51: 673–84.

Guskey, T. R., and Easton, J. Q. (1982). The characteristics of very effective community college teachers. *The Center for the Improvement of Teaching and Learning: City Colleges of Chicago Center Notebook* 1 (3): 36.

Hammons, J., and Wallace, H. (1977). Staff development needs of public community college department/division chairpersons. *Community/ Junior College Research Quarterly* 2 (1): 55–76.

Herzberg, F. (1966). *Work and the nature of man*. Cleveland and New York: The World Publishing Company.

Hocutt, M. O. (1987–88). "De-grading student evaluations: What's wrong with student polls of teaching. *Academic Questions* (Winter): 55–64.

Hollander, P. A. (1992). Evaluating tenured professors: Point of view. *The Chronicle of Higher Education* 38 (41): A44.

Hornbeck, D. W. (1977). Statewide bargaining. In G. Angell, E. Kelley, Jr. and Associates (eds.), *Handbook of faculty bargaining* (pp. 442–65). San Francisco: Jossey-Bass.

Huddle, G. (1985). Teacher evaluation—how important for effective schools? Eight messages from research. *NASSP Bulletin* 69 (479): 58–63.

Hunter, M. (1988a). Create rather than await your fate in teacher evaluation. In S. J. Stanley and W. J. Popham (eds.) *Teacher evaluation: Six prescriptions for success* pp. 32–54. Alexandria, VA: Association for Supervision and Curriculum Development.

Hunter, M. (1988b). Reflecting a reconciliation between supervisor and evaluation—A reply to Popham. *Journal of Personnel Evaluation in Education* 1: 275–80.

Isenberg, A. P. (1990). Evaluating teachers—Some questions and some considerations. *NASSP Bulletin* 74 (529): 16–18.

Jantz, R., White, J., and Bingman, W. (1987). The composite elementary teacher. *Action in Teacher Education* 9 (1): 35–41.

Jasiek, C. R., Wisgoski, A., and Andrews, H. A. (1985). The trustee role in college personnel management. In G. F. Petty (ed.), *Active trusteeship for a changing era* (pp. 87–97). New Directions for Community Colleges, No. 51. San Francisco: Jossey-Bass.

Jenkins, N. N., Barnicle, T. M., Dempsey, G. E., Faulkner, J. T., and Kasson, C. D. (1979). *Formal dismissal procedures under Illinois tenure laws.* Springfield: Illinois Association of School Boards.

Jentz, B., Cheever, D. S., Fisher, S. B., Jones, M. H., Kelleher, P., and Wofford, J. W. (1982). *Entry: The hiring, start-up, and supervision of administrators.* New York: McGraw-Hill.

Johnson, G. S., et al. (1985). The relationship between elementary school climate and teachers' attitudes toward evaluation. *Educational and Psychological Measurement* 5 (2): 89–112. (ERIC Document Reproduction Service No. EJ 320 577).

Kasulis, T. P. (1982). Questioning. In M. Gullette (ed.), *The art and craft of teaching* (pp. 38–48). Cambridge: Harvard-Danforth Center for Teaching and Learning.

Kauchak, D., Peterson, K., and Driscoll, A. (1985). An interview study of teachers' attitudes toward teacher evaluation practices. *Journal of Research and Development in Education* 19 (1): 32–37.

Kauffman, J. F. (1983). Strengthening chair, CEO relationships. *AGB Reports* 25 (2).

Kelleher, P. (1985). Inducing incompetent teachers to resign. *Phi Delta Kappan* 66 (5): 362–64.

Keller, J. W., Mattie, N., Vodanovich, S. J., and Piotrowski, C. (1991). Teaching effectiveness: Comparisons between traditional and nontraditional college students. *Innovative Higher Education* 15 (2): 177–84.

Keller, J. W., and Rabold, F. L. (1990). The importance of teacher behaviors in the classroom. *Journal of Staff, Program, & Organization Development* 8 (3): 161–66.

Kleingartner, A. (1984). Post-tenure evaluation and collective bargaining. Paper presented at the American Council on Education Conference, Periodic Review of Tenured Faculty, Nov., Miami, Florida.

Knight, J. (1986). Tenure and evaluation: Cleaning up our act. *Administrative Action* 1 (2): 3–4.

Knowles, L. W., and Wedlock, E. D., Jr., eds. (1973). *The yearbook of school law, 1973.* Topeka, KS: National Organization on Legal Problems of Education.

Kulik, J. A. (1974). *Evaluation of teaching. Memo to the Faculty, 54.* Ann Arbor: University of Michigan, Center for Research on Learning and Teaching. (ERIC Document Reproduction Service No. ED 092 025).

Kvenvold, J. C. (1989). Incompetence and tenured teachers: A survey of teacher evaluation and follow-up. *NASSP Bulletin* 73 (516): 99–102.

Lampignano, J. (1990). Increasing the effectiveness of part-time faculty. *Vision* 2 (2): 30–32.

Leas, D. E., and Rodriguez, R. C. (1987). Identifying the ineffective university dean. *Thought and Action* 3 (1): 97–102.

Lewis, R. L. (1980). Building effective trustee leadership or how to exploit your trustees. *Educational Record* 61: 18–21.

Licata, C. M., and Andrews, H. A. (1990). The status of tenured faculty evaluation in the community college. *Community College Review* 18 (3): 42–50.

Licata, C. M. (1986). *Post-tenure faculty evaluation: Threat or opportunity?* ASHE-ERIC Higher Education Report No. 1. Washington, DC.

Licata, C. M. (1984). An investigation of the status of post-tenure evaluation in selected community colleges in the United States. Ed.D. diss., The George Washington University.

Lieberman, M. (1985). Educational specialty boards: A way out of the merit pay morass? *Phi Delta Kappan* 67 (2): 103–7.

Littler, S. (1914). Causes of failure among elementary school teachers. *School and Home Education* (March): 255–56.

Lovain, T. B. (1983–84). Grounds for dismissing tenured post-secondary faculty for cause. *The Journal of College and University Law* 10 (3): 419–33.

Mangan, K. S. (1991) Many colleges fill vacancies with part-time professors, citing economy and uncertainty about enrollments. *The Chronicle of Higher Education* 37 (47): A9.

Mangieri, J. N., and Arnn, J.W., Jr. (1985). Excellent schools: The leadership functions of principals. *American Education* 21 (3): 8–10.

Margolese, A. (1982). Dismissal for cause. *California School Boards* 41 (7): 8–11.

Maskowitz, G., and Hayman, J. (1976). Success strategies of inner-city teachers: A year-long study. *Journal of Educational Research* 69: 283–89.

Maslow, A. H. (1954). *Motivation and personality.* New York: Harper & Row.

Mason, B. (1993). Trained teachers and high expectations help children learn to think! *The Phelps-Stokes Fund Dialogue* 2 (May): 1–4.

McCormick, V. (1986). When teaching excellence doesn't pay off. *Education Week* 6 (14).

McDaniel, S. H., and McDaniel T. R. (1980). How to weed out incompetent teachers without getting hauled into court. *The National Elementary Principal* (Mar.): 31–36.

McGreal, T. L. (1988). Evaluation for enhancing instruction: Linking teacher evaluation and staff development. In S. J. Stanley and W. J. Popham (eds.), *Teacher evaluation: Six prescriptions for success* (pp. 1–31). Alexandria, VA: Association for Supervision and Curriculum Development.

McIntyre, K. E. (1984). The merit and demerits of merit pay. *NASSP Bulletin* 68 (469): 100–104.

McLaughlin, M. W. (1990). Embracing contraries: Implementing and sustaining teacher evaluation. In J. Millman and L. Darling-Hammond (eds.),

The new handbook of teacher evaluation: Assessing elementary and secondary school teachers (pp. 403–15). Newbury Park, CA: Sage Publications.

McMillen, L. (1984). A handful of two-year colleges awarding 'merit' raises to outstanding teachers. *Chronicle of Higher Education* 29 (28).

McNeil, J. D. (1981). Politics of Teacher Evaluation. In J. Millman (ed.), *Handbook of teacher evaluation: National council on measurement in education* (pp. 272–91). Beverly Hills: Sage Publications.

Meyer, H. (1975). The pay-for-performance dilemma. *Organizational Dynamics* 3 (30): 39–50.

Morris, A. A. (1992). *Dismissal of tenured higher education faculty: Legal implications of the elimination of mandatory retirement.* Topeka, KS: National Organization of Legal Problems of Education.

Mortimer, K. P., Bagshaw, M., and Masland, A. T. (1985). *Flexibility in academic staffing: Effective policies and practices.* ASHE-ERIC Higher Education Report No. 1. Washington, DC (ED 260 675).

Nash, L. L. (1982). The rhythm of the semester. In M. Gullette (ed.), *The art and craft of teaching* (pp. 70–87). Cambridge: Harvard-Danforth Center for Teaching and Learning.

Nason, J. W. (1982). A sampler from John Nason's the nature of trusteeship. *AGB Reports* 24 (5): 14–15.

NASSP Bulletin. (1986). A *Bulletin* special: NEA's president describes issues in American education, how principals, teachers can improve relationships. *NASSP Bulletin* 70 (489): 52–65.

National Commission on Higher Education Issues. (1982). *To strengthen quality in higher education.* Washington, DC: American Council on Education. (ERIC Document Reproduction Service No. ED 226 646).

National School Board Association. (1987). *Rewarding excellence: Teacher compensation and incentive plans.* Alexandria, VA: National School Board Association.

Nisbet, R. (1973). The future of tenure. In *Change: On learning and change* (pp. 46–64). New Rochelle, NY: Change Magazine.

Norland, C. R. (1987). Report of a conference. *Illinois School Board Journal* 55 (1).

Norman, M. (1984). Advice and recommendations: Improving the work environment for part-timers. *AAHE Bulletin* (Oct.): 13–14.

Olson, L. (1989). Fairfax County, VA, Merit pay loses teachers'-union support. *Education Week* 8 (26): 7.

Olswang, S. G., and Lee, B. A. (1984). *Faculty freedom and institutional accountability: Interactions and conflict.* ASHE-ERIC Higher Education Research Report No. 5. Washington, DC.

Ory, J. C. (1990). Student ratings of instruction: Ethics and practice. *New directions for teaching and learning* 43: 63–74.

Ory, J., and Parker, S. (1989). A survey of assessment activities at large research universities. *Research in Higher Education* 30: 373–83.

Orze, J. J. (1977). Working with the faculty senate in a bargaining context. In G.

Angell, E. Kelley, Jr. and Associates (ed.), *Handbook of faculty bargaining* (504–19). San Francisco: Jossey-Bass.

Perkins, C. D. (1984). *Merit pay task force report*. Washington, DC: U.S. Government Printing Office, Report No. 98.

Petty, G. F. (1986). Courts uphold dismissal. (Editorial). *Illinois Trustee*. (1 Jan.).

Phay, R. E. (1981). Nonreappointment of teachers: A proposed board policy. *School Law Bulletin* 12 (2). (ERIC Document Reproduction Service No. EJ 245 705).

Piele, P. K., ed. (1981). *The yearbook of school law, 1981*. Topeka, KS: National Organization on Legal Problems of Education.

Piele, P. K., ed. (1980). *The yearbook of school law 1980*. Topeka, KS: National Organization on Legal Problems of Education.

Piele, P. K., ed. (1979). *The yearbook of school law 1979*. Topeka, KS: National Organization on Legal Problems of Education.

Piele, P. K., ed. (1975). *The Yearbook of school law 1975*. Topeka, KS: National Organization on Legal Problems of Education.

Poole, L. H., and Dellow, D. A. (1983). Evaluation of full-time faculty. In A. Smith (ed.), *Evaluating faculty and staff: New directions for community colleges* (pp. 19–31). San Francisco: Jossey-Bass.

Popham, W. J. (1988). The dysfunctional marriage of formative and summative teacher evaluation. *Journal of Personnel Evaluation in Education* 1: 269–74.

Porter, A. C., and Brophy, J. (1988). Synthesis of research on good teaching: Insights from the work of the Institute for Research on Teaching. *Educational Leadership* (May): 74–85.

Purkey, S. C., and Smith, M. S. (1983). Effective schools: A review. *The Elementary School Journal* 83 (4): 427–52.

Rapp, J. A., and Ortbal, T. J. (1980). *Illinois public community college act: Tenure policies and procedures*. Springfield, IL: Illinois Community College Trustees Association.

Rebell, M. (1990). Legal issues concerning teacher evaluation. In J. Millman and L. Darling-Hammond (eds.), *The new handbook of teacher evaluation: Assessing elementary and secondary school teachers:* (pp. 337–55). Newbury Park, CA: Sage Publications.

Reich, A. H. (1983). Opinion: Why I teach. *The Chronicle of Higher Education* (19 Oct.): 36.

Rosenberger, D. S., and Plimpton, R. A. (1975). Teacher incompetence and the courts. *Journal of Law and Education* 4: 469–86.

Rosenholtz, S. (1985). Effective schools: Interpreting the evidence. *American Journal of Education* 93 (3): 368–69.

Rotem, A. (1978). The effects of feedback from students to university instructors. *Research in Higher Education* 9: 308–18.

Roueche, J. E. (1983). Excellence for students. In *Celebrating teaching excellence: Proceedings, National Conference on Teaching Excellence and Conference of Presidents* (pp. 29–34). Austin: University of Texas at Austin.

Savage, D. G. (1983). Teacher evaluation: The need for effective measures. *Learning* 12: 54–56.

Sbaratta, P. (1983). Academic deans: Keep the heart pumping. *Community and Junior College Journal* 54 (3): 21–27.

Scherer, M. (1983). Merit pay—the great debate. *Instructor* 93 (3).

Schorr, B. (1983). School's merit pay program draws gripes from losers and winners. *Wall Street Journal* (17 Jun.).

Scott, C. (1975). Collecting information about student learning. In C. S. Scott and G. C. Thorne (eds.), *Professional Assessment in Higher Education.* Monmouth: Oregon State System of Higher Education.

Selden, D. (1978). Faculty bargaining and merit pay: Can they co-exist? *Chronicle of Higher Education* 17 (30 Oct.): 32.

Seldin, P. (1989). Using student feedback to improve teaching. *New Directions for Teaching and Learning* 33: 89–97.

Seldin, P., ed. (1984). *Changing practices in faculty evaluation: A critical assessment and recommendations for improvement.* San Francisco: Jossey-Bass.

Seldin, P. (1982). Improving faculty evaluation systems. *Peabody Journal of Education* 59 (2): 93–99.

Seymour, D. T. (1991). TQM on campus: What the pioneers are finding. *AAHE Bulletin* 44 (3): 10–13.

Shanker, A. (1985). Collective bargaining with educational standards. In *Education on trial: Strategies for the future* (pp. 224–25). San Francisco: Institute for Contemporary Studies.

Slander, F. (1983). Faculty compensation policies. *New Directions for Higher Education* 41: 21–36.

Southern Regional Educational Board (1986). *Career ladder clearinghouse.* Atlanta: Southern Regional Educational Board.

Spinetta, K. I. (1990). Part-time instructors in the California community colleges: A need to revise current policies. *Community College Review* 18 (1): 43–49.

Steinmetz, L. L. (1979). *Human relations: People and work.* New York: Harper & Row.

Stevens, E., Goodwin, L., and Goodwin W. (1991). How are we different? Attitudes and perceptions of teaching across three institutions. *Journal of Staff, Program, & Organization Development* 9 (2): 69–82.

Stiggins, R. J., & Duke, D. L. (1988). *The case for commitment to teacher growth: Research on teacher evaluation.* Albany, NY: State University of New York Press.

Stodolsky, S.S. (1990). Classroom observation. In J. Millman and L. Darling-Hammond (eds.), *The new handbook of teacher evaluation: Assessing elementary and secondary school teachers* (pp. 175–90). Newbury Park, CA: Sage Publications.

Stoner, C. L. (1986). Terminating the tenured. *School and College Product News* 25 (10): 43–48.

Strike, K. A. (1990). The ethics of educational evaluation. In J. Millman and L. Darling-Hammond (eds.), *The new handbook of teacher evaluation: Assessing elementary and secondary school teachers* (pp. 356–73). Newbury Park, CA: Sage Publications.

Strike, K. A., and Bull, B. (1981). Fairness and the legal context of teacher evaluation. In J. Millman (ed.), *Handbook of teacher evaluation: National council on measurement in education* (pp. 310–43). Beverly Hills: Sage Publications.

Sykes, C. J. (1988). *Profscam: Professors and the demise of higher education.* Washington, DC: Regnery Gateway.

Thomas, S. B., ed. (1992). *The yearbook of school law 1992.* Topeka, KS: National Organization on Legal Problems of Education.

Thomas, S. B., ed. (1991). *The yearbook of school law 1991.* Topeka, KS: National Organization on Legal Problems of Education.

Thomas, S. B., ed. (1990). *The yearbook of school law 1990.* Topeka, KS: National Organization on Legal Problems of Education.

Thomas, S. B., ed. (1989). *The yearbook of school law 1989.* Topeka, KS: National Organization on Legal Problems of Education.

Thomas, S. B., ed. (1988). *The yearbook of school law 1988.* Topeka, KS: National Organization on Legal Problems of Education.

Thomas, S. B., ed. (1987). *The yearbook of school law 1987.* Topeka, KS: National Organization on Legal Problems of Education.

Thomas, S. B., ed. (1986). *The yearbook of school law 1986.* Topeka, KS: National Organization on Legal Problems of Education.

Thomas, S. B., ed. (1985). *The yearbook of school law 1985.* Topeka, KS: National Organization on Legal Problems of Education.

Turner, R. R. (1986). What teachers think about their evaluations. *Learning 86* 15 (9): 58–67.

Valente, W. (1987). *Law in the schools.* 2d ed. Columbus, OH: Merrill Publishing Company.

Van Horn, Jr., B. (1984). *Teacher incompetence: A legal memorandum.* Reston, VA: National Association of Secondary School Principals.

Van Sciver, J. H. (1990a). A few tips on teacher dismissals. *The School Administrator* 10 (47): 41.

Van Sciver, J. H. (1990b). Teacher dismissal. *Phi Delta Kappan* 72 (4): 318–19.

Vander Wheele, M. (1992). Principals report teachers lacking. *Chicago Sun-Times* (2 Dec.): 3.

Wheeler, P. W., Haertel, G. D., and Scriven, M. (1993). *Teacher evaluation glossary.* Kalamazoo, MI: Center for Research on Educational Accountability and Teacher Evaluation.

White, D. S. (1983). Can merit pay work in education? *American Educator* 7 (4): 8–42.

Wise, A. E., and Gendler, T. (1990). Governance issues in the evaluation of elementary and secondary schoolteachers. In J. Millman and L. Darling-Hammond (eds.), *The new handbook of teacher evaluation: Assessing elementary and secondary school teachers* (pp. 116–32). Newbury Park, CA: Sage Publications.

Wise, A. E., Darling-Hammond, L., McLaughlin, M. W., and Bernstein, H. T. (1985). Teacher evaluation: A study of effective practices. *The Elementary School Journal* 86 (1): 76–77.

Wise, A., Darling-Hammond, L., McLaughlin, M., and Bernstein, H. (1984). *Teacher evaluation: A study of effective practices.* Santa Monica, CA: The RAND Corporation.

Wolcowitz, J. (1982). The first day of class. In M. Gullette (ed.), *The art and craft of teaching* (pp. 10–24). Cambridge: Harvard-Danforth Center for Teaching and Learning.

Woodruff, B. E. (1976). Trustees must know the law. *AGB Reports* 18 (6): 11–18.

COURT CASES

Alabama State Tenure Commission v. Birmingham Board of Educ., 564 So.2d 980 (Ala. Civ. App. 1990).

Atherton v. Board of Educ. of School Dist. of St. Joseph, 744 S.W.2d 518 (Mo. Ct. App. 1988).

Aulwurm v. Board of Educ. of Murphysboro Comm. Unit School Dist., 367 N.E.2d 1337 (Ill. 1977).

Bates v. Sponberg, 547 F.2d 325 (6th Cir. 1976).

Beck v. James, Superintendent Palmyra R–I School Dist., 793 S.W.2d 416 (Mo. Ct. App. 1990).

Board of Educ. of Argo-Summit School Dist. 104 v. Hunt, 487 N.E.2d 24 (1st Dist. 1985).

Board of Educ. of Chicago v. Box, 547 N.E.3d 627 (Ill. App. Ct. 1989).

Board of Educ. of Chicago v. Chicago Teachers Union, Local 1, 88 Ill. 2d 63, 430 N.E.2d 1111 (1981).

Board of Educ. of Chicago v. Harris, 578 N.E.2d 1244 (Ill. App. Ct. 1991).

Board of Educ. of Chicago v. Johnson, 570 N.E.2d 382 (Ill. App. Ct. 1991).

Board of Educ. v. Ingels, 394 N.E.2d 69 (1979).

Board of Educ. of Benton Harbor Area Schools v. Wolff, 361 N.W.2d 750 (Mich. Ct. App. 1985).

Board of Regents v. Roth, 408 U.S. 564 (1972).

Board of Trustees of Comm. College Dist. No. 508 v. Cook County College Teachers Union, Local 1600, 522 N.E.2d 93 (Ill. App. Ct. 1987).

Board of Trustees of Community College District No. 513 v. Krizek and the American Federation of Teachers, Local 1810, N.E.2d 770 (Ill. 1983).

Bradshaw v. Alabama State Tenure Commission, 520 So.2d 541 (Ala. Civ. App. 1988).

Browzin v. Catholic Univ. of America, 527 F.2d 843 (D.C. Cir. 1975).

Caldwell v. Blytheville, Arkansas School Dist. No. 5, 746 S.W.2d 381 (Ark. Ct. App. 1988).

Catherine v. Bd. of Educ. of the City of St. Louis, 822 S.W.2d 881 (Mo. Ct. App. 1991).

Chung v. Park, 377 F. Supp. 218 (M.D. Pa. 1974).

Cleveland Board of Educ. v. Loudermill, 470 U.S. 532, 542 and 545–46 (1985).

Conley v. Board of Educ. of the City of New Britain, 123 A.2d 747 (Conn. 1956).

Cope v. Board of Educ. of the Town of West Hartford, 495 A.2d 718 (Conn. Ct. App. 1985).

Crump v. Durham County Board of Educ., 327 S.E.2d 599 (N.C. Ct. App. 1985).

DeBernard v. State Board of Educ., 527 N.E.2d 616 (Ill. App. Ct. 1988).

Dunnigan v. Ambach, 484 N.Y.S.2d 373 (N.Y. App. Div. 1985).

Eshom v. Board of Educ. of School Dist. No. 54, 364 N.W.2d 7 (Neb. 1985).

Esther Fortson v. Detroit Board of Educ. (83–47).

Evansville-Vanderburgh School Corp. v. Roberts, 395 N.E.2d 291 (Ind. Ct. App. 1979), reconsidering, 392 N.E.2d 810 (Ind. Ct. App. 1979).

Florida Educ. Code, sec. 231.29(2) (1989).

Foleno v. Board of Educ. of the Twp. of Bedminster, Decision of N.J. Comm'r of Educ. (1978).

Ford v. Caldwell Parish School Board, 541 So.2d 955 (La. Ct. App. 1989).

Gaylord v. Board of Educ., Unified School Dist. No. 218, Morton County, 794 P.2d 307 (Kan. Ct. App. 1990).

Goldberg v. Kelly, 397 U.S. 254 (1970).

Hagerstrom v. Clay City Comm. Unit High School Dist. 356 N.E.2d 438 (Ill. App. Ct. 1976).

Hall v. Board of Educ. of City of Chicago, 592 N.E.2d 245 (Ill. App. Ct. 1992).

Hamburg v. North Penn School Dist., 484 A.2d 867 (Pa. Commw. Ct. 1984).

Hanlon v. Board of Educ. of the Parkway School Dist., 695 S.W.2d 930 (Mo. Ct. App. 1985).

Hatta v. Board of Educ., Union Endicott Central School Dist., 394 N.Y.S.2d 301 (App. Div. 1977).

Hou v. Pennsylvania Depart. of Educ., 573 F. Supp. 1539 (W.D. Pa. 1983).

Ianello v. The Univ. of Bridgeport, (see Carnegie Council on Policy Studies in Higher Education, 1979).

Illinois Education Association v. Board of Education, 62 Ill. 2d 127, 340 N.E.2d 7 (1975).

In Re Fugere, 592 A.2d 518 (N.H. 1991).

Irby v. McGowan, 380 F. Supp. 1024 (S.E. Ala. 1974).

Jackson v. Sobol as Commissioner of Educ. of the State of New York, et al., Respondents, 565 N.Y.S.2d 612 (App. Div. 1991).

Jawa v. Fayetteville Univ., 426 F. Supp. 218 (E.D. N.C. 1976).

Jefferson Cons. School Dist. C–123 v. Carden, 772 S.W.2d 753, 759 (Mo. Ct. App. 1989).

In Re the Proposed Termination of James E. Johnson's Teaching Contract with Independent School Dist. No. 709, 451 N.W.2d 343 (Minn. Ct. App. 1990).

Johnson v. School Board of Dade County, 578 So.2d 387 (Fla. Dist. Ct. App. 1991).

Kamrath v. Board of Educ., Ill. 2d N.E.2d (1987).

Katz v. Board of Trustees of Gloucester County College, 118 N.J. Sup. Ct. 398, 288 A.2d 43 (1972).

Kleinberg v. Board of Educ. of the Albuquerque Public Schools, 751 P.2d 722 (N.M. Ct. App. 1988).

Korf v. Ball State Univ., 726 F.2d 1222 (7th Cir. 1984).

Landrum v. Eastern Kentucky Univ., 578 F. Supp. 241 (E.D. Ky. 1984).

Lehman v. Board of Trustees of Whitman College, 576 P.2d 397 (Wash. 1978).

Lipka v. Brown City Community Schools, 252 N.W.2d 770 (Mich. 1977).

Lockport Area Special Education Cooperative v. Lockport Area Special Education Cooperative Association, 33 Ill. App. 3d 789, 338 N.E.2d 463 (1975).

Lovan v. Dora R. Illinois School Dist., 677 S.W.2d 956 (Mo. Ct. App. 1984).

Malverne Union Free School Dist. v. Sobol, 586 N.Y.S.2d 673 (App. Div. 1992).

Manheim Central Educ. Ass'n. v. Manheim Central School Dist., 572 A.2d 31 (Pa. Commw. Ct. 1990).

Martin v. Parrish, 805 F.2d 583 (5th Cir. 1986).

McConnel v. Howard Univ., 621 F. Supp. 327 (D.D.C. 1985).

McGuire v. Governing Board of San Diego Comm. College Dist., 208 Cal. Rptr. 260 (Cal. Ct. App. 1984).

Meckley v. Kanawha County Board of Educ., 383 S.E.2d 839 (W. Va. 1989).

Meyer v. Board of Educ. of the Charlotte Valley Central School Dist., 581 N.Y.S.2d 920 (App. Div. 1992).

Mims v. West Baton Rouge Parish School Board, 315 S.2d 349 (La. Ct. App. 1975).

Mongitore v. Regan, 520 N.Y.S.2d 194 (App. Div. 1987).

Moravek v. Davenport Comm. School Dist., 262 N.W.2d 797 (Iowa 1978)

Mott v. Endicott School Dist., 713 P.2d 98 (Wash. 1986).

Nevels v. Board of Educ. of School Dist. of Maplewood-Richmond Heights, 822 S.W.2d 898 (Mo. Ct. App. 1991).

N.Y. Inst. of Technology v. Commission of Human Rights of City of N.Y., 38 N.Y. 2d, 28, 339 N.E.2d 880, 377 N.Y.S.2d 471, 478 (1975).

Perry v. Sinderman, 408 U.S. 593 (1972).

Petrella v. Siegel, 843 F.2d 87 (2d Cir. 1988).

Powell v. Board of Trustees, Crook County School Dist. No. 1, 550 P.2d 1112 (Wyo. Sup. Ct. 1976).

Queen v. Minneapolis Public Schools, 481 N.W.2d 66 (Minn. Ct. App. 1992).

Roberts v. Santa Cruz Valley Unified School Dist. No. 35, 778 P.2d 1294 (Ariz. Ct. App. 1989).

Rolando v. School Directors of Dist. No. 125, County of LaSalle and State of Illinois, 358 N.E. 2d 945 (Ill. App. 1976).

Rossi v. Pennsylvania State Univ. 489 A. 2d 828 (Pa. Sup. Ct. 1985).

Rosso v. Board of Educ. of School Directors, 388 A. 2d 1238 (Pa. Commw. Ct., 1977).

Saunders v. Reorganized School Dist. No. 2 of Osage Co., 420 S.W. 2d 29 (Mo. 1975).

Sauter v. Mount Vernon School Dist. No. 320, Skagit County, 791 P.2d 549 (Wash. Ct. App. 1990).

Selby v. North Callaway Board of Educ., 777 S.W.2d 275 (Mo. Ct. App. 1989).

Shaw v. Board of Trustees of Frederick Community College, 549 F. 2d 929 (4th cir. 1976).

Stamper v. Board of Educ. of Elem. School Dist. 143, 491 N.E.2d 36 (1st Dist. 1986).

Stasny v. Board of Trustees of Central Washington Univ., 32 Wash. App. 239, 647 P.2d 496 (1982).

Strain v. Rapid City School Board for Rapid City Area School Dist., 447 N.W.2d 332 (S.D. 1989).

Sutherby v. Gobles Board of Educ., 348 N.W.2d 277 (Mich. Ct. App. 1984).

Swann v. Caylor, 516 So. 2d 699, 701 (Ala. Civ. App. 1987).

Teacneck Board of Educ. v. Teacneck Teachers Ass'n., 390 A.2d 1198 (N.J. Sup. Ct. 1978).

Tishey v. Board of School Trustees of North Newton School Corp., 575 N.E.2d 1018, 1021 (Ind. Ct. App. 1991).

Tomczik v. State Tenure Comm'n Center Line Public Schools, 438 N.W.2d 642 (Mich. Ct. App. 1989).

Wagner v. Department of Education State Personnel Board, 549 S.W.2d 300 (Ky. 1977).

Ward v. Board of Educ. of the School Dist. of Philadelphia, 496 A.2d 1352 (Pa. Commw. Ct. 1985).

Ware v. Morgan County School Dist., 748 P.2d 1295 (Colo. 1988).

Wiley v. Richland Parish School Board, 476 So. 2d 439 (La. Ct. App. 1985).

Worzella v. Board of Regents, 93 N.W.2d 411, 414 (S.D. 1958).

INDEX